WRITERS
ON
WRITING

WRITERS
ON
WRITING

VOLUME II

Edited by
Tom Waldrep
University of South Carolina

Random House/New York

First Edition
987654321
Copyright © 1988 by Random House, Inc.

Library of Congress Cataloging in Publication Data

(Revised for vol. 2)

Writers on writing.

    Includes bibliographical references.
    1. English language—Rhetoric. 2. Authorship
I. Waldrep, Tom.
PE1408.W7715   1985   808'.042   85-1947
ISBN 0-394-36771-5

FOREWORD

Writers on Writing, Volume I, brought to the profession personal accounts of "how I write" by thirty rhetoric/composition specialists throughout the country. The response to these statements overall was positive, with most reviewers and critics perceiving them as honest, revealing, accurate. Graduate and undergraduate students in over thirty universities in the United States and Canada read the volume, and many reported that while an individual's composing process probably *cannot* be emulated, the accounts were helpful because connections can be made and parallels can be drawn. *Writers on Writing*, Volume II, is a continuation of that research on how writing teachers write.

As the Foreword of *Writers on Writing*, Volume I points out, the idea for interrogating rhetoricians about their composing processes began in a graduate class, at the University of South Carolina where I teach. Students in that class were quite perturbed by all the rhetorical theory in that course and wondered aloud if rhetoricians practised what they preached. They needed proof that a knowledge of rhetorical theory would enhance their understanding of the pedagogy, of the practical application of these rhetoricians' theories.

So, in shaping the project I had both writers and young writing teachers in mind. I set out to make the sort of book that would have stimulated me to be a better teacher of writing eighteen years ago when I began teaching, and would in fact have helped me, too, when I first began to think of myself as a writer. I suspected that every young writer and probably many young writing teachers today make for guidance and inspiration a commonplace book recording the dicta of their most admired elders on their art. We record, we gather clippings, we gather good essays and bad ones. *Writers on Writing*, Volumes I and II, may be taken as an extension of such a working writer's commonplace book.

Also, I knew this collection would be valuable if the eminent practitioners who agreed to participate in this project would give us a truthful statement of their own writing theories and the pedagogical application of those theories. I hoped that the rhetoricians would, in fact, define as best they could their theories and tell us how they apply these theories in their own writing. For I knew that the practitioners, often after trial and error, had found out much for themselves. In struggling to write and teach writing, they have discovered their own pulses. And they have also discovered, I believe, the validity of whatever "laws" of composition other rhetoricians in the past have laid down.

So I learned in this study that our attitudes differ toward writing —or at least toward the process that gives us the product. I learned further that as individuals our motivations for writing vary greatly. Some write only to publish—for tenure, for praise, for "a public"—but others write only for self, from an internal *motivating* force that in the end will make the writer less "cranky," easier to get along with.

Toby Fulwiler tells us in this volume,

> I write not because of Kipling or my mother, or because my papers were read in the tenth grade, but because I have to. I write because if I don't I cannot sleep. And if I cannot sleep, I am as cranky as when I don't write in my journal for a week.

Muriel Harris confides,

> I write in response to an inner urge to share something I've learned. From my teaching, research, or reading, an insight might bubble up and take shape, and, like hearing a good joke, I have to run and tell it to the next person. At other times what I have read or heard infuriates me, because I think it is dead wrong, destructive to the theory and pedagogy of teaching writing.

And Harry Brent tells us in Volume I,

> I wander through the woods, occasionally intersecting one of the sacred pathways of invention or arrangement, but never following it for very long. Asphalt roads have their place when you're traveling straight and by clear design, but I like to wander when I write, and create my own roads.

Jacqueline Berke in this volume says,

> I must remind myself that not everyone has the desire, the determination, the willfulness, the willingness, the stubbornness, the quirkiness, that goes with being a writer. That is, with writing for a living, or if not for a living, then writing as a serious and chronic condition for living.

I also learned that most of us writers take words seriously; and as someone has said, perhaps we are the last professional class that does so. And no matter what the reason for writing, many of us writers believe when we pick up our pens and compose at our desks, or our dining room table, or our personal computer, that we put on a disguise that frees us, protects us, or allows us to speak out untimidly. Often desire for articles to be published or for articles simply to be read derives in part from the hope that our disguise will *not* slip, that our perceived authorial persona will *not* be lost, and that the real person behind the words will *not* be revealed.

Listen to Susan Miller:

> Writing is at once a way to be myself and a way to hide myself, and it always was. I was writing columns in high school under another name, Sam. I was writing themes in college, sounding like I had grown up in a family who always went to college, *not* as the coal miner's daughter I was—I am. Even now, I suspect myself of not showing who I really am, but now I have the joy of understanding that I am not constructing a text to imitate me, but a text that will create new parts of me. I really am whoever I am in my writing at this moment. The writing, both the act and the word, *is constructing a me,* not vice-versa.

And Barbara Tomlinson says:

> To do important kinds of writing, to shape the deeper meaning, to push forward the main theme, to write about things that I don't yet understand, I need to be intimate with the text, I must feel myself wholly within the evolving text, and it within me. We are in each others' skin, blood, flesh, self. We—text and I—formulate the text within the collaborative matrix of self, text, and context. As I mark and shape the text, so the text shapes me, marks me, sometimes even scars me.

Yet in spite of disguises, in spite of scars, we continue to write. The essays make it clear that all of us go through the struggle of writing, whether for pleasure or for publications lists, because this "means of communication" gives to us something we *must have. Never* was it my intention to give to the profession a "how-to" book, a book that after one's reading and synthesis, a mature reader would vow, "Well, *this* is *the* way it's done." *Writers on Writing,* Volumes I and II, are simply what I proposed—a compilation of insight and wisdom, revelation, surprise, falsity, disguise, coverup—like many of our accounts of our lives, as Susan Miller suggested in her essay. From all these insights we can develop a better sense of *what is writing*—the act—what has it been, for us, in the past—what can it be, for us, in the future—and how we can allow our students to see that the analysis of others' composing and one's own is as diverse, as exciting, as insightful as *writers* themselves are.

Tom Waldrep

CONTENTS

that I wrote in the fourth grade. It was that piece of writing each of us can remember if we travel back in time far enough—the one that came out whole, as if it resided there just so in our minds. The one that caused your teacher or mother to pronounce you a WRITER.

what I have read or heard infuriates me because I think it is dead wrong, destructive to the theory and pedagogy of teaching writing.

I am conscious at all times of an unfolding plan, of where I am in that plan, and of what remains to be done. Even though I occasionally write sections of a piece out of the order in which they will appear in the final text, I continue to be conscious of what I think will be the final plan. And I try to be sure that the plan in the final text will unfold clearly, so that the reader is aware at all times where he or she is and, if possible, why.

Talk is central to our collaboration in a way that it seldom has been for us as individual writers. We find ourselves talking through to a common thesis and plan, talking through the links in an argument, talking through various points of significance or alternative conclusions. Talk is also central to our planning, which must be both more explicit and more detailed when we write together than either of us is accustomed to when working alone.

My impression is that I know a whole lot more about how I initiate writing than I know about how I keep it going and finish it. . . . The more I get into a project, the more the adrenalin flows and that project becomes the world I inhabit.

The essential factor for me in writing anything that is not routine—that is anything from which I expect to learn—is to create a conversation in my head. I need to hear voices to whom my writing is a response. I want to feel part of a conversation.

I am a compulsive writer. I not only love to write; I *must* write. If a day passes when I have written nothing, I am depressed. If I am expecting to write and something interrupts and keeps me from my task, I feel useless and lazy and somehow spent no matter what I have accomplished otherwise or how much good I may have done in another part of my working life. But several hours of writing leaves me in a state of euphoria. It may be lousy stuff. But it is *there,* and I can make it better tomorrow. I have done something worthwhile with my day.

The thesis of this study then is that most (not all) converts manage the conversion to composing at the terminal because they can plan before writing, not just by writing, or because they can at some point form a mental image of the structure of their text. And the longer the converts have been composing at the computer, the less interested they are in frequently printing out their texts. They do most of their revising on the screen and are often content to leave blocks of writing as long as fifty pages on disks alone.

Writing is at once a way to be myself and a way to hide myself, and it always was. I was writing columns in high school under another name, Sam. I was writing themes in college, sounding like I had grown up in a family who always went to college, not as the coal miner's daughter I was. I am. Even now, I suspect myself of not showing who I am, really. But now I have the joy of understanding that *I* am not constructing a text to imitate me, but a text that will create new parts of me. I *really am* whoever I am in my writing at this moment. The writ-

ing—both the act and the words—is constructing a *me,*
not vice versa.

Writing, for me, is almost never a straightforward, dispassionate matter of presenting information or defending conclusions. I assume—indeed, hope—that writing
will entail an interplay of cognition and affect, of rationality and emotion, of conscious, disciplined effort and
intuition and inspiration.

I don't believe in a single, optimum writing process—
an algorithm we might teach students—because I
rarely follow the same process twice. Even the impulse
to write differs on each occasion, and the motive is
never pure. My most faithful muse is a department
head who asks for a list of publications each year, a week
or so before making her salary recommendations.

I write to be read. I used to keep a journal. I wrote it
as though it would be read after I died, but it was read
a few years ago (long before I die, I hope), and now that
it's been read, I don't write in it any more. Although I
wrote in the journal for it to be read, but was disturbed
when it was read—and I write articles to be read, but
they often are not published—I still say I write to be
read. Maybe I just harbor the *illusion* of being read.

To do important kinds of writing—to shape the deeper
meaning, to push forward the main themes, to write
about things that I don't yet understand—I need to be
intimate with the text. I must feel myself wholly within
the evolving text, and it within me: we are in each
other's skin, blood, flesh, self. We—text and I—formulate the text within the collaborative matrix of self, text,

and context. As I mark and shape the text, so the text shapes me, marks me, sometimes scars me.

WRITERS
ON
WRITING

Elizabeth Bell is associate professor of English and head of the English department at the University of South Carolina at Aiken, where she teaches courses in composition and American literature. Much of her interest involves interdisciplinary writing activities, currently including a project with Ronald Bell to incorporate writing into the secondary mathematics classroom. She has also directed for the past two years an interdisciplinary writing/computer/reading program for elementary- and secondary-school students in south-central South Carolina.

A native of Kentucky with a Ph.D. from the University of Louisville, where she served as Writing Clinic director, Bell has published articles on a variety of topics—from "The Slang Associations of D. H. Lawrence's Image Patterns in The Rainbow*" to a series of approaches for training the peer tutor working in the university-level writing lab. She has recently edited* Words That Must Somehow Be Said; Selected Essays of Kay Boyle *(1985), which reflects her continuing interest in nonfiction and autobiography.*

THE MAGIC CIRCLE: A MODERN MYSTICAL WAY OF LOOKING AT WRITING

Elizabeth Bell
University of South Carolina—Aiken

I even find a perverse kind of solace in the recurring "this-is-the-time-the-words-won't-come" syndrome I encounter each time I begin to write. It is a signal that all is as usual. And although I end each writing session by promising myself I'll never put myself through such agony again, a part of me knows the vow is just a ploy: I won't write again until next time.

Every now and then, an epiphany will fall out of the sky (or wherever they come from) and, with no consideration for time or place, hit a person on the head. A friend of mine, well over the age of consent, once collided with an epiphany in the midst of a party: "Oh! You mix gin and tonic together! That's why they call it a gin and tonic!" Not all epiphanies are of this magnitude, of course, but they all produce that moment of enlightenment which changes everything that comes after. Within the past several months, I've encountered three such flashes of light that have reshaped my perceptions of myself as writer and, consequently, as teacher of writing.

At first, I found this remodeled writer/teacher image surprising. After all, I have been writing in one context or another for the better part of several decades and teaching almost as long. This should be ample time for a healthy bit of knowledge about my motives, my skills, my talents, my problems—at least, I always thought so. But the conjunction of two events—an interdisciplinary writing workshop for faculty members on my campus and a late-night encounter with a damaged floppy disk—convinced me otherwise. Much as it pains me to admit this to myself, all these years I have been a stranger to the me who writes all those "pieces," as well as to the me who teaches all those other writers in my classes.

My first epiphany, which came to me late one Thursday afternoon in December in a classroom filled with a ragtag band of colleagues who had just been challenged to produce a piece of writing to be analyzed (criticized, enjoyed) by the group, involved my perception of why I write. Had you asked me the question in September or at Halloween or even on Thanksgiving Day, I would have said to you, "I write because I enjoy battling with my ideas, fighting with them and shaping them, until I understand them well enough to put them on paper." If a certain degree of smugness emerges from the depths of this answer, it can be chalked up to naiveté on the part of the speaker. The real answer to your question, I discovered, would sound something like this: "I write to be noticed by (adored by, taken seriously by, argued with by) my audience, for I find an inherent thrill in engaging someone's attention." This is a far riskier answer than the first; ideas that don't form well seldom (at least, one hopes seldom) reach the public forum of the printed, typed, written, or word-processed page, but audiences are always a volatile, reacting, evaluating reality for the writer. Because they have the authority and ability to judge one a fool or a genius, and anything in-between, one must approach them with respect. This is especially true for one willing to admit that the audience's range of reactions is a central factor in one's motives for writing.

This realization came about from my recognition that late December afternoon that I was going to write an informal essay that would be read, not by the anonymous or impersonal audience separated from me as writer by the journal page or the speaker's podium, but by real people I knew and worked with every day: the chemist, the philosopher, the political scientist, and the nurse, who would face me across the committee table or the lunch table next week and next month and next year. My first reaction was stark terror at the prospect. These people mattered to me personally in a way an abstract audience cannot. What if, I thought to myself, I sound foolish or, even worse, *shallow* to them?

What followed was an agonizing process of decision making: What should I write about, how scholarly should I sound, how many conclusions should I make, and—yes, I admit it—how long should my paper be? I almost rejected my first choice of topic because I thought it would sound too flaky to my friends. I almost adopted a dry and serious tone of voice because I wanted to convince these people I am a serious person. I almost couldn't write the paper. In the end, several abortive drafts later, I decided to trust my instincts, born of years of experience, and write what I wanted and in the manner I wanted *because*—and I consider this crucial (in fact, the first epiphany)—I felt my idea was offbeat enough to amuse and perhaps even intrigue my readers, my friends. In short, I felt the potential result in terms of audience response was worth the risk of appearing a fool.

By the time we gathered to read our works to each other, I was fascinated by my own reactions. Knowing I had written about an unconventional subject (Godzilla) in a nonscholarly tone of voice which I hoped would sound light but profound, I could hardly contain myself until my turn came to read my essay aloud to the group. Instead of being reticent, as I expected I would be, I found myself surprisingly—nay, astonishingly—eager. Outwardly I behaved with decorum, of course, but inwardly I hardly recognized myself! The mental image I hold of this experience is of a mature-looking, gray-haired first grader bouncing up and down in her seat waving her hand as if to say, "Call on me now! I want my turn; call on me now!" I wanted to engage my audience; for better or worse I craved their attention. And what's more, I realized that my response to *this* audience differed very little from my response to the more impersonal audiences we are accustomed to in our professional personae.

This has been a startling discovery for one who thought she wrote for the sake of ideas. Oh, I still love fighting with ideas and making them my own, finding words to express the concepts I believe deeply but as yet nonverbally, pacing the floor while I consume chocolate chip cookies and diet soft drinks, addressing the eternal verities. This for me is familiar territory. I even find a perverse kind of solace in the recurring "this-is-the-time-the-words-won't-come" syndrome I encounter each time I begin to write. It is a signal that all is as usual. And although I end each writing session by promising myself I'll never put myself through such agony again, a part of me knows the vow is just a ploy: I won't write again until next time. What draws me back, I now realize, is quite simply my infatuation with the audience, the living breathing reason I write, without whom the exercise of putting words on paper is totally and permanently irrelevant.

Meanwhile, that process of putting words on paper occasioned my encounter with the second of my epiphanies. From a habit forged in graduate school, when my children were hardly more than babies and evenings were hectic affairs at our house, I still do some of my most serious writing between the hours of midnight and two, when only the most stubborn insomniacs are moving about. Until just recently, this arrangement has worked beautifully; but now that I find myself enchanted with the computer, I have had to make some adjustments: I have had to undertake the expense of buying a computer to use at home and to tie myself more closely to a specific location—the computer's set-up—just for the privilege of working at the time I'm most comfortable. I have had to ask myself if the adjustments I have had to make are worth the effort.

And this brings us to the night in question. With a morning deadline staring me in the face, I found myself at 1:05 A.M. in possession of an unusable floppy disk, absolutely no spare disks (a situation I have since corrected), and no options available for obtaining a new floppy disk. Even my computer-buff friends would not have taken well an early morning telephone call from someone trying to convince them that borrowing a floppy disk is a useful endeavor at 1:05 A.M. Without a floppy disk, however, one's computer might just as well be a geranium planter.

Having written for a considerable number of years before the computer entered my life, I saw no immediate emergency. I merely uncovered from the depths of my desk drawer the yellow legal pad and ballpoint pen that had served me well in years past. And I began to write, just as I used to, with the inserts and deletions that are typical of my composing. I found myself putting Insert A on the back of page 1 and Insert B on the scrap of paper that was too big to waste. I paperclipped Insert B to page 2, just over the paragraph I marked out with long slashes of blue ink. By the time I decided that part of page 7 actually belonged in the middle of Insert X that went with the content of page 4, I couldn't find it. In fact, I wasn't sure what "it" I was looking for. I was not amused.

I found myself frustrated by thumbing through pages of messed up, marked out, arrow-laden prose in search of a train of thought that sounded logical in my head, but appeared—when I could find it at all —fragmented and haphazard on the written page. This had not bothered me before; I have written this way ever since I was old enough to care about my writing. I had accepted without whimper the inconveniences and scavenger hunts that my method of writing necessitated because I had had, until now, no choice. My method of writing had not altered, but what had changed, I realized, was that now with my word processor I am able to see my work as a clean-copy whole, no matter at what stage of my composing I am. Now as I reread my prose, as I do quite often during the course of putting together my writing, I no longer need to hunt for the transitions that will show me where the next section is. Instead, I can start at the beginning and read through the piece to the end, or I can begin with a section and read until I decide to end it. I value that ability.

I discovered something else personally significant that night. I found that I feel closer to the text of my word-processed writing because I can conceptualize it in more coherent terms than I have been able to do ever before. I can concentrate more completely on the content and the sound of the piece without the distractions of my own disorganization. This epiphany, that the process of being able to see and read one's work-in-process without surface-level distractions can change one's relationship to the writing, is in some ways similar to the gin-and-tonic epiphany of my friend: It is somewhat obvious to anyone familiar with the genre. Any teacher who has read stacks of student papers knows that the neatly written papers, especially if they come toward the end of the stack, enjoy a more kindly reception than their illegible, coffee-stained, more hapless colleagues. Whether or not the appearance of the paper ultimately affects our evaluation of the writing, it certainly affects the way we read it. The same, I discovered, is true of our own writing. Our way of reading our own writing—and perhaps our understanding of the purpose for doing it—changes when we are more immediately able to concentrate on its substantive levels instead of its accidental ones.

Does writing with a word processor help one produce better prose? Only a naif would argue either side of that question in front of an audience of experienced or professional writers. While I don't wish to tackle that issue, I will address a related one that also concerns the value of word processing, not as a panacea to every writing problem or even as an advantage for every writer, but as a practical and beneficial tool for writers who revise heavily as they write. Personal experience has shown me that the word processor makes this kind of writing process less frustrating because it makes what I have already said more accessible. It makes the interior sounds and cadences of my own voice more familiar to me by more readily recording them as I hear them in my mind, without the interruptions inherent in the visible, permanent strikeovers and inserts of the handwritten draft. It makes a clean copy of my work available anytime I want it, at any stage of my writing. In answer to my own question, the adjustments I must make to accommodate the vagaries of the computer are indeed worth the trouble they cause me, for the computer has opened for me a new conception of my writing, one that would be impossible without the technology of the floppy disk and the computer chip.

When I first began this essay, I thought I had two epiphanies to discuss. In fact, if you could see my original drafts (safely tucked away in my backup file on disk), you would see that number prominently displayed in my first paragraph. But as I reread my work, I realized that I saw three different recognitions that are of equal importance to me. I suppose this third one is a variant form of epiphany, produced as a kind of spontaneous generation, for although I have been thinking about my own processes and concerns as a writer, I find that I have also been making discoveries about my processes and concerns as a teacher of writing.

The interdisciplinary faculty writing workshop renewed my ties to myself as student. I experienced in a context more familiar to me in a remote time than in the present, the subtle, tenuous relationship spawned in the classroom between writer and subject, writer and audience. The immediacy of the writing assignment and the audience, and my recognition of their power to affect my daily life, renewed my awareness of the difficult task we give our students, the risks we make them take, every day of their experiences with us. On the other hand, my encounter with my disk introduced me to the joy of "hearing" my writing in a new way, of being able to conceptualize it more readily than I had ever been able to do before. For the experienced writer in me, this new vision reintroduced me to something I had forgotten over the years: the awe one associates with beginning writers who receive the first positive response to their writing or small puppies who hear themselves bark for the first time: It's an astonishing encounter with their own voice, but they know they'll want to make that noise again. My realization of this delicate interplay of the emotional and intellectual concerns that mark the human being engaged in writing convinced me that I teach student writers because I want to guide them toward their own discoveries about the nature of writing and of themselves as human beings who are involved in writing.

My students, after all, share some of the same concerns with which more experienced writers habitually contend. Students, too, want to sound intelligent to their audiences (and they fear the times they don't). They, too, want to engage their audience's attention for a more substantive response than just red marks in the margin of the page and a grade they may or may not have expected. Encased somewhere within every page they write is the student's tacit plea, "Hear me! Hear *me.*" For some of these students, the ones for whom previous attempts at writing have produced an awareness of problems and fears that have become so overwhelming they have stifled the sounds of the students' own thoughts, I can say, "Listen to yourself. Hear what you have to say, for it is important." Yes, the problems will need to be corrected, but only after the message has found its place on paper. For other students who have very clear ideas about their thoughts, I sometimes need to say, "Take me, the reader, with you. I can't follow until you set up more of a guideline for me." Clear, convincing writing is, after all, reader-oriented. For other students, who need only to polish and prune their style and content, I can say, "Make your choices. Decide what effect you want, for it is in your power to create it." From all of these students, I learn about my own fears, my own processes, my own choices.

It is, I believe, this magic circle that exists within the composition classroom, where writer becomes audience and audience turns into writer, where generation of ideas and responses to them mingle, that draws me back year after year to the "same" composition courses I have been teaching since the beginning, with students who allow me to share their processes of discovery anew each time I read their work and who demonstrate to me consistently the value of putting word to paper. I have discovered, in short, that trying to separate my view of myself as writer from my perception of myself as teacher of writing creates a distortion I find misleading.

Conclusions are always difficult to formulate, whether they be the mental ones or the composing ones. When one is dealing with matters as fragmentary but monumental as epiphanies, the problem is even more pronounced. But if I may generalize from the specifics l have described, as indeed I have been doing all along, and if I can make what is patently subjective sound more objective and thereby more logical, I will contend that writers—students or professionals—write the way they do because they find something about the process or the result sufficiently rewarding to counterbalance the agony of writing. For the lucky ones, there is real joy in writing. In addition, writers choose to compose in ways, contexts, and processes that provide a modicum of physical, emotional, human comfort to them during the writing's gestation, for instinctively they want their message—whatever it may be— to find its way into the world, and they will do whatever is possible to help it reach its public form. And finally, writers—if they are to be writers worth reading—continue to learn, to write, to read, and to respond to writing, for to do otherwise would be to lose part of themselves.

Jacqueline Berke is professor of English and director of writing at Drew University, where she has been teaching for more than twenty years. Author of a composition textbook, Twenty Questions for the Writer *(4th ed., 1985), and coauthor with George Hammerbacher of* What Every Writer Should Know About Language: The Story of English and Guide to Good Usage *(1986), she has published many articles on writing and rhetoric, as well as light essays and light verse on a variety of topics.*

As feminist critic she has also published and delivered papers at the Midwest Modern Language Association, the American Studies Association, the Conference on College Composition and Communication, the College English Association, among others. Her special field of interest is mothers and daughters/mothers and sons in literature, with a particular focus on what she calls the new Jewish mother. She is currently working on a full-length feminist critique of this subject: The New Jewish Mother—A Popular Image Revised and Humanized by Women Writers.

WEE WILLIE WINKIE AND WHY I WRITE*

Jacqueline Berke
Drew University

I must remind myself that not everyone has the drive, the determination, the willfulness, the wiliness, the stubbornness, the quirkiness that goes with being a writer; with writing for a living —or if not for a living (does anyone *make a living as a writer?), then writing as a serious and chronic condition of living.*

Why do I write?

Confronting this question in a recent interview, the Canadian poet/novelist, Margaret Atwood, called it a redundancy, like "Why does the sun shine?" The real question, said Atwood, is "Why doesn't everyone write?"

Ah, at one time I assumed that everyone did in fact write, just as everyone read or was read to. Everyone heard the words in the book and then, later on, perhaps in bed at night, heard them again—like a song singing inside their heads . . . singing . . . singing:

Wee Willie Winkie runs through the town,
Upstairs and downstairs in his nightgown,
Rapping at the window, crying through the lock,
Are the children all in bed, for now it's eight o'clock.

Eight o'clock . . . eight o'clock . . . time to go to bed. I'd have had my bath, hot and steaming; hair shampooed and painfully unknotted with the torturous fine comb; then vigorously dried, my mother wielding the towel like a weapon—and chanting:

*This essay was written for Allen L. Weatherby, late of the English Department and dean emeritus at Drew, a man of many good words. "It's all in the ear," he'd say about writing, smiling his warm, easy smile. I remember it well.

11

Rub-a-dub-dub, three men in a tub
And who do you think they be?
The butcher, the baker, the candlestick maker,
They all sailed out to sea.

They all sailed out to sea . . . they all sailed out to sea . . . out to sea,
out to sea . . . look at me . . . in a tree . . . now I'm free . . . one, two,
three . . .

So it went in those long ago days of childhood. The words sailed out
to sea. They tumbled out to sea. They rumbled, stumbled, fumbled,
crumbled, mumbled out to sea. So it went, with Old Mother Goose
singing her silly songs (a dillar, a dollar / a ten o'clock scholar), incom-
prehensible, nonsensical—but who cared? (and there I met an old man
who would not say his prayers / I took him by the left leg and threw him
down the stairs). So it went, with that sickly child, later known as Robert
Louis Stevenson, gazing longingly out the window from the lonely land
of counterpane (how do you like to go up in a swing? . . . oh, I do think
it's the pleasantest thing).
   So it went . . . so it went with A. A. Milne and *Now We Are Six.* (The
king asked the queen / and the queen asked the dairy maid / could we
have some butter / for the royal slice of bread?) Well, of course, of
course (I'll go and tell the cow now / before she goes to bed).

Songwriter Bob Dylan once remarked that "Some people work in
gas stations and they're poets." Listen to this, Bob Dylan: Some people
are kids and *think they're poets* (isn't everyone?) "Poets write of
spring / but I sing my praises / straight to you / cold, hard, long winter
. . ." There it was—cold, hard, long and wonderful winter in New York
City; and there I was, age ten, (not even working in a gas station!) yet
regaling my teacher daily with my poems: "I must tell you this Miss
Foley, I simply must. Yesterday I went up to the Cloisters in Fort Tryon
Park and I looked out over the Hudson River:

far, far beyond the water
wasteland stretching far
   far beyond the water
wasteland . . . wasteland . . .

"Oh my dear!" Miss Foley frowned. "Now that you're in sixth
grade, you musn't imitate."
   "Imitate?"
   Miss Foley looked at me knowingly. "T. S. Eliot."
   T. S. . . . WHO?

On my application to graduate school I would later write—cryptically—that of my early literary influences Edna St. Vincent Millay and Dorothy Parker were prominent. Also Thomas Stearns Eliot.

I was admitted anyhow.

"Would you like to teach a section of freshman composition?" the chairman of the department asked me one afternoon as I arrived in class. He taught Milton, was even named for Milton (J. Milton French), and I thought that some day I too might teach Milton:

Of Man's First Disobedience, and the Fruit
Of that Forbidden Tree, whose mortal taste
Brought Death into the World, and all our woe . . .
Sing Heav'nly Muse. . . .

Sing . . . O Sing Heav'nly Muse . . . Sing O Sing . . .

They did not sing, my students. In response to a writing assignment I had entitled "The trouble with . . ." (surely the students would fill in provocative topics that would raise lively class discussion), one student wrote: "The trouble with the English language is that there's too many words and we don't know what to do with them."

THUD!

Rub-a-dub-dubber . . . O flubber-dub-tubber . . . O wubber-crub-snubber . . . O plubber . . . O fubber . . . O grubber-lub-lubber.

Alfred Kazin quotes Thoreau as saying, "You have to be strong in the legs to write." Such a statement, Kazin concludes, signifies "spiritual self-confidence."

Such a statement gives me vertigo. I hate to raise the gender issue here (somehow it seems so old-hat and me-too at this advanced stage of the women's movement), yet I must say this: Talking about writing in terms of strength and self-confidence and astonishment ("A writer lives . . . in a state of astonishment," says William Sansom in his *Writer's Journal*) strikes me as so relentlessly masculine—so lofty, so self-assured, so tall in the saddle—that I am unable to connect at all; I find it totally alien to my experience and observation.

"The best time for planning a book," Agatha Christie once said, "is while you're doing the dishes." Now *that* I can relate to!

While I was doing the dishes (and doing the dishes and doing the dishes) I planned my textbook on writing. "What *is* good writing, anyhow?" an irritated student had asked me one day at the end of an especially arduous class editing session. She really meant "What in the h——— *do* you like since you obviously don't like what *we* write?" It was my first year of teaching and I had to be on my toes. *What is good writing?* As the question hovered in the air, the students stopped shuffling books and papers and silently, stonily awaited my reply.

"The Gettysburg Address," I shot back, as startled by my answer as they were.

Driving home that afternoon I kept thinking about what I had said. Of course I loved the Gettysburg Address and practically had it memorized (that government of the people, by the people, for the people . . .) What a miracle of language! Notwithstanding, did the Gettysburg Address provide an appropriate standard of expectation for students in freshman composition? To earn an A in my course did a student have to write the Gettysburg Address?

Well . . . uh . . . uh . . . yes.

As a penance for being so mean, so unreasonable, so intractable, I spent a total of three and a half years working on my textbook. In my own voice, based on my own teaching experience, my training as a journalist, my ten years of freelance writing, I would justify the ways of rhetoric to freshmen, to the fit however few. Above all, I would adopt an approach students could understand (for God's sake, I told myself, don't call it a *heuristic!*). After several inauspicious beginnings, I finally worked out a simple, journalistically inspired plan: twenty questions for the writer. Ah, what tantalizing projections followed! Part I would be called "Writing as a Human Activity" (Wee Willie Winkie runs through the town) because that's what writing *is:* a special way of using language on paper, a special way of behaving (upstairs and downstairs in his nightgown); then I'd move on to Part II, "The Limits of Language" because—let's face it—every medium has its resistances as well as its strengths (Rapping at the window, crying through the lock); the challenge—clearly—is to overcome the resistances (Are the children all in bed) and—as I'd go on to show in Parts III and IV—to cultivate the strengths "to the best possible effect" (for now it's eight o'clock).

Eight o'clock . . . eight o'clock . . . time to go to press. What a collage of time units required to produce one book: a one-year sabbatical plus a one-semester leave plus summers and semester breaks and Christmas and spring vacations and mornings, noons, and nights as I could squeeze them in and around teaching and family responsibilities. Whew!

"How do you have the patience, the energy?" asked an admiring colleague, with just a faint hint of derision in his voice, suggesting that beyond admiration he suspected that I must be crazy. My answer confirmed his suspicion. "It isn't hard," I told him. "All you have to be is fanatic, compulsive, and obsessive."

Which, of course, I was and still am. Mercifully, or perhaps more's the pity (depending on your point of view), not everyone is similarly "hung up" on writing. Sure, my students want to write well; and just as sure, many of them *do* write well—better and better and better as they go along. But, I often want to tell them, they could—if they pressed still harder—write *still better.* It's then I must remind myself that not everyone has the drive, the determination, the willfulness, the wiliness, the stubbornness, the quirkiness that goes with being a writer; that is, with writing for a living—or if not for a living (does *anyone* make a living as a writer?), then writing as a serious and chronic condition of living. So be it.

I still love the Gettysburg Address, but other things are going on in class these days. We issue a list of "Touchstones of Good Writing" in the English Department. Students not familiar with Matthew Arnold feel the term is vaguely clinical (like "gallstones," I guess). No matter. In order to earn a passing grade, everyone taking the introductory writing course must learn to write clearly (more or a little less). As E. B. White, my ultimate authority, put it: "Clarity, clarity, clarity, if you must be obscure, be obscure clearly." White's observations are equally apt on the subject of economy: "A sentence should have no unnecessary words for the same reason that a machine should have no unnecessary parts." Beyond clarity and conciseness one would hope for a modicum of cogency (if cogency can be said to come in modicums). Naturally I would raise the flag for *all* the rhetorical virtues: grace, euphony, rhythm, vigor, liveliness, etcetera—in a word, for *power.* But I've learned to set priorities and stand behind minimum requirements. I often think of John Ciardi's assertion that "there is no teaching of writing, only the coaching one can give to self-learners." Good luck, I say, to all of us who coach student writers. It's those indefatigable pushers and plodders, those fellow-fanatic self-learners who pass through my courses that I like to keep track of over the years.

In an essay paying tribute to his teachers who perished in the Holocaust, survivor Elie Wiesel says that "for me writing is a *matzeva,* an invisible tombstone erected to the memory of the dead unburied." We can understand that writing as commemoration has a special significance and urgency for this gifted and haunted writer whose generation —as he tells us—"lost everything, even our cemeteries."

On another level—an existential level, let's call it—I believe writing is a *matzeva* for most writers. For however happy one's past, however bright and blessed, it slips away; it is lost, irretrievable except for memory. No wonder novelist Anita Brookner claims that "for the writer there is no oblivion. Only endless memory." An image, a voice, an event, a face, a place—the word restores, resurrects; the word memorializes. The word . . . the word . . .

> "I knew it wasn't right but I couldn't think of the right word," a
> student admits at a class editing session. "I just gave up."
> "Did you check with the thesaurus?" a fellow student asks helpfully.
> "What's a synonym for 'thesaurus'?" quips a third student (later attributing the line to a TV comedian).
> For a moment we all think, then laugh. Then we go back to what this
> Advanced Nonfiction Writing course is all about: it's about words and the
> thesaurus and Webster 3 and the OED; it's about the endless struggle to
> find the right word, the precisely right word that will work within a precisely defined context.

The difference between the precisely right word and the word that isn't precisely right, as Mark Twain once explained, is the difference between lightning and a lightning bug.

A student confesses in her journal: "I began to write early on in high school when I realized I couldn't do the simplest algebraic problem." "How poignant!" I think, stirred to a confession of my own, a silent confession, as I sit there with editorial pencil poised above the margin. Shall I tell her how it was with me?—my struggle with signs and symbols, formulas, equations, axioms, theorems, triangles, rectangles, parallelograms, hypotenuses (hypotenusi?), square roots, and proofs, proofs, proofs. How my head spun!

What can I say now? What can I say about math and physics and the newly sprung computer sciences? Shall I tell this student that even now (as autumn leaves / drift by my window) I sometimes think I'll have another go at it; audit a course with one of my math colleagues, always so cool and casual, assuming that *anyone* can fathom their mysterious lickety-split formulations stretching from one end of the long blackboard to the other. I wonder, as I wistfully contemplate the prospect of entering their wordless world of x's and y's, whether Wee Willie Winkie will be any help.

Lil Brannon is associate professor of English at the State University of New York at Albany. She is a member of the executive committee of the Conference on College Composition and Communication; of the delegate assembly of the Modern Language Association; and the executive committee as well as the team of consultant/evaluators of the Council of Writing Program Administrators.

She is the author of two books: Writers Writing, *written with Vara Neverow-Turk and Melinda Knight; and* Rhetorical Traditions and the Teaching of Writing, *written with C. H. Knoblauch. Her other publications include numerous scholarly articles and contributions to several books.*

NOTHING BUT THE TRUTH

' *Lil Brannon*

State University of New York at Albany

I write all the time, every day, usually in the morning, but always every day. I write some of my best stuff at work, at my desk, with pen and paper, and plenty of interruptions. I need interruptions. Give me quiet and I go nuts. Give me solitude and I'll vacuum. I fill my writing up with people. And I never stop. Take that back. I did stop once, and learned never to do that again. Stopping is bad only because starting up is so hard. The hardest part is getting started. So if you don't stop, you skip the hardest part. So I don't stop.

It's hard to imagine why anyone would ever want to return to Commerce, Texas—that low down, dry rot, hell of a place. But they do 'cause it's an addiction. And once you set foot in it, you can never really leave it. Something keeps pulling you back, back to the dust and the heat. Pulling you, like the earth itself pulling back every attempt to pave it over and start again. Sink holes—lives become sink holes.

One old timer talking outside the Chat-n-Chew remembered how silly it was for people like me to believe—like city slickers want to believe—that they wouldn't feel the place in their bones. Like those men at the university thinking they could build a swimming pool—thinking they could tame the place, even spending three million dollars on it. But the earth ate it alive in two days.

There's nothing like this place, like Commerce, Texas, and once I was there, I could never leave, never really leave.

A plausible fiction—a story—so who cares if it's true or not? And who is to know? I did live once in Commerce, Texas, and they did— those crazy university people—they did try to build a swimming pool, and I remember the water table being so high that the concrete cracked. But it may have been a tornado that really did it in— blew the roof right off the place—ruined the swimming pool, bowling alleys, racketball courts—the whole thing gone. But the real facts

19

don't matter so much as the story. The story has to be right. The story. After all, who is to say what's real? The eyewitnesses are all scattered—Jeanette's in Lubbock, Joyce in Logan, Jerry and JoAnn, they say, are in North Carolina, and Butch, I imagine, is a rodeo clown somewhere in Oklahoma. I guess someone might call Brenda —last word had it that she was in Commerce—but she would never tell. So I'm safe.

Telling tales is risky business—risky, that is, if you want to know the truth. Facts are a lot easier than the truth. Facts only need witnesses —need corroborating storytellers. I have none here—no one to step forward and say, "Hey y'all, Lil ain't joking. This is the way it is." All I have is the way I remember the story. And if I can fashion it carefully, say it just right, then I may have crafted the truth, however uncertain the facts. So with that as a preamble (or a downright ramble if you want to get technical), let's get down to business. Tom tells me that you want to know how I write.

Can't imagine why anyone would care about that, why anyone would give a hoot, why anyone would be dying to know how I put words on paper, anyone—except Alice, and only Alice because she asked me once, asked flat out when she caught me writing poetry back in Commerce, back then when I'd gone into hiding, been in hiding since my experience with a famous Southern poet back in college. See, I had gone to this small college, this women's college back in South Carolina. Each year the fifteen women in the creative writing seminar got to have their poetry commented on by the distinguished poet who they imported to campus each spring. Every year I was in college I applied to be in that class—loved writing poetry—thought I could spend my whole life doing that. No one told me that most poets get paid in copies of journals (hard to pay rent on that). No one told me to my face either how godawful my poetry was. I should have known, should have inferred, each year when I was turned down for that class. It wasn't until my senior year that I got in, and then probably because I was the only English major who hadn't taken it.

Well, about midterm we sent our three best poems to this famous poet. I thought mine were great, couldn't wait until he came to Converse to discuss them with the class. He came. He came to the class. We sat around a large oak table; he stood at a podium. He began. Miss Smith? One young woman raised her hand. And then he would describe the imagery or his sense of the poem. It was fantastic. I waited impatiently, waited for him to get to mine. He did another, then another, and then Miss Borop?—that was me—I raised my hand. The room changed. He walked from behind the podium over to where I was sitting. Folded my poems. Bent over. Looked me square in the eye—and said, "You need to learn to lie." I was dumb-founded. But somehow I managed to say, "Mr. Dickey, I thought po-etry was about truth." And then he said, "If this is truth, you need to learn to lie."

That's how I learned about truth, how it's important to a good story or a poem to get it right even if it ain't accurate. It's kinda like what I told Alice that day in Commerce. There's no need getting all confused with the facts, if you haven't got the truth in the first place. A story's no good at all if it ain't the truth. That's why I had gone into hiding. I needed time to figure out how to do it. Lie, that is. I needed to learn to lie. And what better way to learn than by writing poems. Like I told Alice—before that day with Mr. Dickey, writing was pretty easy, a simple matter of recording facts. What I did was school writing. Even won awards for it, like the eighth grade poetry writing contest for this gem:

The Duffer

Carefully he gripped his club
and took the proper stance.
And then he viewed the fairways
and noted with a glance
the ponds, the green, and traps.

"Three hundred yards," he thought to drive.
The golf ball at his feet.
He knew before he took his swing
the setting was complete.

Palmer, Hogan, Nicklaus, Snead,
inspired his every mood.
And now without a doubt he felt
he had it in the groove.

The club he swung with mighty power.
His form was great to see.
But when he looked to find his ball,
it still was on the tee.

Now don't get me wrong. There's nothing wrong in and of itself with school writing, nothing except when you begin to believe that it might work someplace else, someplace outside of school. School writ-ing is like one of those stories which ain't funny unless you were there.

It was near Commerce, Texas, sometime after my talk with Alice that I went public again, and this time for good. Read my poems out loud to some ladies in double-knit pants suits at Paris Junior College. Tony Clark and Joe Murphey, the real poets, were why they were there. I was the warm-up. Tony and Joe figured that they had to really want to hear poetry if they stayed through mine. Not long after that Charlie and LuAnn put me on the airwaves in their talk to poets series called *Quiet by the Swamp,* complete with call-in questions, just like Phil Donahue or Dr. Ruth. It was halfway through that show—halfway into my response to some ingrate or lunatic—that I realized there must be a better way to make a living. A poet of the people, a writer writing to the general public wasn't all it was cracked up to be. I decided right there in midsentence that it would be lots easier to become an academic. And so I did.

An academic writer, a writer who spins the facts into truth, is what I am. A storyteller who keeps her presence hidden, her voice in a whisper. I didn't give poetry up altogether. Just reassigned priorities. It's much easier to write statements that only four people in the country will read (though a few dozen more will pretend they have), much easier than answering questions from lunatics or having to read out loud to ladies in double-knit. It feels like it must feel like to the guy on the desert island who writes a letter, puts in in a wine bottle, and tosses it in the Atlantic. Academic writing is the silent treatment. Every now and then someone will say, "Oh, I used your book one semester. Yeah, I used it. I think it was your book. Yeah, it was. I used it." That's how I know my audience. I write to teachers like me. If I understand what I write, then they will understand, or at least believe that they do or pretend that they do or forget that they didn't. Much easier than writing to a bunch of lunatics.

I write because I have to. It's an addiction, writing. If you give up one kind, you have to take up another. So I've stayed with the academic stuff, partly because it's easier than poetry, but mostly because I have to. It's an addiction. Some academics get addicted to reading. Glad I didn't. They're the ones who get in trouble. The BOSS doesn't care how much you read, doesn't reward it. The BOSS promotes the writer—the academic writer that is—'cause he's like the lunatic when it comes to stories or poems—doesn't know the good from the bad. So I'm lucky in my addiction. I'm paid to keep up my habit.

But even if they didn't pay me, I'd probably still do it. Just not on Saturdays or vacations, but still every morning before I go to school. See, until I put words down—black on white (or green on black since I got my computer)—I don't know for sure what I'm thinking. If I keep those ideas in my head, they seem great—seem logical, clear, fluent, articulate, meaningful, and important. When I commit them to paper or screen, I see what I've got—sometimes logical and clear, fluent, articulate, meaningful, and important. Sometimes dull, flat, dumb, silly, trivial, and crude. Take that back. Most of the time dull, flat, dumb, silly, trivial, and crude. And there's no way to predict which is which. I have to write to figure it out.

I write all the time, every day, usually in the morning, but always every day. I write some of my best stuff at work, at my desk, with pen and paper, and plenty of interruptions. I need interruptions. Give me quiet and I go nuts. Give me solitude and I'll vacuum. I fill my writing up with people. And I never stop. Take that back. I did stop once, and learned never to do that again. Stopping is bad only because starting up is so hard. The hardest part is getting started. So if you don't stop, you skip the hardest part. So I don't stop. I write five things at once, so that I'm never really conscious of starting something from scratch and I'm never really conscious of finishing anything either.

I do know for a fact that I've never used any of those prewriting heuristics—no loops, no cubes, no tagnemics, no topoi. But I do freewrite, if by freewrite you mean write like mad while the idea is hot. If I just write, write, write, the language will bring with it ideas. And some of them ain't bad. But I have to make myself do it. There's something in my brain that doesn't like freewriting, doesn't like the messiness of it, doesn't want to write down stuff that isn't good to start with. And it clicks on sometimes, making me stop and check, and erase (or delete from the screen), making me craft each sentence as I go. Early on in writing I keep trying to lose that part of my brain, lose her in the laundry room, or the grocery store, lose her so that I can write to see what will happen. I'm better off early on if she's gone. If I can't shake her, I still write—but instead of pages, I get a few sentences of finely crafted, parallel and logical stuff—sometimes usable, oftentimes not. If I can't shake her, the writing goes slowly, and all I can do is hope I'm headed in the right direction, 'cause nothing is worse than being on a slow boat to China and winding up in Panama City.

If she's shook, I write, not worrying about this or that, just write to see where I'm headed. But I don't write like mad until I think I have my snappy introduction, until I think I know where I'm starting from—not that I ever end up starting from there—but I like to think that I'm starting up where I want to start—on solid ground—on a snappy introduction. I think it was Mrs. Wilder in the sixth grade who said you must have a snappy introduction. And she sits on my shoulder until this day, making me write those snappy introductions so that I can get to writing to see what I think. I never set out to compare/contrast, extend a definition, analyze, argue, explain, enumerate, or any of those rhetorical mode things that you see in some composition textbooks. So I never have an approach or a format in mind when I start. I just write to see what I think, to see what will emerge on its own. Ideas are interesting things—they will find their own form—they will structure themselves—and it's not magic—its the way of those critters. But they can get away from you—ideas. They can fool you into thinking that you've got something when you don't or that you've said something when you haven't. That's why I need people.

My writing is filled with people. Usually those who stop by the office about some other matter and see me writing. I say to them, "Come on in and have a seat, while I finish this sentence." Then I have them trapped, seated right there, seeing me write. Good manners dictate that they have to ask about what I'm working on. So I have an audience right there, seated in my office, captured and primed. Now someone who is there to ask me something can't say my writing is terrible, can't say my writing needs more work. If you are captured, all you can say is that it seems interesting, that you would like to hear it all when its finished, that the idea is intriguing. My captured readers keep me writing by telling me to keep on writing.

Sometimes I make the mistake of asking a critic reader to hear my work too early. My husband's one of those. And so are some people at work. They are the one's who expect logic and order, expect you to have—of all things—organization before you have even settled on the idea. They hear your work as if it were finished, not half-baked and rambling and convoluted like my early writing is. They ask questions, hard questions, questions like "How does this follow that?" or "What do you mean when you say blah, blah, blah?" I get mad. I get really mad. I say, "How can you ask me those questions when you see that I'm just beginning? I don't know how this follows; it just does right now." And they say, "Don't get mad. What did you want me to say? You asked me what I thought." And I say, "I wanted you to say that it was good, interesting, an intriguing idea, that you would like to hear it all once I was finished." And they say, "Well, why didn't you say so. It's good; it's interesting." And I say, "No it's not; you're just saying that because I told you to."

I get mad too if my writing doesn't pass the critic reader's test when I'm ready for a demanding reader, if they spot a hole that I overlooked. I usually blame them, think they're dumb for not knowing what I was saying when it is perfectly clear what I was saying. I get mad because deep down inside I know that I have to change the whole damn thing, that they are right, that I haven't said what I wanted to say. Nothing is worse than having to start all over again when you thought you were done, nothing except starting from scratch. Critic readers have been good for me, even though they make me mad, 'cause they've forced me to do my best work, forced me to push deeper, forced me to discover ideas I didn't know I knew. Without them I'd have settled for less. Close counts for me. Just getting close. My critic readers make me nail it down.

Close counts for me because I circle around ideas; I can feel 'em corralled, and once corralled, I know I have 'em, even if a reader might need a map and compass to find 'em. The crazy thing about academic writing, though, is that readers don't want to work hard, don't want a map and a compass to find the idea, don't want a safari adventure. They want it laid flat out: boom, boom, boom, ideas that are clear and logical. My ideas don't come that way, don't come like Sherman marching through Georgia, boom, boom, boom. Finding my ideas is like a safari adventure—dangerous and exciting, with interesting game and breathtaking sights along the way. The exploration is the fun of it. My drafts, then, are an adventure, are the footprints of my exploration, all the back roads, dead ends, and genuine discoveries along the way. Because they are fun for me, I keep on thinking that they will be fun for the critic reader. But no. No, the critics keep on wanting everything to be logical. So my work in writing is making my ideas logical, making them look as if they came effortlessly in a logical order, making them look as if they make inevitable sense.

Telling tales logically is tricky business—tricky, that is, cause it's often hard to see the truth in all the facts. What details might seem important at the time, what might seem like they lead to the big banana and so seem so very important at the time, can be nothing more than the things that got you thinking, nothing more than important private moments. Or they just might lead to the big banana, just might be the point on which to rest your case. Knowing which facts lead to the big banana is tricky business, 'cause no one except you will know when it's right, and then you only know because you see it. Which is a roundabout way of saying that you know when you know. But just in case I might mess up—discard a fact that leads to the big banana—I save everything, every scrap, word, phrase, doodle—everything. I save it all, even years after the essay has seen print. I save all drafts, all notes, all thinking. I save it because ideas—good ideas—are so hard to come by and are so hard to locate. I keep all my thinking so that if I remember that I thought of something before, I can go back and find it smack dab in the middle of a scrap of paper I saved. Trouble is, though, that I have yet to go back to any of it. Not once.

But I have it all, just in case I need it. And don't worry, I don't lose any facts because of the computer either. I print all the time, print every bit and piece, so that I can have it all out there in front of me. I lose nothing, just in case.

So I have it all out there in front of me. And I try to figure it out, how it might go so that it looks logical. What should I say first, second, later. I ask myself hard questions, those very same questions of the critic reader. "What do I mean by this? How does this relate to that? If I say this, how can this follow?" I work on small chunks at a time, and I have to get the first one right before I can go on to the next. I fill my writing up with people. And I get mad if they aren't hard on me. See, by this time, I know it's good, intriguing, and interesting. What I don't know is if it makes sense to an outsider. So if a reader says something nice, something like "I like it" or "That's interesting" or "What do you think about your text?" I get mad. I want them to be tough—to get me talking. I want them to challenge those ideas I've constructed. I want my ideas to generate talk, to make sense, to provoke. I want a good story. And the only way to get there for me is through the challenges of tough readers.

That's why I write a lot with other people. That and it's never quite as lonely. That and it's just plain more fun. You get to talk a lot. You get to hear yourself think. The best collaborations I've had were those where there was a lot of talk, where we would talk out the ideas and write as we talked, dictate the piece. The first draft would be a conglomerate of stuff—talked-out ideas, sixteen examples, a ramble or two here and there. A draft much like my first drafts—way too long, a few gems hidden within a jungle. Then, each of us would try our hand at making it right—working on this part here, that part there, adding and deleting, whatever it needed. Then we would meet and see what we had and cut and write and add and substract together. But the focus was on talk, the talking out of the ideas, the asking of questions, and the exploring. The essay or chapter was just the by-product of the talk. The talk was the important part. The talk was important because it would generate hundreds of ideas which didn't fit into the paper but which could become papers later on. The talk created a future for ideas. The writing never seemed hard either—time consuming but not hard. There were real deadlines— the next meeting, so I would have to have my part completed. And the work sessions were always intellectual highs, safaris where you always found game, big game.

My work with Cy is the best example. We begin sitting at the kitchen table with pad and paper and ideas which we generated through talk a few days before at work. What's good about the talk at work is that we come at the problem from different places—him from the stratosphere, me from the earth. One newcomer once asked a friend of ours why we couldn't agree on anything. He had only heard the talk. Now, what's interesting about the kitchen table part is that Cy and I are very different writers—I like to corral, he likes to march through Georgia. So he likes to play scribe when we write out loud, so that he works out all those little connections along the way. I make it hard for him, though, 'cause I'm always thinking three paragraphs ahead of where we are writing, and if he says something that might take us in a direction away from where I'm going I *x*-it. He doesn't take *x*-ing very well. Sometimes he gets stubborn and insists on going in the direction he's going in, even though he almost always doesn't know where he's headed. He says the logic dictates that he go in his direction. So I let him, but I write like mad quietly on my own notepad to keep hold of my idea, 'cause I know it is important. After all it's in the corral. Sooner or later we get to my idea—when the logic dictates it. He hates it when I play scribe, can't figure out how I ever wind up with anything approaching logical when I let my writing stay so flabby and loose while I circle round my idea. I just don't pay him any attention, 'cause I know sooner or later I can make it look logical.

When we finish a first draft we know that the idea is nailed down —too nailed down—sometimes dead with overwriting. Talk will do that to you, make you say too much, say everything that's on your mind when half will do. So revision is usually deleting all those things which seemed perfectly reasonable when we said them, but now weigh down a lively idea. It's easier to ditch stuff if I am scribe, 'cause it seems flabby anyway. It's harder to ditch stuff when Cy is scribe, because of his elaborate architecture. It takes some powerful rewriting to unwrite one of Cy's architecturally designed paragraphs. I have to keep my ears listening too, listening really hard for Cy's hubba hubba voice, that voice that sounds boring and scholarly, a certain cure for insomnia. Our voice is different, I hope, different. And I want it to be our voice, a voice talking to teachers. I listen for things like "educational environments" when we mean "classrooms." I listen for jargon or shortcuts like "liberation pedagogy." I'm in charge of listening, of making sure that the writing is ours, of making sure that teachers will understand it, that teachers will want to read it, that it makes sense to teachers. I'm in charge of listening and rewriting in plain language those hard, complicated ideas that are captured so well in the jargon, in the slogans, in the high falutin' language of philosophers.

Once we have it, once it's right and ours, we try it out on reader critics, hard readers, readers who won't let us alone. They argue with us, write down their thoughts right in the margin, filling it up and spilling on to the back of the page. They argue with us, push us, never let us off easy. They say, "If you say blah blah blah, how can you possibly say blah, blah, blah?" They argue at length with this connection or that. They say, "And furthermore, how could you possibly say blah, blah, blah." Their comments send us back to the drawing board, back to the chaos, back, back, back to where we started in the first place. Their comments make us do hard thinking, make us sit back down at the kitchen table and wonder how in the world we could have been so stupid. We write again. Top to bottom. We write again. This time it had better be right. This time it will be as right as we can make it. We won't do this again. This is it. The final draft.

Not all collaborations are as good as the one with Cy. I've collaborated with non-collaborators, collaborated with people who I won't collaborate with again. Those non-collaborations aren't fun, more like work. And when you finish, you hear yourself saying, "It would have been easier if I had just done it by myself," or worse, "I feel like I have done it by myself." If you feel like you did it by yourself, you might as well have done it that way. It's hard to say why collaborations fail. On the surface, they appear OK. On the surface, each person is responsible for whatever he or she is responsible for. But it just doesn't click. The talk's no good. The writing's no good. Someone doesn't see the idea, see it corralled right there in front of 'em. Someone doesn't do his or her part, drags feet, drags momentum, drags it all out. Someone is just plain dumb, hasn't done the thinking he or she should have. It's hard to figure why collaborations don't work, 'cause no one is safe to talk about it. It's just a feeling, a feeling that you might as well have done it by yourself. I hate it when it happens. Haven't been able to predict it either. Lucky for me it hasn't happened but twice. Twice too many.

Given that I write so much with people, I have no one place that's my writing place. I can write anywhere. I prefer writing on my computer because its neater and doesn't take as long. I know it inside out, so I don't have to think that I'm writing on a computer. I can write on other people's computers, though I pay more attention to the computer than my writing. The old fear of making mistakes that's been ingrained in every writer since elementary school, I guess. I can write anywhere. I like noise and distraction, the more the better. My mind focuses better if it's forced to concentrate on the ideas, tune out the rest of the world. It's like I'm in my own world. I'm aware that the TV is on, that the stereo is playing, that a student is sitting there waiting to ask me a question, but my attention is on the idea. I can write anywhere. And I do. I write on the train, I write at school, I write at home, I write in my sleep, I write in the shower or the grocery store. I write anywhere. I also never stop writing, even when I'm not putting words on paper, because when I'm not writing, I'm always still thinking about it. It doesn't go away. Everything anyone says to me is somehow related to whatever it is I am writing. Relevant, everything is relevant. I write anywhere to figure out what I'm thinking.

So there you have it. Just like I told Alice. The truth. The plain truth.

Charles W. Bridges is associate professor of English, head of the Department of English at New Mexico State University, and director of the New Mexico State Writing Institute. He has published essays on rhetorical theory and composition pedagogy; coauthored (with Ronald F. Lunsford) a textbook on the teaching of writing, Writing: Discovering Form and Meaning *(1984); and edited a collection of essays,* Training the New Teacher of College Composition *(1986).*

In addition, Bridges has conducted inservice programs in writing and the language arts for public schools faculty throughout New Mexico and has presented papers at meetings of the Conference on College Composition and Communication, the Modern Language Association, and the Young Rhetorician's Conference.

ON OPENING THE FLOODGATES: HOW I WRITE

Charles W. Bridges
New Mexico State University

The only way to write is to write. Insofar as possible, I set aside mornings for my writing. Three mornings a week I give to the writing I'm required to do; two mornings a week I try to hold for me. This setting time aside for writing is actually the beginning of my process, the start of how I write.

I'm a writer. I also teach writing and administer a writing program—the New Mexico State Writing Institute. A major portion of the institute's work is a summer writing project for teachers of writing in all disciplines at all grade levels. One of the slogans my codirector and I have developed for our project is "Theory and Research into Practice," and that's the approach I want to take to this paper on my writing process—why I write (a theory/research correlate) figures strongly in how I write, the actual practice of my writing.

WHY I WRITE

The reasons I write are many. My administrative work requires that I write memoranda and academic reports (e.g., summaries of enrollments, requests for increased funding for writing courses) for a fairly limited audience of administrators and faculty in my own university. I've coauthored a freshman composition textbook and various professional articles on the teaching of writing. I also write for audiences beyond academe. For example, as a soccer coach and leader of a Cub Scout pack, I prepare newsletters for parents and other Scout leaders. And I fancy myself a fiction writer, with some shorter fiction finished and a novel under way. All told, I spend a good bit of time writing each

31

day and miss the experience when such activities as administrative duties or travel take the time I want to give to writing.

My interest in writing runs deep. In part, I'm interested in writing because my job and my extracurricular activities require that I write. If I'm to do my job effectively, then I must write—and write well. If my memoranda requesting additional funding are garbled, my chances of receiving the funding are nil. If my newsletters to soccer parents don't clearly outline practice times and other requirements, then my soccer season won't proceed very smoothly. Past these kinds of required writing, I'm interested in using writing (1) to discover what I know and then to report those discoveries and (2) to discover what I don't know to stake out territory for exploration. Finally, I write because it's fun. Perhaps it smacks of posturing to say "Yes, I'm at work on a novel," particularly since I'm at best a dabbler in fiction and given that the novel I'm writing is a potboiler, a pulpy spy thriller—but it's fun. I enjoy spending time with my characters as they work through my plot. And it's not difficult to be with this book. The plot I've outlined keeps nagging at me, calling me to the game of spies; I can see situations my characters get into and out of; at times, I can hear dialogue between and among them, so that they assume a life of their own. Creating and then working with these characters is exciting. This kind of writing takes me away from whatever day-to-day problems or tedium I may confront; it helps me keep my sanity.

Because I write for these varied purposes, audience plays a varied role, and I attend to audience at different points in my process, depending on the purpose of a given piece of writing. As an administrator, my audience is preset, and I generally attend to an academic audience early on in the writing. I know the member(s) of my audience personally and so can easily visualize audience as I write. This lets me gauge reactions and responses to the writing and change it accordingly. The same holds true for pieces of writing intended for the parents of my soccer team members and the Cub Scouts in my pack. For papers and texts written for a broader, more generalized audience (e.g., a freshman composition textbook), I create a stereotype and use that typical reader to help revise a first draft. In writing fiction, I first write to have my say, so that I become my own audience throughout the writing. After writing a story, I revise with a particular magazine or type of magazine in mind, so that concern with an audience beyond me figures in revision.

All this writing takes time, which becomes the biggest constraint on me when I write. But the only way to write is to write. Insofar as possible, I set aside mornings for my writing. Three mornings a week I give to the writing I'm required to do; two mornings a week I try to hold for me. This setting time aside for writing is actually the beginning of my process, the start of how I write.

HOW I WRITE

In this section, I want to focus on how I write academic papers for a professional audience. As I said earlier, I use writing to discover what I both know and don't know, particularly in examining topics for more scholarly papers. While the process I use for administrative and extracurricular purposes is actually fairly linear, that for writing to discover is anything but.

My writing process is essentially chaotic, and describing it is something I've attempted on several occasions. At times, I've compared my process to DNA at work, seeing the breaking apart and then the recombining of DNA chains as similar to my breaking apart chunks of text and then realigning them to restructure (and so create anew) a piece of writing. On other occasions, I've described my process as being like a series of funnels laid end to end, to emphasize the limited beginnings of a piece of writing that I would then expand, then contract, then expand, then contract, and so on till the paper was done. Neither the DNA nor the funnel metaphors seemed quite accurate enough, because neither really allowed for the introduction of entirely new material into the piece of writing at hand. Eventually, I settled on wait-till-the-dam-bursts-Nellie as the best descriptor of my process.

One summer, I asked Writing Project participants to draw their writing process, to represent it graphically, using as few words as possible. To represent my own, I hit upon a flood plain. I drew several broken dams on streams feeding into one big lake (the Lake of the Penultimate Draft), with a spillway (Revision) leading from the lake to a pool (Final Draft) at the downstream base of the dam. This drawing, crude though it was, does represent how I write—I store up ideas, then write in a sudden burst till those ideas are exhausted, then let things settle till the ideas build up again, and then write in another burst. This "flash flood" approach holds until I have some semblance of a first draft to revise.

Now, the preceding description suggests that I proceed in a fairly linear fashion, albeit one marked by fits and starts or spurts of writing. That's not exactly the case, because I do have a lot of false starts. To return to the flood analogy, one dam may break, but that doesn't mean the others will break as well. My writing is marked by a lot of false starts and throwing away much of what I've written. But that's a large part of what writing to discover is all about—writing requires the writer to trash up to 90 percent of what he or she has written. "Throw away" or "trash" may not be entirely accurate. Many of the ideas I decide not to use in a particular piece of writing often wend their way into other pieces, so it's probably not so much a matter of tossing ideas away as simply putting them on hold for another day. And yes, some ideas do get trashed in a real sense; some ideas I get just aren't worth keeping. But these false starts are absolutely necessary; they're essential throat clearing for the work to come.

To begin that work, I may use any of a number of informal and formal invention techniques. Generally, I mull an idea over in my head a good bit before committing very much of it to paper. Once it's committed to paper, I take notes, talk to colleagues and myself, read, and raise questions that occur to me about the idea. I freewrite a good bit and, when appropriate, apply the Questions for Analysis, the heuristic procedure Ron Lunsford and I developed from Kenneth Burke's logological formula (see Bridges and Lunsford, *Writing: Discovering Form and Meaning*, Wadsworth, 1984, pp. 36–58). These invention techniques I use at any point I need to while writing a paper—invention in writing is not limited to prewriting; the various techniques I use in prewriting are just as valid for helping me over stuck points during final revisions as they are in helping me get started.

As I generate material, a shape for the paper generally begins to emerge fairly well on its own. I don't worry much about the form until well into the first draft stage, but once there, I get a little antsy if I don't have some idea of what shape the final paper will assume. Committing to a shape is a technique I use for arranging the material generated in my prewriting, and I've found that drawing my paper is a very good way of finding a shape. Recently, I was stuck on discerning a workable shape for a paper describing the rationale and then the structure of a course I teach designed to prepare teachers of writing. The course has several strands, which derive from a central theme—that by employing the best we know of theory and research on writing, we create a student-centered class—and I was having trouble organizing discussion of the strands. I tried drawing a hamburger, but that suggested there was a central meaty issue, with the other elements being simple garnishes for that issue. The breakthrough came when, in one of those heavy rains rare to New Mexico, I saw the paper's shape as an umbrella, with the umbrella providing the overall rubric and each strand represented by raindrops streaming from the umbrella. This drawing worked by letting me see the parts of my course as equally important and necessary, with each deriving from the central theme. (The idea for drawing papers I gleaned from James Adams, *Conceptual Blockbusting*, Norton, 1980).

Most of my writing I do on a word processor, because I'm faster on a keyboard than with a pen and because of physical limitations. (I grip a pen or pencil very hard, and my hand cramps after only a very short period.) I do take notes by hand but try to transfer them to various working files as soon as possible so that I don't lose them. And once they're on a diskette, I have something from which to build a piece of writing, something to expand, something to revise.

When I hit stuck points while I write, I try to blast through them if it's early in my writing day. I stop and read back over what I've written, trying to prime the pump again that way. If that fails, then I try a number of writing strategies till one works: I freewrite about the topic or about why I seem to be stuck, summarize in a sentence or two the point(s) I've made up to the stuck point, speculate about where I want the paper to go next, or apply a formal heuristic (Questions for Analysis). If all those fail, then I leave the writing for a while. I spend a few minutes playing ball with my children, catching an inning or two of a baseball game, or talking with my wife; if I'm at school, then I take a short walk or talk with colleagues. What I do isn't as important as the fact that I don't absolutely force the writing to come. Getting away from it, even for just a few minutes, seems to allow my thoughts to regroup so that I can proceed on returning to my writing. If I am stuck near the end of my writing period, then I leave the problem till the next day.

Once I have a draft, then I enter fully into revision, which forms a major part of my process. And here I want to make a necessary distinction between revising and editing. Revision for me involves major concern with content and structure, while editing involves correctness. Like invention, revision may occur at any point in my process; editing takes place only at the end.

I generally stop revising only when the paper's due. Even though I use a word processor for my writing, I still like to revise from hard copy so that I can see on paper how things look, to get something of a "flesh and blood" feel that I can't get from a computer monitor. As to how I actually revise, I try to let things sit for a while, try not to read a draft on the same day (or even in the same week) that I wrote it. This works to prevent me from reading my good intentions instead of what actually found its way to the page. I read some of the passages aloud, listening for rhythm and the sound of words. Oftentimes I find that something that sounded good in my head and looked good on the page sounds absolutely awful when read aloud, and that means I revise. Whether I read aloud or silently, I mark poor word choice and note sentences and entire passages that seem out of place. I also look for holes in the paper as I read. When I find them, I return to the early stages of my process, doing some prewriting before drafting text to fill them.

When I have a draft I pass it along to colleagues for their criticism, asking them to read for the sense of the piece. Whether I'm satisfied with the draft makes little difference, for I have asked these readers to suggest how to get past troublesome spots I've identified. My colleagues are good readers, and I've found that their questions and advice help me write better papers.

Once I've revised a paper, I edit it. I read back over the draft, looking for misspellings and problems in grammar and mechanics. If the paper is a long one, I'll run a spell check program, which will flag most of the spelling errors. I try not to read for grammatical and mechanical problems while I revise because I want to deal first with the content, the substance, of the piece of writing and then attend to the surface problems. (Granted, this doesn't always work, and I do occasionally find myself editing while I'm revising. Still, I like to make the distinction between revision and editing and try to keep the two separate as much as possible.)

How I write is indeed a complex, recursive process. It's nothing if not chaotic, at times frustrating. At the same time, it's rewarding. I participate as both creator and observer of a piece of writing, and in the creation and observation, I learn a lot about my own thinking and writing. And that learning makes the chaos bearable, the frustration worthwhile.

Mary Croft's teaching credits include assignments at Iowa State Teachers College, a private school for girls in Evanston, Illinois, Southern Illinois University, the University of Oklahoma, the University of Saigon and Vietnam-American Association, and University of Wisconsin at Stevens Point, where she is professor emeritus.

Croft was selected by Change *magazine in 1976 as one of twenty-nine "most effective teachers in the fields of biology, English, and political science in American higher education." In 1985, the Wisconsin Council of Teachers of English awarded her the Frank Chislom Award for meritorious service. The writing lab developed by Croft at UW-SP and named in honor of her became a national model both in operational procedures and in principles in the total university concept.*

She is currently collaborwriting with Joyce Steward a book on "elderwriters," which is intended to encourage senior citizens who are interested in writing.

PABLO, GO HOME AND PAINT

Mary Croft
University of Wisconsin—Stevens Point

*Whenever I accept my task [writing] as a chore or let it become
a chore (and I have, I have!), I am doomed, and what's more, so
is the writing. I feel very keenly about this.*

For years I have characterized myself as a "meat and potatoes" writer.
But to be honest, I cook meat and potatoes—almost any variety in
almost any variety of ways—far more easily than I write. And yet I have
always loved to write.

Preparing to write this article, I dug through dusty boxes of
memorabilia and found I had saved numerous pieces of writing (many
of which I wished I did not have to claim). And so I reviewed my writing
past—where I wrote and what I wrote for.

Such a review has to feature my seventh-grade teacher. Miss Guthoff taught in an interdisciplinary, writing-across-the-curriculum fashion long before there were such phrases—combining social studies,
geography, and writing in one extended project. We wrote in install-
ments, tracing a trip around the world at a selected latitude, describing
a different country each week, sharing our work with the class on
Mondays. There was, as I recall, great excitement and laughter as our
heroes proceeded on their travels. I had Amos and Andy make the trip
along the fortieth parallel. I blush now that it was in dialect, blush also
that it was such bad dialect. Their adventures and misadventures—"Is
Dis Heah World Round or Square?"—were a dream sequence, realistic
seventh grader that I was. Who in depression year 1932 had the money
to travel around the globe? Yet how much we wrote and how much we
learned!

In the eighth grade, still with Miss Guthoff, I wrote my first and only
novel. The heroine (surprise!) was very poor, very brave, very bright—
her only goal to get to college. Well, someone in class borrowed it—and
lost it. I concede it's a far, far better world without that novel. But the

39

attempt at authorship—that was the important part. I loved having written it.

High-school years brought much writing—in class and in journalistic activities. (Yes, copies of the *Thorntonian* and the *Chronoscope* were in those old boxes.) Again a superb teacher, Sigrid Moe, encouraged and assisted and demanded our best. The same was true of history teacher Ruth Steele Buffington, who simply assigned research papers and expected them to be good. And who introduced me to the University of Chicago.

There followed the Chicago years, the first of which included a course "in the writing of clear and effective exposition." Our task was to master "the method"—my label, not theirs. In preparation, we made marginal epitomes; wrote summaries; criticized and developed outlines; combined materials from parallel sources; practiced note taking; etc.—all the familiar activities. Reviewing the syllabus, exercises, and papers of that year from the vantage point of years of teaching writing, I noted: We did a great deal of writing; even our criticism and analysis of examples were presented in writing. We did much summarizing—a discipline too often overlooked now. We did much sentence combining; but instead of the short "kernels" in most such exercises today, the initial sentences were already quite formidable. We had to dress our writing properly. Class period after class period we worked to exorcise the demon colloquialisms, misusages, and idioms in our writing vocabularies. We spent much time analyzing given selections: some was student writing—usually bad, I regret to say; much was professional—always good. We worked with material Mortimer Adler surely approved, probably had selected, such as Prescott's *History of the Conquest of Mexico,* James's *Psychology,* Darwin's *Origin of Species,* and of course, Newman's *Idea of a University.* Finally, our assignments were painstakingly read, corrected, and annotated— not graded.

My major opus for that year was "The Horror Devices of Poe." I had read and analyzed about seventy stories; presented my findings in categories—atmosphere, disease, torture, death, and supernatural events; and illustrated them from the text. The paper (properly documented, all the "ibids" in place) was duly submitted on May 13, 1937, and was duly returned at quarter's end by my instructor with the comment, "Might this information have been more revealing if viewed chronologically? You have ample material to illustrate Poe's use of these devices, but does the use of them vary in time? What do they tell us of his aims in composing stories?" Good comments, good issues to raise about a so-so paper. What a pity, though, that they were not offered in process instead of as judgment!

Our year's efforts were merely preparation for the June English

Comprehensive, a six-hour examination. And then, too, research techniques were not ignored. The afternoon session consisted of taking notes on a given topic from several given sources (the notes were collected and a uniform set distributed); developing an outline (collected, and a uniform outline distributed); then writing and documenting a paper on the topic. Is it any wonder that during the years that followed I could produce research papers on call, concluding each project with the obligatory all-night editing and typing? There was, for example, one on Mary Queen of Scots, another on "The Schoolmaster Thomas Arnold" (all I remember about him was that he was the father of Matthew Arnold). I became so confident in my control of the method that I even took on the poetic theories of George Herbert as found in *The Temple,* and an interpretation of Othello in the light of Elizabethan psychological theories!

All very logical, all very methodical. The routine became ingrained, almost Pavlovian. And, teasing and oversimplification aside, I am grateful for the discipline. It is a good tool for many of the writing tasks that come my way—papers where objectivity and documentation are essential. However, using that method, I process the material; I don't really get engaged. I remain at a distance from it.

Typically, the writing I do is nonfiction—except for the autobiographical parts of this essay, which George Bernard Shaw would have pronounced "the highest form of fiction." Through the years I have written (and continue to write) reports; manuscripts for presentations; correspondence, especially recommendations; critiques of manuscripts; newsletters; and teaching materials—some of which developed into articles and even a book or two. I tried poetry once, during college, but the result was just a bad imitation of Amy Lowell.

So, essentially, I am just a practical, "meat and potatoes" writer. For writing that covers new or unfamiliar material I follow "the method" usually—or a variation. Writing about known material—knowledge that has come from years of experience (lived, read, etc.)—doesn't need that kind of preparation or treatment. It's there to be tapped, and so the tapping process begins. If I have any kind of consistent process, this is probably it:

For shorter pieces I begin by allowing ideas to roil and roll around in my head, usually as I am driving, and preferably traveling over familiar roads—like the seven miles between home and the university. This can go on for some time. I try ideas out, looking at them from many angles. I phrase them, rephrase them, discard them, replace them—all the time "hearing" myself talking aloud in my head. I allow them to play around until the ideas catch and flow, until they have satisfied the inner critic (at least temporarily). Somehow this is necessary to generate the ideas—to truly find my direction, even though I may have thought

I knew what I was doing and where I was going ahead of time. I need to internalize ideas before I can externalize them.

After a period of roiling, perhaps many such periods, after some talking and testing ideas with colleagues, I am ready for my typewriter. There I triple-space the results of the headwork and view it for the first time. Now the writing/rewriting begins.

For this I need physical comfort. My computer-adept friends tell me I will learn to compose and edit with the word-processing program of my computer, that I will prefer it and rarely use a pencil again for editing. I'm not sure. When I am seated in my Siesta chair, feet on the footstool, script and clipboard on my lap, freshly sharpened Number 2½ Mongol pencil in hand, I am among friends, happily anticipating a pleasurable activity. On the other hand, when I sit before my microcomputer, my mood is perforce business. I am at a desk, I am sitting in a desk chair, and I am facing a machine. Moreover, the machine is at work, the whirr chiding me, "I'm ready. Let's get going. What's keeping you?" It hurries me at a time when I don't want to be hurried. Worse even, I feel intimidated. My conscience admonishes me that I am wasting electricity as well as time. I feel compelled to get on quickly with the editing decisions. So I act. But the procedure is inhibiting, the creative juices are soured, the results stilted and common. Thus I rarely use the computer at this stage.

The editing continues apace, with many pauses for reading and rereading what has gone before. (While I was working on this article, mulling over my ways of writing, daughter Mary Ann was practicing the piano, at times repeating a few bars over and over and over. I interrupted her to ask why the repetition. Various reasons, she said: To study the reason why it doesn't work, to figure out why one place always breaks down; to memorize it; to listen to the interpretation; to create a "coming together of the way you imagine the phrase to be with what your clumsy fingers are actually doing. You repeat it until it works." An apt analogy, I realized, for what I was trying to do—and try to do.)

There comes a time in the rewriting process when I reach a point of no return. I find my writing becoming banal, dull, repetitive. Not only are the words not fresh, neither are the ideas. It's like some evenings of grading papers. After a time, my comments become similar, no longer responding to the particular paper and particular student—and what is worse, even becoming sarcastic or sharp. Time to quit for the night. The students and their efforts do not deserve such treatment. In a similar moment of rewriting, deadline or no, it's time to put the script aside. I don't force the writing. It would be, as Don Murray says, like putting a piece of spaghetti through a keyhole.

When I return to it, the next hour after a cup of coffee and a stretch, or the next morning after a night of subconscious effort (sometimes even conscious effort, scribbling on the notepad next to my bed), or a few days later, I must first become reacquainted with this friend I have not seen for some time. So I greet it warmly, ask it some questions about its past, then consider its plans for the future. This, too, takes time. It cannot be hurried. When we are once again on the old footing, close and comfortable with each other, we are ready to move forward.

Now the writing/rewriting begins again, the process is repeated—recursively—and a draft or two or ten later, I am ready to turn to my computer for the final, fine-tuning and then printing.

For longer pieces I begin much the same way to discover direction, but then work in segments, not necessarily in the order in which they will eventually appear. (The order is always in a tentative state.) And I am much more likely to work from files of material on each segment or aspect, then notes from the material, then notes on the notes—working toward order and synthesis and sense. Again, depending on time and circumstances, I am likely to share the work with a friend and further refine.

By now it is very clear that I am a slow writer—and a messy one. The many years of teaching writing—formally in the classroom, informally in student conferences, then years of the writing lab—have developed a lot of "editorship" in me. I instinctively look at *any* writing to see what's good about it and how it can be improved. So when I write, inevitably the editor syndrome takes over. Worse than ever. Because it's my writing and I am on the line—not just with my audience but with *me.* I do and consider, redo and reconsider, ad infinitum—waiting, like Ferlinghetti, "for some strains of unpremeditated art / to shake my typewriter." Thank God for deadlines!

Even so, it is not an unhappy process. Which brings up an aside of sorts: In reviewing a manuscript for a publishing house not too long ago, I recommended rejection, concluding my critique with, "I do not underestimate the demands of teaching writing, but I know that once you accept your task as a chore, you are doomed, and more important, so are the students." Fine-sounding words—very noble and righteous. They apply also to my writing. Whenever I accept my task as a chore or let it become a chore (and I have, I have!), I am doomed, and what's more, so is the writing. I feel very keenly about this. Similarly, I am angered by the attitude still found all too often, as in this statement from the jacket of a book I picked up recently: "The bane in the life of the teacher of English and his students is composition work."

I am a file keeper, not a consistent notebook keeper. To be honest, I'm a file junkie. I save ideas, quotations, anecdotes, techniques, suggestions, notes from conference presentations—whatever is fresh or well phrased or surprising or supporting or usable or . . . These and other files fill twenty-three bank file boxes in my basement (having gone through five office moves in the last two years) as well as five filing cabinets. They comprise my storehouse. I appreciate the need for fairly impersonal and direct writing for certain audiences and tasks. Yet I also have an innate need to go along with Zinsser's precept—just because you work for an institution, you don't have to sound like one. (Another example of my latching on to a good bit!)

So a reference to a *New Yorker* review of a new play on Broadway, *Open Admissions,* becomes part of the conclusion to a report on the minority/disadvantaged program at the University—destined for the Board of Regents. A *Councilgram* story on a job description for a writing lab director, followed by the comment that it sounded as though they were recruiting "God with patience" becomes part of a chapter on the selection of writing lab staff. A poem from the 4 C's journal, "To Jackson Pollock," cleverly illustrating how writing is hard work, becomes the cover for a writing lab brochure—for student distribution.*

To Jackson Pollock

~~Some say that~~ the process
~~of~~ writing is ~~simply~~ a matter
of getting things you can write
not simply ~~taking composing~~
thoughts on paper. ~~It is
difficult Composing~~ Writing
is ~~tough~~ hard ~~to do to
accomplish easily~~ work.

Michael C. Flanigan
Indiana University
Bloomington

All from my storehouse. I find. I store. I try to apply. There is nothing brilliant or earth-shaking in those examples. But they are intended to make my writing more readable and humane and alive. Moreover, adding to my storehouse keeps me alert, growing, learning.

That once again brings up the writing lab. I have realized more than ever in this introspective venture how much I learned and continue to learn about writing, and thus about my own writing, from the lab experience. The sharing, the openness, the involvement (indeed, immersion) in writing, the acknowledgment of fears and blocks and frustrations, the camaraderie—all features that demystify writing and allow it to be a highly satisfying if not easy task.

Similarly I learned and continue to learn from my collaboration with Joyce Steward. Coauthoring teaches much about the realm of writing, the process of "melding" styles, even the concept of style. Joyce and I truly had fun doing the writing lab book. Our views of writing and the teaching of writing were similar—still are! The material, based on years of experience, was second nature to us. And we surely knew our audience—directors and staffs of labs. We entered into the give and take of coauthorship with zest. We approached each other's writing in the same way that we approached the writing that walked into our respective labs through all those years. And we edited and edited until our responses were identical—indeed, anticipated the other's reactions. Work, yes, from inception to final proofing—but what a gratifying experience!

To conclude, I ask my students to brainstorm, to experiment, to risk, to fall, to dust themselves off and try again. I try to ask the same of myself, knowing it is not so easy as my manner to my students implies. The most courageous thing I ever did in my life (well, almost) was getting up the nerve to show a three-page introduction on poetry to a friend and colleague, but also published poet and acclaimed teacher of the writing of poetry, Rich Behm. I needed his assistance/approval, for I was in fairly unfamiliar territory. Rich, good teacher that he is, gave it. I was reminded of the statement another colleague, novelist Larry Watson, made recalling his early writing days: "At times I was overpraised. But that praise was what I needed at that time."

So I continue to write. The story is told that during an evening at the Paris home of Gertrude Stein, Picasso read some of his poetry. The silence that followed was broken at last by the hostess: "Pablo, go home and paint." There are many, many moments when, trying to write, I feel I should go home and cook meat and potatoes.

Frank J. D'Angelo is professor of English at Arizona State University, where he directs the Ph.D. graduate emphasis in rhetoric and composition. He is past chair of the Conference on College Composition and Communication, a former member of the executive committee of the National Council of Teachers of English, and a past chair of the writing division of the Modern Language Association. He has recently served on the board of directors of the Rhetoric Society of America and on the publications committee of the CCCC. He is currently an associate editor of the Rhetoric Review *and of the* Journal of Advanced Composition.

D'Angelo's books include A Conceptual Theory of Rhetoric *(1975) and* Process and Thought in Composition *(1985). He has published more than fifty articles in professional books and journals, on such topics as rhetorical theory, the teaching of composition, stylistics, imitation, paraphrase, fables, proverbs, graffiti, doublespeak, and subliminal appeals in advertising.*

THE ART OF COMPOSING

Frank J. D'Angelo
Arizona State University

Like Mozart, Gibbon, and Russell (but more modestly, of course), I plan and deliberate beforehand with a view to subsequent action. As I compose in my head, I "hear" myself composing, as if I were reciting my lessons in high school in a formal manner, repeating aloud, saying the same things over and over, going over the same ground (or "places" as it were), laying a foundation, or erecting a scaffolding for what is to follow. It's as though I were an actor, practicing my lines in private, in preparation for a more formal or public performance.

I am a Mozartian composer. Mozart is said to have composed an entire musical composition in his head. When given an assignment, he would think about it for long periods of time, hum melodies to himself, try out variations in his head. Then, when he was ready to write down his ideas, he would put the musical notes down on paper as quickly and as easily as he might compose a letter. Beethoven, on the other hand, would score a composition many times—making false starts, rejecting themes, revising, crossing out, working laboriously, slowly.

Like Mozart, I prefer to work in loneliness and seclusion. I, too, like to work in solitude. I usually write on a long table in my office at the university when no one else is around. I seem to need a lot of space to spread out in and freedom from interruption. Not only is the table large and spacious, but my office also has abundant space. Sometimes I write in the early morning; sometimes in the afternoon. I seldom write at night because at night I usually think about what I will be writing the next day. When I write, I prefer to have an uninterrupted span of time, so I do most of my writing during the semester break or during the summer.

I write with a blue felt pen on a large yellow tablet. For some reason, the physical act of writing is important to me. As I bear down on the paper, I feel a physical sensation akin to that which Janet Emig has described as "carving or sculpting . . . in wood or stone." With pen in hand, I feel as if I have more control over my ideas, and I take an almost aesthetic pleasure in forming the letters, words, phrases, sentences, and paragraphs.

I write because I feel I have something to say. Given world enough and time, I get great pleasure from writing. But given the constraints of time and deadlines, I find the process agonizing. I could never write for a newspaper. I compose best when I have full presence of mind, self-control, poise, calmness, and tranquillity—in brief, when I have composure.

I write mostly for academic audiences—college teachers, high-school teachers, college students—but I have on occasion written for more general audiences. I have written on a wide variety of subjects—magazine advertising, proverbs, paraphrase, imitation, style, fables, graffiti, doublespeak, literacy, the teaching of writing, and rhetorical theory.

I have seldom had writer's block. This does not mean that problems never arise *as I compose.* But they seldom arise *as I write,* because I am a think-write writer. Since I do most of my composing in my head, I usually discard incomplete or unfruitful ideas *before* I begin to write.

Usually the subjects I write about come out of my reading or teaching, but from time to time someone may ask me to lecture or write on an assigned topic. When I am given a topic, even though I might have some knowledge of that topic stored in memory, I begin to compile an exhaustive bibliography of books and articles on the subject. Then I read from the storehouse of materials I have collected, taking copious notes, thinking about what I have read, making connections with things I have previously read or with ideas I have previously stored in my mind. I find I can never read enough about my subject. I must read and take notes until I have an abundance of ideas, a cornucopia of matter, an overflowing tide of plenty. I am reminded of Erasmus' saying that "there is nothing more admirable or more splendid than a speech [or discourse] with a rich copia of thoughts and words overflowing in a golden stream."

As I read, take notes, and think about what I have read, I find my mind ranging over a wealth of ideas, a veritable thesaurus of words and concepts, looking for some sort of ordering principle, some way to see one thing in terms of another. Although I do not self-consciously go through a formal checklist of inventional devices, I find myself more or less consciously using analogy, etymology, definition, and division into parts in my reading, my note taking, and my thinking.

Unless there are constraints of time, I usually do not sit down to write until I have thought through the material reasonably well, know pretty much what I want to say, roughly the order in which I want to say it, and even the conclusions I wish to draw. *Writing is seldom a process of discovery for me.* However, composing always is. For me, the process of composing is broader than that of writing. As I read, take notes, think about what I have read, put things together in my head, arrange them and change them, I am composing. Ordinarily, I discover what I mean, or I make meaning, *before I begin to write* I discover what I mean as I write only in situations where I am suddenly forced to write immediately. When I am forced to write before I am ready—before I have acquired enough information about my subject and before I have thought through it thoroughly—I find the act of composing my thoughts in writing very difficult. Then there is more posing than composing, more pausing than poise-ing. When I am thoroughly prepared, however, the words and ideas pour forth easily and copiously.

During the prewriting period, which may take days, weeks, months, I read and reread my notes, take new notes, think about what I have read, lie awake at night turning over ideas in my mind, reflecting, pondering, making connections, giving play to my imagination, planning, arranging, casting, recasting, putting things in order, composing and disposing ideas. There seems to be more than an accidental association between my reposing and composing. In order to compose thoughtfully, I must first compose myself, take on a certain posture, which is just as much an attitude of body as it is a frame of mind.

The term that best describes my method of composing is *premeditated composing*. This is a term used by scholars of Greek epic poetry to describe the kind of composition that the singer of tales goes through inside his head before he begins to recite. The English historian Edward Gibbon used this method to compose his monumental *Decline and Fall of the Roman Empire*. Gibbon "premeditated" long passages of his history, working them over in his memory until he had almost perfected them. Then he wrote them down. In *Memoirs of My Life,* he gives this account: "It has always been my practice to cast a long paragraph in a single mould, to try it by ear, to deposit it in my memory; but to suspend the action of my pen until I had given the last polish to my work." The British philosopher and mathematician Bertrand Russell composed in a similar manner: "Now, for many years past, he had learned to write in his own mind, turning phrases, constructing sentences, until in his memory they grew into paragraphs and chapters." Russell, through long experience in thinking and writing, could plan, arrange, and hold in his memory entire chapters of prose in advance of his writing it all down.

Like Mozart, Gibbon, and Russell (but more modestly, of course), I plan and deliberate beforehand with a view to subsequent action. As I compose in my head, I "hear" myself composing, as if I were reciting my lessons in high school in a formal manner, repeating aloud, saying the same things over and over, going over the same ground (or "places" as it were), laying a foundation, or erecting a scaffolding for what is to follow. It's as though I were an actor, practicing my lines in private, in preparation for a more formal or public performance. I find that I prepare for class in the same way—going over my notes in my head as

I lie awake at night, putting them into some kind of logical order, *planning* the introduction to the class period, the body, and the conclusion, *visualizing* the whole plan, *talking* the ideas over in my head, enumerating the parts, recounting them in some order, returning to them again and again.

When I write, I seldom use a traditional outline, but I do use various schemes. I seldom write these down, however, because through reading, memorizing, writing, formal education, and training I have internalized plans, patterns, plots, scenarios, designs, frames, and forms of all kinds. In my writing, I seem to be able to draw upon these schemes in a more or less conscious manner. As I write, I *hear* myself composing, as if I were composing aloud, and I audit and edit internally as I compose. As I write, I seem to be able to *visualize* the plan of a piece of writing. This plan, this design of the whole, seems most important to me. I am reminded of Schopenhauer's advice to writers in his *Essay on Style:* "Write the way an architect builds, who first drafts his plan and designs every detail." As I write, I stop from time to time to read what I have written, perhaps make a few superficial changes, and continue to write again. I need to read and reread what I have written, not so much to remember what I put down on paper, as to maintain a kind of *flow* of ideas and a sense of the whole. I seem to sense a kind of internal rhythm as I write.

I can write for long stretches of time, usually without interruption, if I have planned well before I write. The only constraint is physical tiredness. If I am interrupted while writing, before I can continue I must reread everything that I have written, not just a paragraph or two. I seem to need to get *some sense of the whole* piece of writing again. I also have to get back into the flow and rhythm of writing.

When I finish the first draft, I reread what I have written, making mostly minor changes. Whenever I write, I try to produce reader-based prose in my first draft. (Not all of the editors to whom I send my writing think that I do, of course.) Most of the articles that I submit for publication are published in the form in which I submit them. As for the others, the advice of editors usually is to condense them more. (I admitted earlier to a fondness for copiousness.) I hate to revise. I would rather write a completely new essay than revise extensively a completed one. Robert Frost echoes completely my sentiments about revising: "I have never been good at revising. I always thought I made things worse by recasting and retouching." Whereas for some writers, what they first put down on paper gives them hints for new directions to take in their writing, for me, what I put down on the page inhibits me. I can't seem to go beyond the confines of what I have already put down on paper.

I have little doubt that my early education has contributed to the way I write. I had eight years of a Jesuit education. In high school I took four years of speech; four years of English, Latin, and math; two years of a modern foreign language; two years of history; and four years of religion (ethics, religious doctrine, etc.). In the first year of speech class, I memorized famous speeches, poems, and passages from plays. In my second year, I analyzed poems, speeches, and passages from plays and gave dramatic readings. In my third year, I composed and delivered original speeches. And in my fourth year, I gave extemporaneous speeches.

In my English classes, I memorized rules of grammar, parsed sentences, and diagramed them. I also memorized lists of words, their forms, etymologies, and meanings. The same person who taught me English also taught me Latin, so that what I learned in English was reinforced in Latin class. In Latin class, I also memorized rules of grammar, parsed sentences, translated from Latin into English and from English into Latin, and learned etymologies of words.

In my English and Latin classes, I memorized passages of literature, read aloud, and recited the daily lesson. In all of my classes, I had to outline the lesson of the day, take notes, copy things out, paraphrase, and imitate. In almost every class, I had to defend or refute a thesis. There was very little original composition at first, for the idea in that early education was to stock the mind, train the memory, inculcate orderly habits of mind, and instill ethical and moral ideas.

Although I did not realize it at the time, even my religious studies had some connection with rhetorical training. In religion classes, as well as in chapel, I was encouraged to memorize prayers, reflect, meditate, and form images in my mind. In penance hall (appropriately named)— a classroom to which students who cut up in class had to go for two hours after school—the punishment was to memorize poems, prose passages, or passages from plays. If you could memorize the assignment in less than the time allotted, you would go to the prefect's desk, recite your lines quietly, and then leave. Needless to say, I became quite skillful at memorizing.

When I went to college, much of what I had learned in high school was reinforced. Not only did I continue to take courses in English, speech, and classical and foreign languages, but I also added to these logic, metaphysics, philosophy, rational psychology, and ethics. I see now that I had the kind of education that Quintilian describes in *The Education of the Citizen-Orator.* In all of those years, I had inculcated habits of mind and developed resources that I am still using today. I guess that accounts for my interest in topical systems of all kinds, tropes, thesauri, encyclopedias, books of proverbs, maxims, quotations, and so forth. I know that some critics of education today would consider my early education and training highly artificial. But that which is artificial is not necessarily unnatural, stilted, or forced, but artful, skillful, and inventive. For in the final analysis, the art of composition depends on how well we compose ourselves, through studied conduct and skillfulness in adapting means to ends.

Ken Donelson is coeditor of the English Journal *and professor of English at Arizona State University. He writes mostly about young adult literature, about censorship for the secondary English curriculum, and about the problems of teaching high-school English. He has authored or coauthored several books and several hundred articles.*

OH, LORD, IF I CAN ONLY GET A PERFECT DRAFT ON THAT FIRST PAGE

Ken Donelson
Arizona State University

While something in me forces me to write, I hate the act of writing. Other writers know precisely what I mean, but my students are often surprised that any writer could feel as I do. Anyone who writes knows what Red Smith meant when he wrote, "Writing is easy. I just open a vein and bleed."

Why do I write? For no rational reason I've ever been able to figure out or explain to others. I write because I need to write. It's that simple— or that complicated. Some compulsion or quirk or virus makes me write. Nothing ever makes me like to write. That's a different matter, one that borders on masochism, but I know that I must write. Maybe it's that I'm more fascinated by myself and what goes through my mind, or my guts, than I am by anyone else's ideas or visceral reactions. Some rhetoricians talk about writing as discovery, and maybe that's it. There was a time when I worried about justifying my writing to other people. That hasn't been true for years, but maybe that's a product of my galloping senility or intellectual myopia.

And I write for pay, as all writers do. Sometimes the pay is real and immediate money. Once it was for promotion or tenure. Now it's more likely to be doled out in dribbles as merit pay. Sometimes pay comes as letters responding to something I've written, and it often comes in my imagination as a warm feeling that someone out there is reading my stuff and thinking, "God but this is great (or witty or wise or scintillating or something even nicer)." Since I rarely get all that many letters about my writing, I assume—or need to assume—that the masses out there are struck dumb or inarticulate by my words and are unable to write to tell me that. That's pay, of sorts, even though it's created by my imagination and not reality. I simply cannot imagine an English teacher worth a damn who doesn't write and doesn't have something to say that others might care to hear. As we are all in debt to others in our profession for bringing ideas to our attention and for making us react, so we all need to repay that debt by doing the same for those who follow us. That may seem immodest at times, given the giants that we learned from, but even our feeble and fumbling efforts are far better than nothing at all.

The writing I do can be loosely divided into three parts. First comes the correspondence that comes with being a coeditor of the *English Journal* and handling some administrative jobs. While we use a form rejection letter for manuscripts we can't use, I do occasionally write rejected authors who I know have good articles in them, even if the present articles aren't that. And several sections of *EJ* (notably the "Too Good to Miss" and "Recommended Authors" features) demand that I keep in touch with would-be authors who haven't yet come through. I correspond with publishers frequently on all sorts of things, just as I correspond with present—or future—undergraduate and graduate students here at Arizona State University. As one of a small network of people who till the fields of young adult literature and school/library censorship, I'm usually way behind in the letters I owe those people. And I respond with reasonable dispatch—defined as I see it, not as friends do—to friends who send me their manuscripts for my reaction. (That's not paid by me in kind since I hate to get criticism of my work.) And there are always personal letters that deserve to be written yet rob me of time for my own writing.

Second comes the time I spend editing and tightening and rewriting (always in moderation and with the best of intentions) articles we've accepted for *EJ*. My record for speed in editing so far is something less than an hour for a first-rate article that needed little more than proofing. My record for slowness was something better than twenty-four hours, spread out over several days, on an article of real worth written by someone for whom English at times seemed to be a foreign language. And there are always students waiting to see me who foolishly believe that I can offer some help for their writing problems.

Third comes the real writing I do, though it may be the least important part of my job to others, articles and books, usually aimed at secondary English teachers. That comes from my background as a high-school English teacher in Iowa for thirteen years, my work with Bob Carlsen, and my doctorate in English Education at the University of Iowa. I believe, not with an uncanny instinct but a highly developed egotism, that I have something to say that secondary English teachers need to hear, or at least might be willing to listen to. Some of this writing begins with reading professional material and reacting to it. More often, it happens with a random thought or collection of thoughts/impressions that appears from nowhere I can clearly identify, and that leads to rapidly scrawling on whatever is handy (a matchbook cover, a paper napkin, the back of a church announcement, toilet paper, Kleenex) and as speedily as I can manage it a retreat to a quiet place with ample paper where I can do more with these fragments. Quiet is what I'd like, but I've learned to write wherever I am, and one of the articles I'm proudest of began as a thought and then a rough draft in a noisy rock music dive in Milwaukee. The floors were sawdust-covered, and as dancers went by me they stared (I was told by an amused friend) at me writing, as I was clearly oblivious to anything save the words spewing out before me and an occasional gulp of beer to keep me going.

Moments like that always puzzle me, for only rarely have I been able to go back and reconstruct what led to these sudden insights and bursts of writing. Sometimes the thoughts lead me later to something worth developing. Sometimes they prove dead-end and frustrating because they looked so promising. Sometimes they are obviously the product of a diseased or weird mind and they go no place and never deserved to go any farther. I probably should be more curious, but I've always been grateful to God or the beer or the companionship or whatever it is that spontaneously lets me get started with writing. Incidentally but I hope obviously, I've never confused any of this with visits from a loving or pawky Muse.

Many of my published articles began as speeches, which I usually give from notes. Infrequently, I've taped a speech on the off chance that someplace as I rambled on I'd say something clever or synthesize ideas that had been floating around in my brain or subconscious for months. Then my secretary transcribes my words. That I would recommend to any speaker/writer, if nothing else than as an exercise in humility (and sometimes humiliation). When I first did that, I learned what I should already have known, that speech and writing are two quite different forms of discourse, and that while rambling and repetition may be mildly forgivable in speech, they're not in writing. But if the tapes embarrassed me, they also provided me with the beginnings of an article, often vastly better because I'd done some thinking on my feet about the topic. I've never given the same speech twice—though many of my speeches clearly derive from earlier talks or articles. Doing a speech more than once always seems unfair to my audience, and besides it forces me to turn the speeches into articles or shredded paper.

While something in me forces me to write, I hate the act of writing. Other writers know precisely what I mean, but my students are often surprised that any writer could feel as I do. Anyone who writes knows what Red Smith meant when he wrote, "Writing is easy. I just open a vein and bleed." Smith was a marvelous writer on sports and life, but he apparently had it easier than many of us. At least he could find a vein most of the time. I stare at that blank piece of gloriously white paper in the typewriter before me, paper so pure that I hate to sully it with my puerile words and often do nothing but stare for hours at a time.

Years ago, Woolcott Gibbs (I think it was), the dramatist and fine drama critic of the *New Yorker,* observed that the only person he knew who liked to write was now properly employed as a gas station attendant. I've heard more writing instructors than I care to admit tell students about the *joy* of writing, but how can anyone who writes think of writing as joy? Only people who do not write can talk with a straight face about the *joy* of writing. Writing can be, and often is, necessary or demanding, maybe even satisfying, but never joyful.

Even with my first novel, written when I was nine or ten under the influence of and imitating *Herb Kent, West Point Fullback,* writing came hard for me, though my mother thought the 40-page book impressive. Later, when I wrote my second and last novel—a heavily Proustian and Kafkaesque effort which due to intellectual shoddiness and literary pretentiousness was vastly inferior to my first work—at the University of Iowa, words came not one bit easier.

But if I cannot imagine the *joy* of writing, neither can I imagine a time when I do not write. By the time this article was typed, in a semifinished form, I had spent perhaps three days working on it nearly full-time, but I began it in several ways six or seven months ago. During the intervening time, I jotted down ideas here and there during a camping trip, during a convention at Philadelphia, and at odds and ends moments in Boston and San Diego and sundry other places. And as I worked on this, I stopped repeatedly to work on articles that were more immediately pressing or that seemed, for the moment, to be more inviting or more important or more intriguing, all pulling me this way or that for attention. Whether that's a sensible way to write, I have no idea, but it works for me.

I know that writing is not joyful and I'm not convinced that it's a natural act, certainly not in the sense that eating or making love or scratching a dog are natural, but I'm dead sure that writing comes with my territory. Because that's one of my givens, I'm curious what other writers have to say about their compulsion and delusions. So I read the *Paris Review* interviews and any other sources I can find, shake my head in dismay at the weird foibles of others, puzzle over the sensible advice of Jim Moffett and Don Grave and Don Murray, and wonder why I cannot follow the patterns and practices so carefully and intelligently provided by those hundreds of rhetorics that flood the market.

I remember particularly puzzling over Martin Nystrand's *What Writers Know: The Language, Process, and Structure of Written Discourse* (Academic Press, 1982) and being surprised—horrified may be a better word—with all the things writers supposedly know about what they do when they write, much of which I either did not know or care about and could not imagine any real writer ever caring about, most of it written in forbidding and jargon-ridden prose that I could not imagine real writers ever using. I've never been asked to do a rhetoric (proof positive that there is a loving God and that publishers occasionally have glimmers of common sense), but I read many of them as they appear. I've yet to find any help for me or my writing, but I continue to be impressed that so many seem so sure about how to teach writing and how to write.

When I was a lowly high-school English teacher, I was at first convinced by the deluge of writing texts that some people out there knew something about how to write that I did not know. But the longer I taught in both high school and college, the more I doubted that anyone had an answer to the question "How do we write?" and the more confident I became that people who claimed that they had *the* ten (or thirty) steps to effective writing were either borderline lunatics or out-and-out charlatans.

I can, of course, suggest to my students several approaches or gimmicks or paradigms that seem to work with others, not because those are right, but because sometimes almost any way of getting writing under way is better than no way at all. But I long ago learned what most writers learn, that the approach or gimmick or whatever you choose to call it that works best for an individual writer must be discovered by that person. Nobody else can do it for him or her, and that's both encouraging and frightening—encouraging because it *allows* us to find our own path (or paths) to writing, frightening because it *forces* us to find that path. Even then the writer is better off knowing several ways to get off dead center and under way, partly because different kinds of writing may demand different approaches, partly because one approach may fail and another approach may get the writer started. In writing as in sex or any other sport, it pays to have a second method if the first one fails.

If sometimes I'm excited by some notes I've made, the excitement disappears once I'm seated before my IBM Correcting Selectric II and ready to write. Sweat appears before any words do. Let me explain how I write, not because it's sensible—I've been told often enough that it isn't—but because it eventually works for me. I begin with a tentative first sentence (which often vanishes after a few drafts), retreat to my desk to try to figure out why I wanted that sentence, glance over assorted notes that somehow will appear later in the article, read some clippings that I've vaguely thought of quoting from (I'm an inveterate clipper-outer of odds and ends from newspapers and a storer-upper of quotes on music or literature or whathaveyou), and fumblingly and stumblingly get some words onto the paper. If that sounds vague, then that's the way it is—one of my students once called it Donelson's *mystical method* of writing, but both words strike me as ill-chosen. At the end of this article I'll try to be more specific about my mad method by showing how I wrote the first paragraph in an "Editors' Page" for the *English Journal* that Alleen Pace Nilsen, my coeditor, and I have the wonderful opportunity to do (or get stuck with doing, whichever seems appropriate) eight times a year.

Once I make a mistake on that first page, that page ceases to have value, save to be copied or have words and phrases extracted from it; and once the next copy is a bit further along than the first, the offending draft is crumpled up and tossed with a high-arched basketball shot into the wastepaper basket. Once there, that draft awaits its companions, which are rarely slow in coming, until the wastebasket is full (or errant shots cover my office floor). My personal best for number of drafts before I completed the first page was 73 tries (or drafts, if you want to dignify them). How do I know that? The article had gone badly, as you might guess, and I was swearing loudly when my secretary appeared. She snickered, I glared, and then she counted the 73 balled-up pieces of paper. In truth, it's rare for more than 25 balls to be tossed, just as it's even more rare for less than 10 to be discarded.

I never move on to page 2 until I have a perfect draft of the first page. *Perfect* is here defined as something I think has some merit and has no goofs, typos, misspellings. Friends have kindly, or rudely, pointed out that my insistence on that *perfect* draft is an evasion, since I may, Freudian-like, make a deliberate (?) error to stall me, and that's an uncomfortable possibility that may have some truth to it. But the system—if anything so haphazard or sloppy can be termed a system—works for me. By the time I've finished with page 1, I have ideas and phrases and even sentences aplenty that I'll use later in the article. By the end of page 1, I've worked out a plan for the entire article, and I'm far more comfortable with myself and my work. Granted, that first page may take hours to do (sometimes days), but once it's done I'm on my way.

Other pages can cause problems but none so frustrating or so terrifying as page 1. The pages that follow go much faster, or perhaps it simply seems so since I've broken my writing logjam.

What happens if I stall, and nothing seems to be forthcoming? I often panic or go for long walks or get a cup of tea or swear a lot. If I'm especially frustrated, I'll take a walk. There's something of a groove in the hall outside my office where I've repeatedly paced like a wounded writer.

I've been told that I ought to brainstorm before or as I write, but I've never understood what *brainstorming* meant. There's enough going wrong with my head when I try to write that I need no other mental disturbances. And somehow that term has always seemed uncomfortably reminiscent of those horrible days when I was saddled with taking Introduction to Psychology and listening to a professor speak jargon and force us to regurgitate it on tests.

If I'm really desperate about my writing, I'll usually turn to writers I admire and envy and read from E. B. White's *Charlotte's Web* or *The Second Tree from the Corner,* Frank Sullivan's unfairly neglected classic *The Night the Old Nostalgia Burned Down,* or George Gissing's *The Private Papers of Henry Ryecroft.* Or maybe Thoreau's *Walden* or Dickens's *Bleak House* or *Dombey and Son* or *Our Mutual Friend.* Or often the Bible, not from religious impulses—it's hardly fair to blame God for the writing mess I'm in—but because it's wondrous at times to get back in touch with the King James version and good English prose.

As I said earlier, I've learned to write under almost any conditions, but if I'm taking notes or making early stabs, it has to be in pen, never pencil—pencils are reserved for editing and nothing else. I'd prefer to have classical music in the background at all times, and we're lucky in Phoenix to have KONC, a round-the-clock supplier of great music. I've been told that music disturbs some writers, but that's their problem. I can't do without it, either to listen to or type to.

But if pens—always black and preferably fine-lined—are useful in taking notes, an electric typewriter is essential for drafting and redrafting, in other words the real work of writing. Many of my friends use word processors and wonder that I ever get my writing done, my approach is so plodding, any question of quality of writing aside. They wonder when I'll buy a word processor, but so far I've resisted. I may be one of a dying breed of Neanderthals, writers who need to type to feel that real writing is happening, but since I've managed to get several books and monographs and several hundred articles written and since my system continues to work for me, the word processor still has no appeal.

(One small worry about technology and word processors and writers—how will writers who use the magic of word processors, where final products look so lovely and apparently untouched by any changes along the way, leave their working papers, their drafts, behind so we can study what happened as the writer moved from this draft to that draft unto the final and published draft?)

I'm sure there are writers out there who hunger for criticism, but I've never met one yet who really wanted criticism, though I've met God's aplenty who wanted praise. Anyone who writes knows that sooner or later manuscripts need to be mailed and criticism will follow —though out-and-out acceptance letters are nicer—either as form rejection letters or as comments from anonymous reviewers. I prefer the former, and I've never found the latter at all helpful, sincerely as they presumably are intended.

Some writers apparently ask for criticism from a spouse or a lover. I can't think of anything less intelligent to do with writing. Asking for criticism is the fastest way to destroy a human relationship I can imagine. If I'm working on some piece of writing—as I always seem to be —at the office and I inadvertently mention that to my wife, she used to ask, "What's it about?" That sounds like a quite sensible question, but since I'm often unsure what my writing will turn out to be—and it stands a fine chance of turning out to be nothing at all—it's not a question I want to address when I go home. I once asked her to read what I hoped was the last draft of an article and to tell me what she really thought of it. That was stupid because she did just that, pointing out this weakness and that unhappy sentence. More than that, she had the effrontery to tell me that one paragraph was unclear, "ambiguous" was what she called it. Well, to make a long and tense story short, the weakness was a clever bit of irony she hadn't grasped, the unhappy sentence was quite fine, thank you, and the "ambiguous" paragraph was clear to even the most casual reader. So much for criticism from her.

When I tell my graduate classes that they should never ask anyone they love or even like to criticize their work, that indeed if they really want someone to criticize their work they ought to pick a disposable acquaintance, they laugh appreciatively at my little joke. But it is not a joke. Most writers do not want criticism, no matter what they pretend, until it's forced on them by an editor or publisher.

Grammar may not be worth teaching—I certainly would argue that it's not—but it's almost a cliché of teaching that the fastest way to learn grammar is to be forced to teach it. In a slightly parallel way, I think I learned more about writing and what distinguishes good from mediocre or poor writing from becoming coeditor of the *English Journal* than I had from all my earlier writing and teaching experience. People who send manuscripts to *EJ* are usually college or high-school English teachers, people presumably aware of what writing is supposed to do and presumably able to write effectively. Such is often not the case, as I soon learned. I learned that introductions, the longer the better, are essential; that jargon is rampant (*EJ* contributors seem especially enamored of *process, in-depth, input, output, viable, meaningful,* and *relevant*); that stuffy words like *utilize* and *facilitate* (which rarely mean anything more complex than *use* or *help*) make writing pompous and uninviting; and that if using three examples is good, using thirteen is even better.

I also learned a few other things that have proved even more helpful to me as a writer and a teacher.

As coeditor, I'm required to write the "Editors' Page" every other month. My coeditor and I try each time to write something intelligent about the state of English teaching, and a few years back it was my turn. I tend to procrastinate when I'm faced with deadlines, but I have learned that time passes and deadlines arrive. I work best under the pressure of time, or so I've convinced myself. Whether it's true I have no idea since I've never tried another way.

And so it came to pass that Monday had arrived and the editorial was due late Tuesday afternoon. I'd been reading and thinking about merit pay in secondary schools, I'd read newspaper stories, and I'd scribbled out some notes. Like many other people, I think merit pay is great in theory and nearly impossible to apply in practice, at least if we want to maintain whatever morale of good teachers is left near the end of the year. And extraordinarily fine teachers, those most of us would agree deserve merit pay, are often against the idea.

Before I turned to the ever-waiting and by now leering type-writer, I considered criteria for merit pay (those I'd use, those that have been used, and still others that have been proposed but not yet used), and I wondered and worried about precisely who would apply those criteria and exactly how they'd be applied, rewarding the lucky and kissing off the rest. I worried that too often English Department chairs in high school are chosen because they "yes" administrators, and identifying the meritorious has too often meant rewarding the toadies. I wondered if originality and independence and sincerity might go unrewarded because some administrators seem happier with conformity and seem constitutionally incapable of rewarding anyone who makes waves.

In one of those fortuitous bursts of writing which but rarely happen to me, I had completed the last paragraph, barring a tiny change or two. Now all I had to do was write what came before that last paragraph, and I was home. Complicating the problem, as it always did, the entire editorial could be no longer than 72 lines (one printed page).

I won't bore readers with everything I changed as I wrote, but here are a few changes that took place in the first paragraph of the 22 drafts. I've indicated by the number preceding each paragraph the stage of each draft.

My first draft reflected what I was then most concerned about, that President Reagan, like most politicians, saw education as little more than an issue for reelection, not as a real issue that affected teachers and school boards, one that needed to be faced rather than played with. So I began.

> 1. Until a few months ago, no one could have accused President Reagan of being fond of education. But time and chance and the need to curry favor may change us all, and Mr. Reagan's fallen in love, and

That seemed a bit windy and what was left of the 72-line total was slipping away so I tried something a bit faster, not much but just a bit.

4. Up till a few months ago, no one could have accused President Reagan of being fond of education, but times and passions change, and now he's fallen in love, and improved education through merit pay is her name. In Knoxville this past June he said, "If we want to achieve excellence, we

Somewhere about the fifth or sixth draft, I grew discouraged. I wanted to keep some of what I'd written, but I sensed that the material on Reagan was out of order and needed to pop up later. One last attempt, the seventh draft, I stooped to beginning with "The political football for 1984 is likely to be . . . ," but that was a tired enough image to make me return to my desk for half an hour.

During that interval, I went back to my notes and reread Ellen Goodman's column in which she insisted on misunderstanding why teachers fear merit pay, and that depressed me even more. If people as intelligent and perceptive as Goodman can't understand, what hope was there for my editorial? I also reread a clipping on former Secretary of Education Terrell Bell and his support of his boss. I didn't expect that to encourage me, but strangely enough it did. Bell's analogy of secondary-school merit pay with merit pay for college teachers struck me as ludicrous—and dangerous—but it was a place to begin. So the eighth draft began with that. If it proved little better than what I'd written before, at least it got me back before the typewriter and ready to try again.

The thirteenth draft, after several miserable attempts, got me on a tack that seemed workable, and by this time the elements of the editorial that I'd discarded as openings began to fall into proper place later in the piece.

13. Education almost always gets ignored at election time, but that may change in 1984. Given the doomsday documents about the plight of the schools and political opportunists looking desperately to find an issue to grab voters, education in general (and how bad it is) and merit pay in particular (and how it will remedy the badness) are likely to

The drafts that followed number 13 advanced the editorial hardly at all, but they included lines I was able to use later in the piece. I suspect that these intermediate drafts were intentional/unintentional stalls, written to fill in time until I could see my way to my final draft, or one very close to it.

By the eighteenth draft I'd dropped *doomsday documents* from the paragraph. I have no idea whether other people have used it, but it's a term I've used repeatedly in early drafts of several articles—and subsequently dropped in every article. Maybe it's that the phrase seems foolishly melodramatic. Maybe it's yet another example of Donelson's overkill. Whatever the reason, the phrase was removed.

Four more drafts and the first paragraph was ready. The 22 drafts took me, as I remember, about six hours to do, but much of that time was taken up by staring—one of my hobbies—by pacing outside my office, and by returning to my desk a few feet from my typewriter to look at notes and clippings.

And here is the final draft of the entire editorial as it appeared in the December 1983 *English Journal.**

EDITORS' PAGE
COLLECTED WISDOM ABOUT MERIT PAY
Ken Donelson

Education usually gets ignored come election time, but 1984 may be a bit different. With all those reports lamenting the plight of public schools and all those politicians desperately looking for hot issues to grab the folks back home, the badness of American education *(the problem)* and the goodness of merit pay *(the solution)* are likely to become next year's political clichés.

No one knows that better than President Reagan. Up to the last few months, few could have accused him of being smitten by education. Then came spring (when a young man's fancy lightly turns to thoughts of re-election) and the final report of the National Commission on Excellence in Education, and he found someone he could love and use, and her name is merit pay.

Love does make us blind, and if his passion for merit pay won him followers—"Any Democrat who opposes merit pay for teachers is going to cut his throat" was the way one ex-teacher put it (June 9 *New York Times*)—his reasoning has been open to question. In a speech at Hopkins, Minnesota, on June 9, he suggested that money for merit pay could be found if schools cut other programs of "much lower priority," though what programs would be cut was left for anyone to guess. Then he added, "Teachers who grade students ought to be able to grade each other," but since he's never taught, he wasn't aware that grading kids has always been something teachers get stuck with, never something good teachers enjoy doing and always something good English teachers know is uncomfortably subjective. (In her August 21 syndicated column, the usually sensible Ellen Goodman parroted Reagan when she wrote, "There is something amusing about the way that teachers, of all people, resist being graded. The same people who would defend their own objectivity are sure that any merit plan handled by the administration would go to the principal's pets." And we do worry about that.)

A few days later in Knoxville, Mr. Reagan called for an increase in state taxes to give bonuses to superior teachers, justifying that by saying, "If we want to achieve excellence, we must reward it. It's the American way." Teachers might be forgiven if they wonder why they're expected to pioneer a radical notion that's never taken hold in American life and is more myth than revealed truth. Perhaps we all ought to get paid what we're worth, but if so, how will Congress or the administration fare?

Secretary of Education Terrell Bell dutifully followed his boss and endorsed merit pay but with slightly different reasoning. Bell repeatedly cited the use of merit pay in college as a reward for good teaching. Colleges pretend that tenure and promotion and merit pay go to people outstanding in (1) teaching, (2) public service, and (3) scholarly activities. Anyone who's taught in college knows better. People who publish get the goodies, and teaching performance has nothing to do with anything. That may be sad, but it's true.

Despite all that, I do believe in merit pay if I (or other good teachers) judge our peers. That's the only way it will work, and it may not work even if we don't use principals to review teachers for merit pay. Suspicion and rivalry kill education, and both are encouraged by merit pay. At the very least, teachers this year need to get other voters to consider the effects, good and bad, of merit pay.

December 1983

How did this one piece of writing help me as a writer? Any bit of writing helps me to understand myself and how writing happens, just as every bit of writing is for me an exercise in humility, the finished product falls so far short of my aim.

How did this help my teaching? In a fit of inspiration after I'd concluded the writing, I was curious about the number of drafts I had gone through, so I emptied the wastebasket and counted them. I'd forgotten how different some of the drafts were, and for a few moments I savored my frustrations and stops and starts as I can do only when the deadline is over and the thing is mailed. I realized that I had something that might intrigue a class if I had the guts to show my students— particularly graduate students I'm encouraging to write for publication since their futures may rest on their bibliography—what I had begun with and finally arrived at. Wearing my rhetorical hair shirt to class posed some dangers, I suppose, but since we'd talked before about problems in writing, I'd shown them examples of what I'd published, and most of them had examined early drafts of work by Frost or Hemingway or other important writers, I felt the risk was worth taking. Besides, by then I could laugh at some of the dumb things I'd done in early drafts. It may seem dangerous for any of us to share our writing problems and our several drafts—warts and all—with young writers, since it makes clear that we are fallible and mortal. Maybe it's time they learned that about us. Maybe it's time we remembered it about ourselves.

We might even talk with them about how our writing begins, where and how we floundered, and what problems we faced in completing the job to our satisfaction, if that's an appropriate word for something as eternally cruel and unfinishable as writing. Will that impress students? I hope not, but it might make them think of us as writers, not merely teachers. Teachers may be able to help. Writers surely have a better chance of helping the young. More important, we might even be able to help ourselves.

Founder and editor of Rhetoric Review, *Theresa Enos has taught writing at Southern Methodist University since receiving her Ph.D. in rhetoric from Texas Christian University in 1980. Her essays on rhetoric and the teaching of writing have appeared in various publications, and her* Sourcebook for Basic Writing Teachers *has recently been published by Random House. In addition, she has lectured and presented workshops on corporate and legal writing and has presented numerous papers at professional conferences on rhetoric and composition.*

In 1983, she won an award for excellence in teaching; in 1985, she received the Modern Language Association's award for best journal design. Presently, she is working on a reader for a course in professional writing that focuses on a liberal arts approach.

WRITING, A DRIVING FORCE

Theresa Enos
Southern Methodist University

[My writing] all began (curiously, I'm thinking now) with an essay about travel, exploration, and discovery that I wrote in the fourth grade. It was that piece of writing each of us can remember if we travel back in time far enough—the one that came out whole, as if it resided there just so in our minds. The one that caused your teacher or mother to pronounce you a WRITER.

> March 16, 1986
> U.S. Highway 69
> Enroute from New Orleans
> to Fort Worth

Dear Tom,

Clicking off cruise control, I slow down to about 45 as I drive through Woodville, Texas, known mostly, I believe, for its dogwood snow every spring. The dogwood is pretty, but your request is worrying my mind. You see, when you asked me to join others who are writing on how they write, I joked back about not really wanting others to know how I write and feeling like such a fraud and wondering if you had read *The Impostor Phenomenon.* But part of that response wasn't light humor; I had seen the names of those invited to participate in your Volume 2 . . . Jim Corder, Frank D'Angelo, Peter Elbow, Maxine Hairston, Jim Kinneavy, Richard Lanham, Richard Marius, Dick Young . . . writers I've been admiring and trying to learn from for the last six years. And I began to feel anew that unsettling restlessness that pokes and jabs at me whenever I assign myself—or get assigned, as in this case —a personal essay, a professional article I hope to get published, or a conference paper.

Now, ten miles northeast of Woodville, in my car's encapsulated environment, I am able to keep that stomach-hammering imp at bay

—that perverse thing which at home urges me to get up from my desk, when I've hardly sat down there, to go feed the fussing wrens on my patio, then leads me on out in my backyard to pull up some invading henbit, then impels me to water the pyracantha that's dead anyway, forces me to trail around unfettered. Helps me escape my assignment, you see. But in my car I can write; I can't walk out to find my distractions. Whenever I mention that I write while driving, the response is you've-got-to-be-kidding laughter. But it's true; I do write while driving, just as I am at this moment, exploring in hopes of discovering something that I can shape and send to you. And since my mind already is traveling about as fast as I am (cruise control is back on 63), I know I'll discover something before I get home. And even if you decide that what I eventually send is not what you want, it really is all right, you see, because I'm discovering that *drive, travel, explore, find* connect in ways I've not perceived before, even though I've been doing my exploratory writing this way for a number of years.

But right now I need to follow a divergent path, back to what I said before about the impostor phenomenon. For me it all began (curiously, I'm thinking now) with an essay about travel, exploration, and discovery that I wrote in the fourth grade. It was that piece of writing each of us can remember if we travel back in time far enough—the one that came out whole, as if it resided there just so in our minds. The one that caused your teacher or mother to pronounce you a WRITER. The essay that made me want to believe I was a WRITER told how I imagined Balboa felt when he finally discovered the vast ocean at his travel's end. Sometimes I wish I'd never composed "Balboa Gazing on the Pacific" because I've been trying to live up to Miss Bates's anointment ever since. Teachers' words can make magic happen; but since my fourth grade whenever I face some writing project, I think maybe—surely?—Miss Bates made a mistake and I am an impostor. Once in a while I'll rummage through my keepsake cabinet to find that yellowed piece of ruled paper and read again her words encouraging me to read Keats's "On First Looking into Chapman's Homer," pointing out a similarity in theme and imagery, and promising me future rewards for writing. At ten I'd never heard of Keats, but I listened to my teacher and read the sonnet and knew I wanted to be a WRITER. But never again has a piece of writing come out whole as that one did. I've kept on, but mostly feeling I've never made it to that place again. So that's why I brought up the impostor phenomenon.

Now getting back on the road I'm supposed to be traveling, I have plenty of time on this trip back home from the 4 Cs to explore the way I write. I think how we begin to write depends in part on the way we view our worlds. Although I recognize the oversimplification here, I'll call these different perceptions the "Classical" mind and the "Romantic" mind. The Classical mind, in my generalization, strains toward establishing limits around a group of thoughts, a universe of knowledge. In this mind, ideas seem bound in time and spatial order. (I seem to imagine your interruption here, perhaps suggesting I'm recalling studies of the bicameral brain; and I see the connections, but I'm thinking more of "mind" than "brain.") To the Classical mind, the "world" of an idea is known, and all information within its boundaries is taken into consideration. This mind, in composing, narrows *from* a universe of material. Writers who nearly always have a body of material already at hand probably profit from outlines that help organize their body of information. They can "narrow the subject, limit the topic" as we sometimes tell our students, perhaps too soon and too often. I tend to think, though I may be wrong, that most WRITERS already have their "available means"; freewriting and exploring might lead them to impatience. I wonder if they can use the inventive techniques they offer to their students?

But I include myself in the probably smaller group (smaller anyway in academia, I wonder?) who "see" an abstraction suddenly made visually whole, who experience a sharply etched gestalt. To avoid immediate restrictions, I tend to move outward and begin to build ideas associatively. I do preliminary writing to try to trace that flash of intuition, working outward to discover some universe that is there. Whether or not it's true, Tom, I imagine my struggles to find something to say to be more painful than others'. But perhaps we all feel like impostors when we're struggling to write.

I don't want to belabor the connection here with my restless urgency to go beyond boundaries and my writing while driving. But besides the reality that writing itself is a driving force, the process intensifies when I drive to school or a conference or even a vacation destination.

My way of writing began when I started teaching at a university fifty miles from my home. Being a native of Fort Worth, a city with its western heritage intact and a comfortable sense of community, I was reluctant to move to Dallas, a city that in most ways is much farther from Fort Worth than the geographical thirty-two miles from city limit to city limit. So I have made the fifty-mile trip twice each teaching day for six years now.

I began noticing even that first semester how rich for me were those two hours a day, especially the morning drive. Getting in my car and snapping its seat belt across me, I'd hear Rex (my car's computerized voice) assure me that "All monitored systems are functioning." And with this signal my mind would begin functioning, exploring ideas, as I sped toward Dallas on Interstate 30. Sometimes, when I'd have a particularly tough writing project going, I'd take I-20 because I-20 is eight lanes and not very heavily traveled at the time I'd be driving to school. That's how the ritual began.

At first I tried a cassette recorder so I wouldn't lose thoughts coming as fast as the miles going beneath me. But I'm one of those "eye-minded" people who experience difficulty in "seeing" a concept or remembering a name unless it is written down. I've always spelled quite well, but even so at times when asked how a word is spelled, I feel unsure of my answer until I write out the word. Do you know what I mean? That cassette recorder acted as a constraint because I can't synthesize thoughts by talking them out. Besides, it interfered with another ritual, listening to my cassettes of ZZ Top belting out the miles.

Then during this productive driving time, I tried jotting down key words and phrases on a note pad. I tried thinking out a draft and then writing it from memory later. Nothing worked but actually writing while I drove. So now this is how I begin a writing project. The mechanics are neither difficult nor dangerous. I keep a yellow pad or spiral notebook in my lap, or sometimes on the console separating the front seats. I don't write constantly but in spurts and chunks as my mind travels and explores, explores and travels. With power steering, cruise control, and the triangular-spoked steering wheel, maintaining control is easy. And I usually write when I'm on interstates—and not during rush-hour traffic. I do, thank you, drive safely, seldom taking my eyes off the road unfolding in front of me.

I don't need to see the words unfolding beneath my pen. But when I begin the painful process of revision at home, behind my desk or in front of my IBM PC, I do need my discovery draft. More than this, I have to type it out even to be able to see it. Only then can I begin the first of five or six or seven drafts before I come up with something that I'll turn loose, fearful all the while. Damn that perfect fourth-grade essay anyway.

Actually, *not* watching myself write this first discovery draft, not watching the words and phrases as they tunnel through channels of both mind and pen, allows me to continue exploring as I drive forward. In contrast, when I attempt to discover a discourse at home, I'm much more likely to stop in the middle of a sentence to change a word or some phrasing. And often, when I do this, I know I can then only try to reconstruct the thought I had. Each time I stop there's a sense that something has hidden itself from me, that I've lost consciousness of what my mind was doing just at that moment—or where it was going. But in my car not staring at that piece of paper, that blank space to be filled, I am free to travel, thought rapidly generating thought as I travel in both senses. (I need to look again at that protocol analysis of "blind" writing. Do you remember that study?)

And I'm not consciously concerned with audience in this preliminary stage either. Usually, I have only the urge to write, to travel and explore along the way there, knowing (or hoping anyway) that for me, like Balboa, there will be something vast at journey's end. The driving force both releases and eases that familiar and dreaded urgency. I must get from somewhere to somewhere. I might not—usually don't—end up at the place I thought I was headed for or follow the particular road I thought would take me there. But I do find something there—always.

My best writing? When I have the opportunity to drive to some of our conferences, as I've done this week from Fort Worth to New Orleans and back (1,184 miles), I take advantage of what I recognize as my creative time. Ironically perhaps, my mind roams freer when I'm strapped in a traveling capsule. I need the isolation. The landscape surrounding me and my vehicle aids rather than hinders my mind to become more active in its exploring. I've traveled through all kinds of landscapes and perceived their effect on my mindscapes. For one thing, I've discovered I'm a desert person. The spacious beauty of those isolated landscapes allows my thoughts to move outward, across boundaries. I've found the most on those long stretches taking seven to ten hours to drive, especially the journeys beginning in Fort Worth and then broadening westward and northwestward. This kind of time, concentrated and ensconced with me in my space, a room truly my own, has been even more productive than the hundred-mile trips to and from my classroom.

So you see, Tom, revision is especially hard work for me because I have to face those MACHINES, not the world opening itself up to me with new and marvelous vistas every few minutes. I suppose you could say I'm mostly traditional when I revise. No longer can I imagine revising and editing without my PC and Microsoft Word. (Funny how the word *traditional* already can include word processors.) You'd think all those years when typing earned me money that I'd be a whiz composing on a keyboard. Oh, I do my class preparation and tons of correspondence quite efficiently on my typewriter or PC; I just don't like to turn my mind over to machines at first, when I'm doing what I call WRITING. Perhaps because of those years when typing was part of my job, I now view typing as merely mechanical. I can't create; I can't discover anything. For me, the pen is indeed an extension of my brain. Maybe I just don't like the image of my IBM Selectric or PC being like my brain —much less my mind. I don't *want* to know which button to push to find something. I want to travel and explore, to be surprised when I find something I suspected was there all along.

That an encapsulated environment generates an encapsulated idea may seem a trifle odd, but don't you think it makes some sense? Somewhere around Baton Rouge on I10 this idea just came from nowhere (so it seemed anyway), the idea that metaphor and reality merge when

I write while driving. I've been exploring the idea ever since. (I'm now on U.S. 175, a few miles northwest of Jacksonville, Texas.)

So even though I'm not continuously writing as my tires continuously turn on the way back to Fort Worth—or wherever my destination —still my mind makes its own revolutions. Certainly no finished product comes from this kind of writing, but I usually get down most of the material I end up using. What usually does come from this writing is some purpose enlarged through exploration. When I get home, I put the pages aside because I dread trying to re-create that excitement of discovery. I hate revision, maybe because I haven't yet found a way to revise while driving. Later, when I've got both nerve and stamina—or when the deadline gets too close—I begin the mechanical word-processing procedure, hoping each level of drafting and revising will rise toward synthesis rather than descend into chaos. Somehow, doggedly, I continue until I end up with something tighter and about two-thirds shorter than the discovery draft I began with. It's like traveling back almost to where I started, isn't it? But I know what I didn't know—or couldn't find—before.

Perhaps I'll never discover a Pacific Ocean because I don't—or can't—go far enough. And never can I be the writer I want to be. I'll continue reading and revering Keats and admiring and respecting my colleagues in rhetoric and composition who write with such humanity and grace. But still I know Miss Bates lowered a beautiful burden onto me, a weight that so far I've been willing to carry because by it I am strengthened.

Well, I'm almost home, Tom. Waxahachie by way of U.S. 287 is within thirty miles of Fort Worth. Home. Thank you for inviting me to make this explorative journey.

Cordially,

Theresa

Theresa Enos

Michael C. Flanigan is Earl A. and Betty Galt Brown Professor of Rhetoric and Composition at the University of Oklahoma, where he has been director of writing for five years. Prior to moving to Oklahoma he was director of composition at Indiana University. He has run workshops on teaching composition and on general teaching strategies at the University of Stockholm and at several colleges and high schools around the country.

Flanigan's numerous publications include articles in College English, The English Journal, *and* Theory into Practice. *He has authored or coauthored five books.*

REACHING ACROSS THE GAP: HOW I WRITE

Michael C. Flanigan
University of Oklahoma

My present writing process reflects earlier experiences I've had as a writer. I attend to audience; I do not write just for myself, though as I write I find that I order knowledge, learn to make connections, think about ideas more deeply, and search for the words, images, and experiences that will elicit in others ideas that I want to communicate.

My sister Mary and my brother Leo were the first two audiences I wrote for. Mary and the boys (four of us) were separated when my father joined the Navy at the beginning of World War II. Mary stayed with my mother while we went to St. Francis's Home for Boys to get discipline, uniforms, and cleanly ways. I was five, the youngest in the five-hundred-boy school. I remember how much I wanted to write my sister, so after our daily lessons of reading and penmanship (the rest of school is forgotten) I would return to the dorm in the evening and practice. I wrote and wrote and wrote. All the initial writing was practice—to get my penmanship right, to string words together for sense, to punctuate, to fill a page, then another and another until a pad was gone.

Finally I wrote a letter to my sister. I filled a page with How are you? Hope you are fine. Miss you. Love you. Leo, Pat, and Pete are fine. Leo is growing trees from sticks. Please write. I was not confident of my first attempt at written communication, so I stuffed the letter with jokes from magazines, some buttons I had collected, and a holy medal. All things I knew my sister liked.

Within a week my letter was answered. Besides a thank you for the gifts were descriptions of Mary's new school, how she was learning to ride a bike, and hosts of other information about herself and our mother —three full pages. She asked one question: How does Leo grow trees from sticks? I didn't know. He just told me. I knew I had to find out. When I asked, Leo explained in minute detail how he picked the right branches from trees, cut them, soaked them, and on through a whole fascinating process that I repeated as best I could in my next letter. I also followed my sister's example and told about bits and pieces from our lives at the "military school." Our correspondence continued for over four years until we boys were sent to see my father in Spokane in 1946. The letters stopped on both ends. A few months later the family was back together.

In 1950 Leo went to Korea. Again the urge to write, to create a reality of home for him, overtook me. I wrote every day for two years until he came home. The letters focused on things I knew he would want to hear about: the state of the house he was building when he left, the orchard he helped plant on Uncle Vic's farm, the mountains he loved, friends we both knew, relatives, and a host of the details that made up his life and ours together. He rarely wrote back, but no need. I was obsessed with keeping words floating through the air. Anything became a possible letter topic—and had to, under the daily assignment I had given myself. I began to see subjects in the smallest events, changes, ideas. When he returned I stopped writing anything, quit school, and "bummed" around the country.

What this early letter writing taught me was to focus on audience. Communication is not possible without common understandings, backgrounds, experiences, knowings, mental processes. Yes, we can learn what appears to be new, but it is only appearance.

Minds use the same kinds of mental processes Aristotle described in the common topoi. When we use language we describe, analyze, compare, and so forth. We bring new understandings, new information, to life by relying on what others already know and what we know about them. In focusing on audiences and trying to elicit images in their minds we are trusting that common threads hold communication together. We make up images, analogies, and other symbolic realities to trigger intellectual and emotional "responses" that allow audiences to reconstruct, to connect to, what we have constructed in words. The match is never exact; it is not exact for any two readers. But if the images, ideas, symbols are familiar, there will be correspondence. Language is a triggering device; it is not reality. It is learned from the experience in a community of others who give us varying images of what reality is to them, and then we in turn construct our own notions of things.

Often the symbols we accept to describe reality blind us to seeing —sensing in detail. We accept other people's words for what we take in through our senses, and the result is that the words confine us. Hughes Mearns notes this phenomenon in typical student writing when he says, in *Creative Power:*

His phrases are copied, too. All his streams ripple, all his lakes are silver (so is his moon), and his trees whisper in the gentle—guess what? Breeze? Right! His rain always beats down or it falls in torrents; his evening shadows are purple; his whippoorwills call mournfully in the solemn night. (My whippoorwill is a healthy, optimistic idiot screaming, *"You* come here!" to his lady friend up the hill, who yells back, "You come *here!* "For hours they keep it up with amorous obstinacy: *"You* come here!" "You come *here!"* *"You* come here!" "You come *here!"* And they just never get *any*where. It's me that's mournful. No; I *don't* mean I. I mean ME! About one a.m. I'm shying rocks at their roosts and saying things aloud. Solemn night? Anything *but* a solemn night.)

His fire shadows dance, his twilights fade, his tall ladies are stately, his little girls romp, his eyes have a twinkle in them, all his smiles are roguish, and all his laughs are merry.

There is no life in any of that language anymore. It has been completely used up by others long ago. (pp. 131–132)

Such confinement, or blindness caused by accepting the words of others, is even more apparent in bureaucratic and governmental language, often constructed with the purpose of hiding meaning as much as possible. This does not mean that Hughes Mearns's students or bureaucrats have no sense of audience. The children Mearns speaks of are often playing it safe or trying to please their teachers. They have read enough simplistic literature from texts their teachers selected to know what will please their audience. Bureaucrats on the other hand frequently try to avoid personal responsibility by using language that will lull audiences into believing that what is being said means something it doesn't; this is especially true when we look at the language the military created to mask reality in Korea and Vietnam. (A "police action" sure looked like a war to those who were there.)

I continued to write letters through a need to keep personal contact with relatives and friends. I still write them, even though the phone sits, telling me to save time. Letters were the first way I learned that writing is a means, if done with some skill, of getting an audience to identify with feelings and ideas I believe are important. In personal letters we know our audiences well and can marshal our words and ideas into a shape they will recognize and accept. I like to think that I stumbled upon a method of self-education as a writer that has been used for centuries by some of the greatest authors I admire. They were letter writers, and consummate ones at that—think of Petrarch, who found and wrote letters, Virginia Woolf, James Joyce, Henry James.

Actually, it wasn't until years later that I realized that basic to most good writing is the need to identify with audiences so that they in turn will take the time to read what is written. Before I could understand this, I had to do considerably more writing—and of a different kind.

In college I began to branch out. I had dropped out of school after the ninth grade, "drifted" around, joined the service, and when I was twenty-two met Bernie McCabe (an English teacher) who persuaded the authorities at the then Western Reserve University to let me in. One of my first courses was English 101, and my teacher was Ms. Reed. She started us writing about what we knew—stories from our own lives. Her constant advice to us was, "Write about what you know. Don't tell me about things you've no experience with." I trusted this small, thin, 60-ish woman right off, so I wrote about getting drunk with a friend and rolling my car over six times before it came to a halt on the front porch of a house. I started with dialogue, slid us off our bar stools and ended with us pulling ourselves upside-down through the body-tight smashed car door window frame into the legs of a waiting policeman. I had misgivings when I turned the paper in. I had told about what I had experienced, but I wasn't sure Ms. Reed would approve. Five minutes before the next class ended she handed the papers back. Mine read, "A over F. See Me!"

In her office that night she told me I had written a lively story, and it had rung true. She liked the dialogue, description, the way I made her see and experience the movement, the obvious friendship and our abandon. But my spelling was atrocious, my punctuation almost as bad. In other words, get a dictionary and handbook and clean up my act. Learn to proof. If I didn't, she warned, she just might drop me from class. Weeks later when I told her about my direct approach of trying to memorize the dictionary and handbook she laughed and told me, "Just carry them with you. I don't mind if you use them in class." I did throughout our two semesters together.

Ms. Reed continued the first half of 101 having us write about ourselves, giving us impromptus, showing us how other writers (professionals) handled similar experiences, and then she had us write argumentative papers about what we knew—of course supported with evidence. She taught us how to do research, using a source book, on the Brook Farm experiment, and then helped us pick topics we cared about to research in the library. She encouraged us, conferenced with us, pushed us, but always the theme was write about what you know or care about. That's what people will want to read. She was a tough but open-minded audience.

Throughout the rest of undergraduate school I relied on Ms. Reed's basic tenet: Write about what you know or care about. Each time I was given a writing assignment in history, sociology, philosophy, or English I would find something I was curious about—whether it was burial customs around the world, a comparison of Grant and Lee as generals, the effect of the Stamp Act on the House of Burgesses in Virginia, causes of juvenile delinquency in Cleveland, or writing imitation stream of consciousness à la Virginia Woolf. Of course I did not know these topics as I knew events from my own life, but I was curious about them. I wanted to find out about them, and I have to admit, I wanted to show what I knew about them to my teachers. Writing became a way of ordering and understanding what I studied and researched. I learned to use primary sources, evaluate sources (historical letters, notebooks, newspaper accounts), weigh evidence, raise questions, become critical. These all became a part of my experience—what I knew and cared about.

In graduate school I continued to refine what I had learned as an undergraduate. Most of my study then concentrated on literature. I learned to do scholarship, especially reading and studying what others had said about the works under consideration—along with learning to read closely. My teachers for the most part wanted a demonstration that a thorough scholarly search had been done, and then anything else we wanted to do in our papers was up to us, so I worked to find a point of view that was unusual or a way of seeing the same thing in a different light. For example, in one course when I chose to do a paper on "Empedicles on Etna" I wrote a paper called "Thirteen Ways of Looking at 'Empedicles on Etna.' " I found twelve readings of the poem and then added my own. Perhaps this was not great scholarship, but it was the only way to make the poem finally mine. Eventually I wrote my dissertation under the guidance of Wallace W. Douglas. He was a taskmaster for a tight, lively prose style—something I did not master in the dissertation and still find difficult today.

My first public writing was done in college when I wrote columns for the school paper. My column was called "The Liberal View" and ran alongside one called "The Conservative View." We were assigned issues to discuss each week: What is a liberal/conservative? Labor unions. Birth control. Voting rights. Neither of us saw the other's response until it appeared in print. Oddly, our views were similar, if not in absolute agreement, on most issues. The conservative turned out to be too liberal. When the editor could not find a conservative willing to write, I was given my own corner—"Flanigan's Corner." Things went fine for a few weeks as I wrote about racial issues, apathy on campus, and such. Then I made an audience mistake. A high-ranking university administrator wrote a book of poetry. I read it and decided to review it. My review was less than kind. The newspaper review board consisting of two faculty advisors, the editor, and other students refused to publish it; they said the review was not balanced, had no place in the paper, bordered on libel. I held my ground, insisting that students would be interested and that my review reflected how bad the poetry was. I also threatened to quit; that was my last day on the paper.

When I went public again I had been teaching at Euclid Central

Junior High School a year and wrote an article about a thematic unit on coming of age that I had written and taught. That was the beginning of twenty years of publishing that I have done on pedagogical issues— both problems and possible solutions. It has been natural to write about what I do, read about, and think about. Ms. Reed would be pleased.

My writing comes out of my work. As I learned to observe and train composition teachers I wrote articles on how to observe and conference with teachers so their own natural talents and styles could be best developed. I wrote about setting up training programs. Broke that into parts on teaching revision, using groups for collaborative writing, using a process approach to develop ideas and eventual papers—ideas should continue as long as I work. Like so many of my colleagues who are concerned about improving teaching I've had to read learning theory, instructional theory, and theory about my subject matter—composition and rhetoric. I had to go back to the ancients, look closely at eighteenth- and nineteenth-century theory and practice, read as much current research as possible—all of it with the idea that such work would help to improve and inform educational practice. So reading and practice are the bedrock of what I write about.

Usually an idea for writing comes to me in the midst of trying to solve a problem in my own teaching and administration. If I think I've found something worthwhile, I want to share it with fellow teachers and administrators. I believe I've come to know these two audiences through my own teaching in schools and universities, through professional meetings, through reading journals dealing with similar issues, and through hundreds of conversations both oral and written. I begin by writing notes to myself, often whole paragraphs that will later appear in some form in the finished piece. I jot down anything that appears to relate to the idea. Of course a good many of these related ideas don't fit once the piece begins to take shape, and its shape is determined as I write, though I have a tentative outline in my head that often shifts as new ideas or memories surface.

When I begin to write with intention and direction I work in two ways: either quickly through the whole draft or slowly over weeks and even months. I seem automatically to choose either to be a "carver" or a "molder" as A. Alvarez explains these terms in his review "Flushed with Ideas":

> Ezra Pound once divided writers into carvers and molders. The molders—Balzac, Lawrence, Whitman—work fast, not much worried by detail or repetition or precision, impatient to get down the shape and flow of their inspiration, while the carvers—Flaubert, Eliot, Beckett—work with infinite slowness, unable to go ahead until each phrase is balanced, each detail perfect. (p. 22)

Most of my writing recently has been slow, for frequently I find as I anticipate the *act* I do other things. In the seven or eight focused sittings to write this piece I've written over two dozen letters, cleaned the house thoroughly three times, made soups enough to last months, gone shopping several times for miscellaneous items, and simply engaged in as many avoidance activities as possible. But once I run out of excuses, sit and begin writing, I dive deeply into myself—into a world that at first is uncomfortably disordered. As I concentrate I begin to see a direction—sometimes the initial direction is abandoned. For example, in writing this piece I had first decided to start with writing about how I write. It just didn't feel right. So then I started with a quotation from John Ciardi about how all writers tell *lies* when they begin to talk about their writing. That seemed to go nowhere. Finally it occurred to me that audience was central in my writing from the first writing I did. The direction I wanted to go became clearer.

Once the writing starts moving in a direction I feel confident with, I keep my audience balanced in my mind with the ideas that occur to me. I keep asking, Will this make sense? Do I need an example? Will this connect with their experience and understanding? For example, in writing this article, when I described the accident I wrote about for Ms. Reed, I decided that because this story was embedded in a story about Ms. Reed you, as a reader, would not need a full description of the story. I wanted to give enough detail, but not so much that it would intrude. I felt you would make the connection. In other words, am I reaching across the void which separates us? Am I making a connection that will ring true? I think about teachers I know and try to speak to them. I try to make the audience as real as possible by remembering the things I've heard and read that other teachers have said or written. As I think about what happens as I write, I don't believe I discover anything so much as I see relationships I had not been aware of before. Odd bits buried away in experience present themselves in a new light, and I realize that these connections may connect with my audience.

The first draft, done on yellow legal pads (I've never learned to think at a typewriter, though I envy the speed of those who have) has hundreds of revisions in it by the time I reach the end. Often, even before I finish the draft, I've read it to or had it read by several friends. The finished first draft is always read by others. I listen to their criticism, noting problems, possibilities, and successes, and then return to the draft to make major and minor changes. Usually the changes required are not severe, because of all the early response I've had to the developing piece.

This process seems to bear out the kind of collaborative revision that I advocate in my teaching. I seem to need audience response as often as possible as a piece develops. I then can see what makes sense, what is connecting to the experiences of others. Most of my students seem to agree.

Obviously my present writing process reflects earlier experiences I've had as a writer. I attend to audience; I do not write just for myself, though as I write I find that I order knowledge, learn to make connections, think about ideas more deeply, and search for the words, images, and experiences that will elicit in others ideas that I want to communicate. I do not write about what I don't know or care about. My writing comes from my daily life as a teacher, administrator, reader, learner. The act of writing helps me structure a world I might not *know,* if it were not for the words on paper. They seem, often as I read them later, to say, Maybe this is what's real.

Bibliography

Alvarez, A. "Flushed with Ideas." *New York Review of Books,* May 13, 1982.

Mearns, Hughes. *Creative Power.* New York: Doubleday, Doran and Company, 1929.

Toby Fulwiler is director of writing at the University of Vermont. Before that he taught for seven years at Michigan Tech, where he became a writer. With Art Young, he is coeditor of Language Connections *(1982) and* Writing Across the Disciplines *(1986).*

He is currently working on a book on writing meant to answer both large and small questions.

PROPOSITIONS OF A PERSONAL NATURE

Toby Fulwiler
University of Vermont

I write not because of Kipling or my mother, or because my papers were read in tenth grade, or because I have to. I write because if I don't, I cannot sleep. And when I cannot sleep I'm as cranky as when I don't write in my journal for a week.

1. I have trained myself to need to write. I think of writing, along with reading, as a literate addiction. I could untrain myself, I think, but I don't want to.

2. In 1967 I called myself an English teacher; in 1977 I called myself a writing teacher; recently I have begun to call myself a writer who teaches English.

3. As a writer I am better able to withstand the slings and arrows of English Department politics, though I am not sure I could tell you why.

4. When a friend reads something I have written, I want most for that friend to hear my voice. When other people read my work, I want them to believe me.

5. When I have time, or something to figure out, or a fresh cup of coffee, I like to write in the leather-covered notebook given to me by Laura, with the Mont Blanc Diplomat given to me by Don Gallher. I call the notebook a journal; the Diplomat writes almost as well as my ten-dollar Pelikan.

6. On United Airlines flights from Burlington to Chicago, I take off my shoes, buckle up, and write with my journal on my lap. Sometimes flight attendants pause and ask what I am doing, and I feel both silly and pleased at the same time.

7. I majored in English at the University of Wisconsin because I hoped that Joyce, Yeats, Eliot, and e. e. cummings would explain life to me. Later, in graduate school, I learned that life was a series of very small questions. Now I teach my students to ask their own questions and write their own answers.

8. It took me three days and a fair amount of anxiety to learn Wordstar on my IBM PC. I damn near ruined a spring break. I taught it to my fourteen-year-old daughter, Megan, in three hours. I tell myself that I am a very good teacher.

9. Laura says that because I write daily in my journal I do not share with her all my thoughts. She's probably right. But so am I.

10. When I was quite young, my mother would read stories to me from Kipling's *Jungle Book*. That was before we bought our first television. (Later, I remember hating Walt Disney for what he did to Bagheera, Baloo, and Kaa.) Listening to jungle sounds made me a writer.

11. When I was quite young, my mother used to write stories and send them to the *New Yorker*. They always came back, but sometimes they wouldn't come back for a long time. Watching my mother write made me a writer.

12. Twice in high school English classes, in Mrs. Muehl's tenth grade and again in Mr. Bush's twelfth, essays I had written were read aloud to the class. I acted like it was no big deal.

13. Twice, too, in "Letters to Editor," I misspelled words in public. When I misspelled "plagiarism" the editor put "sic" after the word, John Simon called me names, and I wished I was still in high school.

14. Annie, my eleven-year-old, keeps a "School Diary" on the computer. In it she writes about what she learned in school each day, and Laura and I write back to her. She does this because I agreed to raise her allowance from two dollars to four. I wanted her to learn early about audience and purpose.

15. When I compose with keyboard and screen, I compose differently than with pencils on pads of lined yellow paper. Instead of writing for seven pages at a linear crack, I now compose from the inside out, reentering my first paragraph and subdividing my way out. I used to write like a tapeworm, now I write like an amoeba.

16. I heard Paul Mariani explain, at the end of a complex piece of poetic interpretation, that he wrote literary criticism because he "had to." I wonder if he, too, taught himself to need that. If not, I wonder where it came from.

17. In third grade Tom Meheon used to ask me to draw rabbits for him. My rabbits weren't that good, but Tom thought they were better than his. He was wrong, you know, but at the time, neither of us knew that.

18. When I write at home, I listen to a radio program from San Francisco called "Hearts of Space." My friend Mike Strauss, who teaches chemistry, says he does the same thing. In fact, once I saw him sitting on a bar stool, a Sony Walkman wired to his ears, writing something. Together we wrote an article called "Expressive Writing and the Teaching of Chemistry." (I can just hear Mr. Bush asking me where, in this paragraph, is the topic sentence. And I can hear myself answering: It's a fragment.)

19. Harry Brent wrote, in Volume 1 of *Writers on Writing,* exactly the piece I wished I had written. Especially the part about the bedside reading. I've been excited and depressed ever since. The only things left for me to write were fragments.

20. Elaine Maimon, Maxine Hairston, and I ate red snapper and watched Jose Greco together in Tampa, Florida, one week before Tom's deadline for this book. We all figured it was OK to be late with our manuscripts since, together, we comprised 8.4 percent of the book. If you read this we were right. If not, deadlines are more serious than we thought.

21. I went to bed at midnight after naming these fragments "Twenty Propositions . . . ." Within twenty minutes of hitting the sack I had discovered four more pieces in my head, with more coming. It is now 4:10 in the morning. I have been writing propositions all night.

22. In the spring of 1982, I agreed to write a short book on composition for Bob Boynton. I told him it would take me the whole summer: before I could write the book, I needed to fix the boathouse so that I would have a place in which to write. It is 1986 and, except for the ceiling, the boathouse is nearly done and the writing is going well.

23. In 1971 I sat down each morning in the cafeteria overlooking Lake Mendota at the University of Wisconsin with a chocolate donut and my journal and wrote about writing my dissertation. One morning I wrote for three hours and discovered Chapter One. All this was before I ever heard of Ken Macrorie, Don Murray, Janet Emig, or James Moffett. You see, it was wondrously easy for them to speak great truths to me.

24. In 1967, when I knew nothing of COMPOSITION or RHETORIC or THE COMPOSING PROCESS, I used to tell my freshmen a good trick to start a piece of writing: "Plan to throw your first page away."

Now, nineteen years later, I tell freshmen about "freewriting" and wish I had written a book called "Writing Without Teachers."

25. In Chico, California, I learned about using team journals. For two days at a writing workshop, twenty-four of us passed notes to each other through these journals. "Greatest thing since sliced bread," I thought: Note passing made legitimate.

26. When Megan was in seventh grade and I asked her English teacher if they ever shared each other's writing in class, she told me "Yes, they correct each other's spelling." I got up, stormed around the room, and told her that the only real writing they did in that class was passing notes back and forth. The next day Megan said, in a rather flat voice: "Thanks Dad."

27. All fall Annie brought home vocabulary workbooks from her sixth-grade English class. They wrote nothing else. That's when I made the deal with her about writing the school diary on the computer, proving, I believe, that I am capable of learning something.

28. It is now 5:00 in the morning: I have restarted the fire, put on a Paul Winter tape, and made a sandwich from cold pot roast. I think that writing propositions is the greatest thing since sliced bread and a good footnote to the piece Harry and I wrote in Volume 1. What's especially nice is how propositions explain fragments and solve the problem of transitions.

29. I am now hopelessly entangled in a lie. It is no longer early that morning, but two weeks later, and I have tinkered mercilessly with my early morning language. It is now better, but less true, since the time and tense are all wrong. Before tonight, of course, everything I wrote was true.

30. I write not because of Kipling or my mother, or because my papers were read in tenth grade, or because I have to. I write because if I don't, I cannot sleep. And when I cannot sleep I'm as cranky as when I don't write in my journal for a week.

Richard C. Gebhardt is professor of English and assistant academic dean at Findlay College in Findlay, Ohio. He has edited Composition and Its Teaching: Articles from CCC During the Editorship of Edward P. J. Corbett (1979), and has published essays on composition theory, the teaching of writing, fiction, and the teaching of literature in a wide range of journals and essay collections.

Gebhardt's "Balancing Theory with Practice in the Training of Writing Teachers" won the 1978 Richard Braddock award as the outstanding article on composition published in any journal of the National Council of Teachers of English. He has served on several editorial boards, has presented a number of papers on composition, literature, and professional concerns, and frequently leads workshops. From 1979 to 1983 he served as secretary of the Conference on College Composition and Communication, of which he is an active member.

CONFIDENCE IN WRITING'S COMPLEXITY

Richard C. Gebhardt
Findlay College

*I know that I do not write in any one way. Rather, how I work
on a writing project seems to be determined to a large extent by
what I write about, why and for whom I write, how long I have
to write, and quirky factors (hunches or luck, for instance) I
neither understand nor worry about. Even more sharply, perhaps, how I write is influenced by whether, during a given drafting session, my cerebral or my behavioral tendencies take control
of the writing.*

The most important result of composition research, I tell students who
plan to be teachers or writers, is that it can save us from silly simplicity
—from believing that there is *a* "writing process," from doubting ourselves when we do not follow it, from trying to impose textbook pro-
nouncements on our students and then criticizing them when they
don't write that way. That's an arguable hypothesis, I know, but one
that is pragmatically attractive to advanced students who are trying to
reconcile the differences between, say, Sharon Pianko's research showing that pausing to reread and reflect is critical to effective writing
("Reflection," *College Composition and Communication* 30 [1979]:
275–278) and Sheridan Blau's conclusion that some people seem to
write better if they can't even see their developing texts as they draft
("Invisible Writing," *College Composition and Communication* 34
[1983]: 297–312). The hypothesis also helps clarify my practices as a
writer. For as I have worked to create and capture ideas in words—first
with pen and pad, later at a typewriter, most recently at the computer
in my office or the one in my study—I have come to realize how true
Donald Murray's words, in *A Writer Teaches Writing*, are of my writing
practices: "There are no absolute laws of composition. Each principle

of writing may be broken to solve a particular problem in a specific piece of work. The only test a writer applies to a page is the craftsman's question, 'Does it work?' " (Houghton Mifflin, 1968, p. 1).

I don't mean that I'm a rhetorical nihilist, or a communications outlaw who breaks rules for the sake of breaking them. But I know that I do not write in any *one* way. Rather, how I work on a writing project seems to be determined to a large extent by what I write about, why and for whom I write, how long I have to write, and quirky factors (hunches or luck, for instance) I neither understand nor worry about. Even more sharply, perhaps, how I write is influenced by whether, during a given drafting session, my cerebral or my behavioral tendencies take control of the writing.

TWO EXPERIENCES

At Michigan State University in 1968, I was writing a dissertation on Ernest Hemingway and teaching composition as a graduate teaching assistant. In the one role, I was struggling with the tangled messiness of my own writing, while in the other I was discovering the idea of freewriting. Surprisingly, the two experiences fit together. I found that once I got started drafting, writing would continue, as ideas flowed along with ink out of my ball-point pen. I was, to overstate the case, coming to understand writing as a nonlinear and behavioral process. And then I had an experience.

After worrying for most of the afternoon over a transitional paragraph between two chapters, I gave up in disgust, started dinner, turned on the news, had a beer, took a bath. And while I relaxed in the tub, just the transition I had not been able to write clicked into place in my mind. Naturally, I jumped out of the tub, dripped to the desk, and made some notes before the thought could fade.

No, that was not the start of some new theory of naked composition. But the experience did make me think differently about my writing. Where had that illusive transition "come" from? Clearly, my relaxed brain had found its way subconsciously through tangles that had baffled my conscious mind. This discovery was part of writing; after all, it helped me discover and communicate ideas on paper. But it was so obviously mental and nonbehavioral, that I realized the idea of writing I had been forming—that writing creates ideas and not the other way around—could not be fully accurate. The bathtub experience, that is, forced me to broaden my understanding of how I write, as well as my concept of writing.

A dozen or so years later, I was drafting what in time became an article called "Initial Plans and Spontaneous Composition" (*College*

English 44 [1982]: 620–627). I began the first draft by analyzing two contradictory passages, one of which I agreed with and one of which I planned to use as a foil to help me argue in favor of a spontaneous, nonlinear idea of composition. This is what I wrote at one point in that early draft:

> . . . So it seems clear that King's linear theory of composing cannot encompass the issues Mandel raises. It does not, that is, account for diversity in the phenomena of writing; it does not weave into its theoretical fabric the practices of people who know that they do not move through a conscious pre-production period of thinking, planning, organizing, and incubating.

While I was reworking that draft, a funny thing happened to my original plan for the article. I had just started retyping the first line of that part of the draft when I saw different words come out of my Smith-Corona: "So it seems clear that *neither* King's linear description of the writing process, *nor*. . . ." Immediately, I sensed that the article was changing direction. And I knew that I would have to revise my original plans for the article when, a few seconds later, I watched my typewriter replace a *period* marking definite closure with a *semicolon* opening the way to more balanced criticism:

> King's linear explanation . . . does not weave into its theoretical fabric the practices of people who know that they do not move through a conscious pre-production period of thinking, planning, organizing, and incubating; Mandel's nonlinear view excludes the writing practices of those who know they *do*.

INITIAL IDEAS, SPONTANEOUS DRAFTING

My experience drafting "Initial Plans and Spontaneous Composition" reveals a truth about my approaches to writing, but not the whole truth. To an outside observer, I know I often look like a very efficient free-writer. For I often begin a writing project as I did this one: by turning on my computer, loading the word-processing software, and just starting to draft. Even more often, I follow the unexpected turns words can take as they appear on my screen, or I get a hunch to change the emphasis of a paragraph even as my fingers continue to lay down letters on the screen. For instance, I began this paragraph thinking I was writing a conclusion to the previous section. As I drafted, though, I sensed that the truth-but-not-the-whole-truth idea could help carry me farther into my practices as a writer. So I hit the return key to stop this paragraph a few lines ago (after "lay down letters on the screen"), ran the cursor up to insert the "Initial Ideas, Spontaneous Drafting" head-ing, and then ran it down to start working on the next paragraph. After I had roughed out the next couple of paragraphs, I ran the cursor back and added these four sentences of illustration.

Such spontaneous composition, I've already indicated, is not the whole truth of my writing. For when I begin to write, I usually have in mind an initial concept for the project and a sense of my future readers. And sometimes I have a great deal more, as another writing experience may suggest. In 1975, I was working on a short review of a new novel. As I read Michael Brownstein's *Country Cousins* (Brazaller, 1974), I noticed similarities to fiction by William Faulkner, Kurt Vonnegut, Jr., and Henry Miller, and I found myself wondering, what if those authors had collaborated on a novel? When I rolled paper into my typewriter and started to draft the review, that thought was so forceful—as a thesis, an implicit organization, and a principle by which to select illustrative details—that it took me only about twenty minutes to write the rough draft of this brief review:

> If William Faulkner, Henry Miller, and Kurt Vonnegut could collaborate on a book today, it might resemble this bizarre first novel . . . . Faulkner might contribute the small town/rural aura; the slightly insane main character, Martin Kilbanky, with his dream of building a lasting edifice on the family farm; and the sycophantic Bill and Marge Parsons who exploit Martin and his mother. Miller might add the outrageous sexual exploits of Marge and Martin—including 54 hours of uninterrupted sex in the kitchen, on the stairs, on the porch. Vonnegut might add the simultaneous and parallel planes of existence that Martin dimly perceives; the plus-sign and minus-sign creatures who visit Martin in a peanut-sized spacecraft; and Martin's final dream of being a hunted deer or bear or beaver in a bulky animal suit. And Vonnegut might also add the matter-of-fact flatness of explanations and descriptions, the uncontrolled exposition, and the unexpected and slightly askew language . . . that contribute so much to the style and texture of the novel."
> (*Choice* 12 [1975]: 68)

The controlling force the initial idea exercised over that review is hardly typical of what happens when I write. Nearly always, my initial intention for a writing project gets me going—gives me words to put on paper or screen when I first sit down to draft. Then *if* that intention continues to make sense to me—especially if drafting confirms it as a useful guide to follow—it serves as a reference point when my drafting runs out of steam or I need inspiration to begin a new writing session. Usually, though, I see new connections while I draft, or a new slant comes to me when I break for a cup of coffee, or I wake up knowing that the tack I was taking the night before needs some adjustment, or

I get some hunch that I should be doing things a little differently. So I usually revise, or at least fine-tune, my initial concept many times before I finish a writing project.

So far, this essay is turning out to be fairly typical of the way I write. Before I wrote the first word, I knew I was going to do something with the no-one-way-to-write idea. After all, my assignment was to try to explain how I write, and I knew from personal experience that my approach to writing is both cerebral and behavioral. I had even sharpened my point of view on those experiences writing several earlier articles and conference papers. So my initial plan for this essay was sharply defined and reasonably detailed, and it helped me draft pretty efficiently until I neared the end of the "Two Experiences" section. I ended one drafting session there, knowing that the section was not done. When I began writing the next day, I recalled my initial intention, and that helped me find the truth-but-not-the-whole-truth idea. But as I explained about three paragraphs ago, spontaneous drafting then replaced the initial concept as the driving force in my writing, leading me to reorganize the paper and suggesting some initial plans for this section. Those plans helped me start drafting, and once I started I saw some new connections—such as how I could use my experiences drafting this particular section of the essay to suggest how initial ideas and spontaneous drafting work for me when I write.

ATTITUDES, APPROACHES

Initial ideas and spontaneous drafting, I've been suggesting, are both important to my writing. Initial hunches about thesis or overall intention usually help me get started on a drafting session. Observing and reacting to the words that appear during drafting nearly always influence what happens then—the gradual growth of ideas through changes in emphasis, switches in sequence, discovery of illustrations. Those sentences really are fairly accurate, but they look too pat, as if writing "just happens" for me.

Sometimes, writing seems to work just that way, as it did once when a weekend of computer writing took me from a few scribbled notes to a 22-page third draft of what eventually was printed as "Sentence Combining and the Teaching of Writing Process" (in *Sentence Combining: A Rhetorical Perspective,* ed. Donald Daiker and others, Southern Illinois University Press, 1985). On occasions like that, writing goes for me much the way I describe it in the "Initial Ideas, Spontaneous Drafting" section: it flows dynamically and efficiently toward a completed draft as an initial concept triggers a flurry of words, the drafting of which brings new insights that trigger more words, etc. But when I reflect honestly on my practices as a writer, I know that writing probably works that way for me—that is, *when* it does—because of a number of my attitudes and approaches to writing.

Confident Eclecticism

Knowing that my approaches to writing fluctuate between the cerebral and the behavioral seems to protect me from blocking anxieties when I tackle an essay like this or start to work on the memos and letters that are always waiting on my desk. If I don't have an idea that is clear enough (or narrow enough, original enough, important enough, etc.), I don't worry too much. Sometimes, I try to think my way to a start or I talk about the project with one of my colleagues, and more often than not that brings an initial idea of what I want to do in a writing project. Then, usually, I start drafting in the direction of my fuzzy intentions, as if the article or memo will write itself.

When the foolishness of that delusion dawns on me, as a drafting session degenerates to fruitless rereading, I consciously do something to alter the situation and get a drafting flow started again. Sometimes I just stop and let my mind work on the block without me for a while (as I did last night when I took my dogs for a run in the snow, since I couldn't seem to get past the end of the "Initial Ideas, Spontaneous Drafting" section), or I use some informal invention procedures. For instance, I may jot down the main points of the completed part of a draft as quickly as I can, hoping to fool my fingers into putting down a couple of new ideas, or I may look for a good quotation, hoping that once my fingers are busy typing those words they'll just keep going. Or I may look in my existing draft for some key words or an underlying pattern that can carry me into the troublesome new territory.

For instance, as I wrote "a number of my attitudes and approaches to writing" three paragraphs ago, I did not know what I would write next. I did know, after I reread the sentence, that I wanted to treat attitudes and strategies together in the final section of this essay. I also knew that I would not have much space to do this, and that I wanted the last section to seem at least somewhat connected to the rest of the essay. So I skimmed back, looking for ideas that might help me move ahead, and I noticed the cerebral/behavioral motif beginning with paragraph two. I realized almost immediately how much I switch back and forth between writing with my brain and writing with my fingers; when I held that thought close to my intention to deal with attitudes, I realized that a lot of the self-confidence I usually feel when I start new writing projects grows from my knowledge that behavioral and cerebral approaches both work for me. So an idea I found by looking back helped me put "Confidence and Eclecticism" down on the screen as a possible subheading and then move forward into that topic.

Changing and Revising

Knowing that I can "write" with my fingers (actively drafting in front of a computer, for example) or with my brain (using no writing tools and, possibly, no conscious thought) influences how I think about revision. A decade ago, I would have said that I wrote rough drafts fairly rapidly (often guided by jotted lists of key ideas) and then revised methodically through several more drafts. Indeed, that was what I did —or at least what I realized I was doing. Aware of the cerebral/behavioral dichotomy in my writing, I thought until 1978 that my drafting was basically behavioral, though punctuated by flashes of insight from my brain, but that my revising was a much more mental activity. Then I started reflecting on my own writing practices in light of research being done by Nancy Sommers, Sondra Perl, and others. And I realized that active *creation of a draft* through the coordinated efforts of hands, brain, and eyes and conscious *efforts to modify a draft* are a lot more similar than I had thought. By 1982, I saw it this way while I was drafting a conference paper that eventually became "Changing and Editing: Moving Current Theory on Revision into the Classroom":

> The terrain of revision is the whole writing process, not just an enclave of refinement at the end of the process. "Revision" is re-writing and editing an existing text, but it also means changing in the midst of drafting. Drafting is a kind of growth that can only occur as writers sense a need to change things and as they incorporate changes into the developing text as they write. In re-writing and editing, the writer devotes a lot of focused time to making changes in a text. During drafting, the writer makes similar changes—but spontaneously, during eye-blink-long pauses and brief re-scannings.
>
> (*Rhetoric Review* 1 [1984]: 78–88)

Once I acknowledged intellectually how central change is to drafting, I began to notice just how much time in my "drafting" sessions actually goes to making the kind of changes I once thought should be part of "revising" sessions. By now, this awareness has became part of my eclectic approach to writing. If I can blast through a several-page section in nonstop writing driven by a strong initial concept, fine; I'm comfortable leaving the typos, the nonsequiturs, and the under-developed and overstated passages for later reworking. But if, during a drafting session, my mind keeps slowing my fingers as my eyes notice contradictions that should be cut or interesting threads that should be picked up, I just work more methodically, while one corner of my brain reassures me that the revision sessions will go faster.

The amount of "revision" that takes place in my "drafting" has increased in the past few years, partly because I have experienced some success with it and partly because I am doing so much of my writing with a computer. Now, when I sense the need for a change as I draft (perhaps the feeling that I've left out a good example that didn't occur to me until my fingers had moved on to another point, or the hunch that I should shift the section I'm on back to an earlier point) I know I can do something about it with a couple of movements of the cursor and a few other keystrokes. Before 1983, I could implement such stray thoughts during a drafting session only by crowding handwritten additions between the typed lines or by filling margins with notes and arrows—wondering, as I punched holes in the paper writing on the uneven top of my typewriter, whether I'd be able to decipher my notes later. Typewriter writing, that is, had some built-in disincentives to making the kind of spontaneous changes I increasingly find coming to me as I draft at a computer.

Writing Causing Writing

It's striking to me how often in writing this essay, I looked for ideas in my earlier articles and pulled examples from recent drafting sessions or experiences on earlier projects. On reflection, I realize that one of the most frequent ways I get started on a project—or restarted in the middle of one—is by reflecting on writing I have done along that general line before.

For instance, I've written dozens of new-course proposals to Findlay College's Educational Policies Committee. So now I really don't begin that sort of writing project "at the beginning," but against a background of detailed memories about content, length, appearance, and likely reader-response, and with a very powerful initial plan about how to use those memories as I draft. Indeed, any earlier proposal that I've saved on a computer disk is a sort of rough draft for a later proposal. Similarly, I really did not begin this essay "at the beginning." Two of its underlying concepts (change as the heart of drafting, and the effectiveness of initial ideas and spontaneous composition) derive from articles published in 1984 and 1982. Some of the illustrations in this essay (the bathtub transition and the review that wrote itself, for instance) are experiences I had written about before, and my opening sentence paraphrases part of a paper I read at the 1980 National Council of Teachers of English convention.

I don't mean to suggest that the articles and memos I write are built up of "boiler plate" passages, like those personalized mass mailings we all get every day. But I am very aware of the fact that working on one writing project often turns out to be a sort of prewriting for some later piece. Writing is a way to learn, we've been telling students for years. It certainly has proved to be that for me—and also a tool to help generate more writing.

Muriel Harris is associate professor of English and director of the Writing Lab at Purdue University. She has edited a collection of articles on writing labs and has written two textbooks for writing courses: Practice for a Purpose *(1985) and, with Thomas Gaston,* Making Paragraphs Work *(1985).*

In addition to writing prolifically, she has served as consultant and outside evaluator for writing programs, for publishing houses, and for computer software development, and as a member of the ERIC/RCS evaluation committee. In 1984, she received an award from the National Writing Centers Association for extraordinary service to writing centers. Her most recent book, Teaching Writing One-to-One, *will be published shortly by the National Council of Teachers of English.*

HOW I WRITE: A COMPOSING PROCESS PROFILE

Muriel Harris
Purdue University

Why do I write? Aside from all the writing dictated by day-to-day business needs, I write in response to an inner urge to share something I've learned. From my teaching, research, or reading, an insight may bubble up and take shape, and like when I hear a good joke, I have to run and tell it to the next person. At other times, what I have read or heard infuriates me because I think it is dead wrong, destructive to the theory and pedagogy of teaching writing.

In Purdue's Writing Lab, as I watch students write during a tutorial, I know that I am not merely interested in but fascinated by the composing processes I see. And I hope that these students have benefited from observations of how I write and from our conversations about writing processes. But despite all this, to dwell on the topic of how I write as the subject of a whole essay teeters on the border of trivia, smacking of those gossip columnist reports that tell us breathlessly what some would-be celebrity or other had for breakfast. Who cares? For those, of course, who investigate or think about how people write, there is merit in case study, but the question still nags at me. Are we any closer to understanding composing processes by knowing that some people like felt-tip pens and that others prefer legal pads to backs of envelopes? What is the significance of preferring a dining room table to a desk? Then again, I share in the very human sense of enjoyment which is the result of having recognized ourselves in others or having noted differences. And so I convince myself that there is some merit in describing how I write.

But other questions sit on my shoulder and whine at me. Since the most likely readers of this essay are other writers and teachers of writing, will I describe what I think I should be doing in the process of composing or, in noting what I really do, reveal the ghastly truth—that I neglect considerations of audience, edit prematurely, care not a whit for the Pentad, and commit all kinds of other faux pas or symptoms of immature or inexperienced writers? Besides, even if I were to sound like the rhetorician's ideal at work, what kind of writing should I describe? We all know how many different writing tasks consume our lives and how different the writing processes are for each of these. Business correspondence, reports, and memos, the daily prose that must get spewed out, is the stuff of one kind of writing. Informal correspondence is another, as is the composing of professional discourse for articles, book chapters, and books or the creative free play of personal expressive writing. But for the purposes of this essay I will put aside the question of different kinds of discourse and indulge myself in what interests me most about my writing processes and those of others, the cognitive differences each person brings to composing tasks. It is into this vast pool, the murky waters of how brains function so differently to arrive at written products, that I like to peer.

To plunge into the various cognitive styles—or preferences or information processing modes or whatever terminology we prefer—I am tempted to start with an Erma Bombeck–style classification, one of those grossly overexaggerated, overly generalized stereotypes that somehow ring true to experience. Despite the exaggeration, despite the need to cast aside all the grays and look only at the clearly defined extremes of black and white, such generalizations seem to tell us something about reality that the cold eye of responsible research (which, after all, must fill in all those shades of gray) misses.

So, in that vein, let us consider two distinct types of composers, the Ys and the Zs. Ys are highly organized types, they know where a piece of writing is going when they set pen to paper (or start their cursor dancing on the screen), and their revisions are minimal. They seem to see the direction of a piece of writing after working it out in their minds so that their first drafts have shape and form. They may rework their drafts, but it is more a matter of honing and polishing than rehauling. (The former head of my department is such a composer, a writer of superb and widely published prose. His first typewritten drafts are so close to final versions that I wonder what meaning he attaches to the word *revision*.) And then there are the Zs. Zs blunder ahead. They plunge into a first draft with a general sense of their topic, but they don't know for sure what shore they will wash up on. First drafts are merely the first explorations of what will emerge several drafts later as the piece begins to take shape. Zs have a deep appreciation of William Faulkner's description of writing as being like nailing a chicken coop in a high wind—one grabs onto any board he can and nails it down fast.

It is a truism of nature that Ys marry Zs and Zs marry Ys. This is not a sex-linked characteristic, for I know both male and female Ys, and in most cases their spouses are Zs. The only known scientifically verifiable correlation of this is that Ys load the dishwasher. Maybe their perception of space and shape or a drive for orderliness leads them to the neat, compact placement of dishes among all those little peculiarly bent wires. I'm just guessing here because I am a confirmed Z, and we Zs of the world would rather just stuff things into the dishwasher as we go, just as we function best by plunging into our writing tasks without a closely articulated sense of how a sentence will end or what each paragraph is going to contain. What else does this Z-ness mean? It dictates the need for drafting and more drafting; it sometimes means jotting down notes randomly and then imposing order afterward; it means *large doses* of *aha*s as we begin to see what we think by watching what emerges on the page (or CRT screen). But this doesn't hold for all of our writing, just the larger, longer, more extended pieces of discourse. And that now calls for some exploration of what I write.

What do I write? A lot of it is formulaic. As Writing Lab director and a member of the faculty, I have a constant need to whip out memos, reports, announcements to teachers, instructional materials, letters of reference, evaluations, reviews, class exercises, purchase requests, recommendations, and so on. As Writing Lab director I also respond to requests for information about writing labs. Having been in this business of writing labs for almost a decade, I am considered an old hand, such is the infancy of the field. And as editor of a monthly newsletter for a group of writing lab directors that now numbers over a thousand, I churn out endless wads of correspondence, edit manuscripts, and respond to a variety of questions.

This brings up a touchy matter, for some of what I write in these categories requires disguising the real message in a way that is not too offensive. How does one tactfully reject the manuscript of a peer—or suggest large scale revisions? What is a decent way to decline offers to speak at conferences I have no time to attend or to contribute an essay to a project I am not wildly interested in? The rhetorical stance is equally difficult when writing a memo to our composition staff where the real purpose is to force them to stop misusing our writing lab. I can't really write memos that begin, "Hey out there, you feelingless clods, stop ordering students you don't want to cope with to go to the lab— as if it were some sort of dumping ground for the basket cases. And don't decimate their egos and desecrate their pages of writing with messages that say 'This is garbage. You don't belong in this class. Maybe the lab can help you learn how to write.' " Would that I were also able to send out memos that announce the lab's refusal to work with students who appear with vague referrals that say "This student has writing problems. Please help." Finding one's stance, seeking a way to couch the real message behind acceptable comments, is a major difficulty, one that sends me into spirals of draft after draft until an appropriate stance emerges.

A totally different type of writing is writing-for-speaking, those occasional formal conference talks that require a manuscript (either to keep me rigidly within a time slot or to offer up to the person preparing the conference proceedings). Generally, I prefer at conference presentations to talk from outlined jottings on note cards that serve as memory prompts, but when a manuscript must be produced, I prepare a rough equivalent of the notecard-type outline and then write as if I'm talking to the audience. I want very much to retain some measure of sounding like I'm talking and not reading aloud. Since speaking to my audience in my head is a useful generative device (one that Flower and Hayes recommend in "Problem-Solving Strategies and the Writing Process," *College English* 39 [1977]: 449–461), such writing flows along easily. I revise mainly by reading aloud what I've produced after a writing session, shortening sentences that are too long for verbal presentation, adding some human-sounding talk, and leaving openings for some ad-lib comments later. Conference-talk writing, especially for invited presentations, also flows along fairly easily because I'm usually recasting the same message I've blathered on about before. That, after all, is why someone bothered to ask me in the first place, to sound off on something I know about. So this kind of writing requires mainly a recasting of the message in terms of the particular audience to be addressed. Having developed a set of scripts that I can trot out, this kind of writing is produced quickly, without heavy revisions.

How do I write? Obviously, I talk to myself in my head, catching on paper the words I hear as I go along. For "real" composing, that kind of generating of text where I'm not recasting (or merely repeating) familiar messages, my Z-ness emerges. For the journal articles, books, book chapters, research proposals, and other forms of extended discourse where I know the premise of what I want to say (and the general content of each section of a paper or chapter of a book) but not the sentence-by-sentence road map of how I will get there, I seem to follow an uneven path to the last version. (I use the word *last* here because I have never produced a final version of anything, in the sense of having worked it over to whatever perfection I am capable of. I merely decide at some point that the impending deadline or a sense of exhaustion dictates that I turn it over to someone else. And I rarely reread my own words when they appear in print—they seem like strangers who have little connection to me; and besides, by the time they appear in print, I can't remember having written them. Thus there is no urge to tinker further with what feels like someone else's prose.)

That uneven path to writing usually begins somewhere in the monologues that run through my head or in the conversations I have with colleagues. As an idea takes shape, I may need to do some reading and note taking or I may fill up a few sheets of paper with scratch outlines. These rough outlines sometimes need to be reshaped a few times until the general structure looks workable. Then, it is time to plunge into prose formulations, the actual writing. As I start, there is usually a pleasant sense of anticipation, like starting off on a journey. Then, as I write, a need to recopy begins to blunt that pleasure. Before I learned the joys (and infuriating hang-ups) of computers as writing tools, first drafts would involve tedious recopying as sentences got reworked, additions became inserted, and trial runs were scratched out. At some stage the page was such an unreadable disaster zone that time was spent recopying to see what I had, and as that recopied version became a similar casualty of additions and revisions, it too had to be redone. Now, with the joys of word processing, I can write a portion, changing as I go, print it out, mangle the hard copy with more changes, and put in the revisions to be reprinted. Occasionally, when deadlines force me to it, I attempt to compose on-screen with minimal notes—and sometimes I succeed. Generally, though, the computer has freed me from the tedium of recopying by hand (having never adequately mastered the art of typing) and easily gives me clean copy to see what I have. I've become a hopeless word-processing addict, unable to write by hand anything other than quick formulaic bits of writing for our secretaries to type up. (Providing readable copy for a secretary was yet another bane of my existence, since my handwriting, in my haste to get things done, has deteriorated into weird hieroglyphics.)

The kind of preparation that goes on before writing sometimes involves rereading literature in the field and always includes a lot of mumbling to myself. This goes on at those times when my hands are engaged but not my mind (cooking, doing laundry, etc.), or when I'm not consciously involved with what I'm doing (taking a shower, exercising, etc.) and my mind is free to wander. Questions, phrases, connections between ideas, flaws in a train of thought, even weaknesses of some arguments I've been putting together drift to the surface. There is an urge to jot down some notes quickly before my inadequate short-term memory loses what has just floated through my consciousness. It often seems as if having phrased something in a particular way during these mental meanderings, I not only can't recall the phrase but must also go on to seek a new way to give expression to the idea when getting it down on paper. Another kind of preparation, in the middle of a large project, is rereading what I've written in a previous session. I'm unable to go forward until I can place myself back in the middle of what was being written previously. But then this rereading of text as I write is something I do often, despite having observed student writers who compulsively reread so often that they may need six or seven of these running starts before completing a sentence.

In the middle of a writing session, while drafting, I note that sometimes when I'm stuck, mulling over options, or not sure where I'm headed next, I find myself suddenly leaping out of my chair to move around (usually in the direction of the stove for a cup of coffee or the refrigerator for something to nibble on—writing and dieting are antithetical acts for me). As I mill around, a phrase will surface in my head or a way to go forward will occur to me. I have no idea why, at such times, motion is more helpful than merely sitting still. Several years ago I remember hearing an esteemed member of our profession of writing teachers say that, in her observations, "writing bouts" tend to last about forty-five minutes. Perhaps my sudden desire for motion may occasionally also spring from restlessness at the end of such "bouts." Maybe some day I'll remember to time these interludes.

As I write, sentence has to follow sentence. I can't go forward until I'm satisfied that I've done at least a semi-decent job with the sentence on the page. But I often don't have a clear idea of the end of the sentence when I launch into it, nor am I sure what the next sentence will be until I'm into it. Sometimes, the writing proceeds smoothly, but there are other times when I bog down and proceed as if swimming in molasses—slow, arduous forward motion. It may be the difficulty of realizing in words what I want to say that causes this, but other conditions can also bring me to a halt. I cannot write indoors on a glorious, sunny day (gloomy, cloudy days, on the other hand, seem to invite the cosiness of hunching over paper or curling up in front of a computer screen), and I cannot write when there are voices nearby (family, radio, TV, etc.) because I need to hear my words as they reverberate through that internal corridor in my head.

My revisions are of two distinct types, a fact that I try to share with students I meet in our Writing Lab when they are in need of revising strategies (too many textbooks seem to do little more than exhort in pious tones the need for revision and then leave the now guilt-ridden student to figure out how to accomplish this "hallmark of a good writer"). I'm not sure that what I describe is useful to the students I've talked to, but it does suggest that they try to consider the need for different approaches at different times. For large-scale revisions, the kind of overhauling that needs to go on with the truly bad prose that wanders, fails to say anything useful, or is irrelevant, I have to rewrite away from the draft. If I look back at it, trying to salvage anything, I become enmeshed by it and lose sight of the new direction I was headed in. When something better is produced, I dump the previous attempt, usually without rereading it. Another, different, type of revision can be done in the margins, as inserts, or above crossed-out phrases. Here, the draft was reasonably on track but needed reworking. I seem to do this best with hard copy rather than on screen at the computer. This may be habit, but I need margins to scrawl in, and I need to see more of the text than is available on screen at any one time.

Revision that is performed on text already drafted seems more often, for me, to be additions rather than deletions. I see something more that needs to be said or some dimension of complexity that has to be added to what was too simplistic in the previous formulation. When I feel the need to insert a large portion of text—or sometimes even just another sentence—it often seems impossible. Having, to the best of my ability, carefully tied each sentence to the next, I find myself incapable of opening a wedge between them to insert something. Some revision, I notice, is for sound. I reread to enjoy the roll of a phrase or catch an awkward rhythm. While all of this is going on, I'm also editing to catch grammatical errors, misspellings, and other minor infelicities. I'm one of those who are so intolerant of surface error on the page that I stop even to correct typos on first drafts. I am enamored of clean copy and enjoy holding the printed pages, even of an early draft, just to feel them in my hands. When the need for minor changes becomes evident, I even reprint in order to have clean copy. Thus my favorite writing tool is a computer. Given this propensity for zeroing in on grammatical errors, I have to sit on my hands sometimes to keep from grabbing students' papers and correcting them—an inappropriate act in general and especially dumb when the student and I are discussing large-scale matters such as refocusing the topic for a rewrite.

Why do I write? Aside from all the writing dictated by day-to-day business needs, I write in response to an inner urge to share something I've learned. From my teaching, research, or reading, an insight may bubble up and take shape, and like when I hear a good joke, I have to run and tell it to the next person. At other times, what I have read or heard infuriates me because I think it is dead wrong, destructive to the theory and pedagogy of teaching writing. My reactions are often caused by a sympathy for students mishandled by our profession, a sight I see too often when teaching in a writing lab, which is a unique vantage point. In the lab, where students come from a variety of classrooms and where we often, in the process of diagnosis, ask about writing habits and notions that may have been formulated back in high school, we see the writer in terms of his or her history of writing instruction. And what we see too often is teacher-induced error—for example, the student straining to cram his thoughts within the rigid frame of the five-paragraph essay, the student so traumatized by red marks that the act of writing has dissolved into avoidance of error, and so on. My need to speak out is often the stimulus that starts a line of thinking or research which leads to more writing. Or, on a more positive note, I see some successful technique at work, ask why, and follow that until it leads to something that ought to be shared, in writing, with others.

As I pursue a topic, long before the stage of writing, it progresses in part from conversations with colleagues, from reading what has been done on the subject, and from a curious selection process that goes on. During the weeks or months when I'm focused on a subject or question, my regular journal reading seems also to focus on that subject, as if other areas of concern are temporarily suspended. I suddenly note interesting connections between other people's work and whatever I've been thinking about. Things seem to leap off the page of other material and become relevant, or I find exactly the right article that I should be reading in the current issue of a standard journal. It's an unconscious selection process forced into action by the question I've been considering.

When the written product from all of this mulling, thinking, talking, reading, drafting, and redrafting finally takes shape and becomes a manuscript, complete with title and ready to be shipped off, there is an empty feeling. All the irritation and frustration of putting it into writing are over; however, so is the pleasure of something taking shape. But the act of writing is also a form of relief. Sometimes, when something agitates me, causes more than the normal amount of dissonance (or whatever it is that gets writers into motion), my mind begins to roil, as ideas struggle to take form in language. Getting some of this mental conversation down on paper is a relief, an emptying out of a churning head. If I don't turn to paper, I continue to spin my mental wheels uneasily. Externalizing my thoughts becomes a way to look at them, but I suspect that just the act of writing them out has a therapeutic effect.

And so, for me, writing is a necessary act of communication. It is also sometimes a sedative, occasionally a source of enjoyment when I reread and like what I've written, all too often a source of frustration as the words and phrases I want don't surface, and usually a means of finding out what I think. I doubt that in admitting to this mixed bag of reactions and feelings I am saying anything different from what most writers feel about writing. Unfortunately, too many of our students, caught up in the reality of "I-have-to-write-a-five-hundred-word-comparison-contrast-essay-by-Friday," know none of this side of writing. Their frustration is in not knowing what the teacher wants, their enjoyment lies in being done with the assignment so that they can get on to something else, and their only purpose is to get a decent grade. When we've figured out how to conquer these obstacles, maybe we can also interest them in thinking about how and why they write.

Richard L. Larson is professor of English at Herbert J. Lehman College of the City University of New York, where he was formerly dean of professional studies. He has taught at the Harvard Graduate School of Business Administration and at the University of Hawaii at Manoa.

A past chair of the Conference on College Composition and Communication, he completed in 1986 a term as editor of College Composition and Communication. *He has written essays on rhetoric, testing, and the teaching of writing.*

WHY IT IS UNIMPORTANT HOW I WRITE

Richard L. Larson
Herbert H. Lehman College of the City University of New York

I am conscious at all times of an unfolding plan, of where I am in that plan, and of what remains to be done. Even though I occasionally write sections of a piece out of the order in which they will appear in the final text, I continue to be conscious of what I think will be the final plan. And I try to be sure that the plan in the final text will unfold clearly, so that the reader is aware at all times where he or she is and, if possible, why.

Readers of this essay should not expect to learn anything about how "writers" compose, or anything that will constitute advice about their own composing. I do not know, and I doubt that anyone knows, how "writers" compose: each writer draws in his or her own way on a repertoire of composing activities, in response to different situations that invite composing. And each writer must decide for himself or herself how to proceed when faced with the need, or impelled by the desire, to compose written English. I am not sure, therefore, why I was invited to contribute to this volume. Readers hoping for suggestions from this essay that they can apply to their own work will, I am convinced, be disappointed; they will find in it an account of idiosyncrasies that no other person would wish to adopt (and with good reason). They might want to move on right now to the next essay.

But I have at least a hunch about why this volume of essays and its predecessor were undertaken, with comments from many persons (almost all of them more prolific, more effective writers than I) on their writing. There is abroad now in the profession the view that teachers of writing emphasize in their teaching—and if they do not, they should —the "process" of writing rather than the "product" of writing, and that in some way the practices of people who write regularly or like to write or have to write can inform the curious and needy reader about how that reader might engage in the "process." It was Maxine Hairston, I think, in her essay "The Winds of Change: Thomas Kuhn and the Revolution in the Teaching of Writing" (*College Composition and Communication,* February 1982, pp. 76–88) who first argued directly that what principally differentiates research on writing and the teaching of writing in the last fifteen or twenty years from earlier work is their attention to "the composing process" or "the writing process." Hairston applauded that interest as a "paradigm shift," comparable in our field to the shift in scientific thinking that came about when people recognized that the earth revolves around the sun instead of the sun around the earth. Hairston is obviously right in noting that much attention in recent teaching and research about writing has been given to the composing process. But I do not think that what we have seen is more than a shift in the focus of attention among teachers and researchers. The fundamental changes in what we value in writing and in how writers write that the phrase "paradigm shift" might lead us to look for are, in my view, not to be found.

The shift, such as it is, has been at best partial. When the Copernican revolution took hold, probably few people continued to teach and write and conduct experiments as if the earth were at the center of the universe. But in the teaching of writing we don't see many signs that either teachers or writers have abandoned their concern for the effectiveness of a piece of writing as that writing moves on its way to its reader to become part of a transaction in which meaning, implication, value, and resonance are created. (Hairston includes on her own list of the features of her "new paradigm" centuries-old rhetorical concerns for the effectiveness of the finished text.) I have not heard many readers of written texts inquire, while interpreting or judging a text, by what process it came into being, and whether that process was or was not wisely adopted or felicitously pursued. (Researchers and some teachers may ask students to keep logs of the procedures they followed in composing a particular text so that the students can evaluate the effectiveness of those procedures; I have asked for such logs myself. But almost always the text can be judged, and is judged, independently of the processes that brought it into being.) And when writing is tested, it is the final text that is judged, not the route taken by the writer to arrive at the final text. The "new paradigm," that is, has not altered the way in which texts make their way in the world. Does it then deserve to be called a "new paradigm"? Might that designation not equally be applied to the recognition that what readers bring to a text—the knowledge, attitudes, orientations, configurations of previous experience that they have developed as they moved through life—affects how they perceive and understand a text, and in effect leads them to "create" that text?

Furthermore, the shift has not necessarily altered the act of writing or the way the act of writing is perceived by its practitioners. Ever since human beings began composing texts, orally or in writing, they have engaged in processes. The processes by which oral epics were composed did not have the services of a friendly observer to record, code, classify, interpret, and analyze them with the aid of a computer and a statistical package, but they were no less processes, of great historical and artistic interest. What is the classical rhetorician's five-part plan— embracing invention, arrangement, expression, memory, and delivery —if it is not a frozen representation of one view of how composing can occur? (Who knows, indeed, how many orators followed the sequence, or whether the sequence is simply—like other plans in the textbooks of today—a way of organizing instruction?) For decades, scholars have been interested in the successive versions of well-known poems, if the versions that preceded the final printed text could be retrieved from the poet's papers or from letters to friends. When I was an undergraduate, one of the conspicuous monuments in literary scholarship was John Livingston Lowes's *The Road to Xanadu,* a study of how the themes and images of "Kubla Khan" may have entered Coleridge's consciousness —surely a part of the "composing process" behind that poem. The more one reflects on historical evidence, the more one can doubt that in our profession there has been any sort of "paradigm shift."

What *has* taken place, as I have noted, is a shift in emphasis, in research on writing, and in teaching. Where in past years research on writing was limited to studies of the features of completed texts and of the revisions made in their texts by well-known published professional writers (the latter are still a center of attention), researchers now try to observe, or obtain data about, composing as it is taking place. And such data almost always illustrate the acts of invention and revision: the taking in, configuring, and shaping of ideas; mental revision, before words are written down; and scribal revision, after words are first written down. Correspondingly, in instruction, teachers give more explicit attention to invention—many times using procedures first identified and described in classical antiquity—and to revision. Ever since they started writing, writers have engaged in invention; if there is a shift in approach to invention today, it is, I think, toward a greater interest in "nonconceptual" procedures such as freewriting and the keeping of journals. (I borrow the term *conceptual* to describe not only classical procedures but also tagmemic heuristics and similar planned inquiries, from Frank D'Angelo's title: *A Conceptual Theory of Rhetoric.*) Also, probably since writers have been writing, they have been revising, sometimes more than once. If there is a shift in the teaching of revision today, it is in the encouraging of multiple drafts, perhaps with comment from the writer's peers on earlier drafts. In fact, if one wants to generalize about the impact of altered foci on the teaching of writing, it lies probably in the increased attention being given by teachers today to *guiding* students' revision, even guiding the authors to a substantially modified understanding of what they have to say. Writers have probably always known that one often discovers one's ideas while trying to utter them. Our much-touted "paradigm shift" may consist largely in our new willingness to let students share our awareness that revision reflects and assists discovery, and to help them act on that knowledge.

But as the evidence of history and of our own experience quickly confirms, different writers invent and revise, and traverse all the other procedures they follow in composing, differently. And the same writer will invent and revise and traverse all the other procedures of composing differently depending on the "rhetorical context" (the relationship of writer, subject, occasion, purpose, and reader) for each writing. These are the reasons why nothing I say in this essay can, or should, have any impact on my readers' ways of composing. (What I've said on earlier pages *might* however have some impact on how they view the teaching of writing, if they believe me.) Jack Selzer has noted this diversity forcefully in his essays "The Composing Processes of an Engineer" (*College Composition and Communication,* May 1983, pp. 178–187) and "Exploring Options in Composing" (*College Composition and Communication,* October 1984, pp. 276–284), though some teachers have told me that what he says is so obvious as to be hardly worth saying. Selzer points out that an executive engineer bidding for a substantial contract, working against a tight time deadline and drawing on a backlog of experience with previous contracts and proposals, composes very differently from the way a writer might compose according to the model privileged in much instruction in writing today, and he sensibly asks teachers to recognize that writers can successfully follow a variety of procedures.

Maxine Hairston, whose detection of a "paradigm shift" in the teaching of writing during the 1970s I have, in my earlier remarks, attempted to qualify, has recently written a speculative essay that builds recognition of this diversity of procedure into a theoretical model of composing. In "Different Products, Different Processes: A Theory About Writing" (*College Composition and Communication,* December 1986, pages 442–452), she identifies three "classes" of writing: "maintenance" or "message" writing (e.g., brief transactional memoranda to colleagues and tradespeople); more complex writing that is still, in her words, "self-limiting" (the writer knows, before starting to write, what he or she will say; the proposals written by Selzer's engineer are an example); and "reflective" writing, speculative and exploratory, in which the writer seeks and has genuine opportunities to make discoveries while writing. Hairston recognizes, of course, that the classes are not watertight, and that the same piece of writing may be at times self-limiting, at times reflective (at times, perhaps, even message) writing. And she knows that the same people undertake different kinds of writing, and writing that embodies a different "mix" of kinds, every day or every week. She knows it because she has observed herself doing the different kinds, and she has talked to colleagues who report the same experiences. Further, she knows that teachers should teach in recognition of these obvious facts and not expect students to write every paper according to the same procedures, to be judged by the same standards, and with the same expectations of discovering ideas and insights as they write. She knows, in short, that the simplistic message which many teachers have taken after observing the shifts in emphasis in recent research on composing is exactly that: simplistic. And she knows, though she does not say it, that references to *a* "process-centered curriculum," to *the* composing process, and to "the process method" (which abound in our textbooks and in the jargon of some teachers and of some leaders of teachers workshops) are, as often uttered, misleading and indefensible. She knows, though again she does not say so in these words, that writers need to find, for themselves, their own procedures, just as writers have had to do since the beginning of writing.

Hairston knows another principle, though again she does not assert it is these words—a principle that underlies her discussions of the kinds of writing. This principle is that writing is *about* something, that it has content, that it reflects inquiry, that it proceeds from the interpretation and synthesis of data—that whether the content is essentially known before the writer writes or is discovered during composing (or revising, which cannot indeed be separated from composing), writing communicates ideas, perceptions, speculations, proposals, convictions. As the profession talks, and teaches, about "process," it loses sight of this principle. And it needs to rediscover, and act upon, this principle. To talk almost exclusively about how I, or anyone else, composes is, I think, to misplace the emphasis we should be seeking. Along with recognizing the diversity of procedures for composing, we should be insisting (to our students—and, if my experiences as editor of *College Composition and Communication* give any indication, to ourselves) that what is composed have substantive value. And we should be seeking ways to reach, test, develop, support, and validate ideas that meet such a standard.

These are the goals, along with reasonable lucidity of plan and reader-based clarity of statement, that I try to reach in my own writing. I do not view myself as a professional writer, and, generally, I do not view myself as a good writer. I have rarely written for money, and recently I have not written much scholarly work. I write no fiction, poetry, or other "fictive" writing. (I value these forms, of course, but I have almost no chance to attempt them.) For ten years, most of the writing I did at my college was transactional administrative prose: committee reports, proposals, budget justifications, personnel evaluations, and the like. Before becoming editor of *College Composition and Communication,* I compiled bibliographies, writing compressed summaries of the content of others' scholarship. After becoming editor, I began another kind of transactional prose: correspondence with prospective contributors to the journal, interwoven with an occasional "Editor's Note" designed to interpret for readers how I saw the contents of an issue of the journal. Such scholarly writing as I undertake is utilitarian and interpretive, intended to organize and clarify the state of knowledge in a field within rhetoric or the teaching of writing.

Because of the pressure of time (preparing committee reports on deadline, preparing grant proposals by a deadline, responding individually to contributors to a journal), most of my writing is, in Linda Flower's term, "first time final" typescript. (That statement applies also to large stretches of the present essay. The essay no doubt shows it.) For the most part, I write a piece or a letter once and once only. I write on the typewriter (only)—at home, in my office, even, occasionally, while traveling (with a truly portable typewriter). On a letter, the "revision" I can manage is usually restricted to what can be accomplished with correction fluid; I have yet to learn to use a word processor, and for most of my term as editor I have had no secretarial help with the journal. On essays and editor's notes I have time to move passages around, to add information, to add ideas, to recast sentences, occasionally to rewrite a paragraph. Usually I have time for no more, unless the essay is not being produced on demand, or on deadline, and can be allowed (as just one piece on which I have worked in five years could be allowed) to remain in draft form while I learn more about my subject and what I think about it. I am in the position of Selzer's engineer (or of Hairston's unremittingly Class Two writer), except that the stakes in what I write are usually not as high as for Selzer's engineer.

How do I respond to these conditions, which in effect preclude my being concerned over a long period of time with the artfulness of a piece of writing? First, I try to learn and put in order what I need to know in order to attempt the piece of writing I'm working on. For a bibliographical essay, I try to be sure that I have read the items to be discussed and have arranged them according to a conceptual framework that will be illuminating. For a letter to a contributor, I try to be sure that I have thought out, in advance, what I intend to say, and why, and what (if anything) I will propose to the contributor. For a committee report, I try to be sure that I have in hand the information I need in order to complete the report. I make notes, often, of what I want to say; but I practice no heuristics and do not consciously follow any strategies of invention. I have gathered in advance of writing the materials I needed, and I have thought about them enough to have decided how

I will handle them. I may later find, of course, that my preparation is incomplete, and that I need more information. But I try to minimize the likelihood of discovering that, not because I do not want to seek additional information, but because I am working under pressure of time.

More, perhaps, than some writers, I plan in advance how I will move through my material, from beginning to end. As far as possible, I try to decide what steps I will take, what moves I will make to accomplish what I set out to do. This does not mean making an outline; a few ordered notes on the back of an envelope will usually do. Naturally, the plan changes as I proceed. Having taken a step, I see more clearly than I could while planning what that step has accomplished and how the next step might be elaborated, contracted, altered, or replaced in view of what is already completed. But I am conscious at all times of an unfolding plan, of where I am in that plan, and of what remains to be done. Even though I occasionally write sections of a piece out of the order in which they will appear in the final text, I continue to be conscious of what I think will be the final plan. And I try to be sure that the plan in the final text will unfold clearly, so that the reader is aware at all times where he or she is and, if possible, why he or she is there.

Once the draft is done, in accordance with the original (or an altered) plan, I usually have little time to revise. I reread, trying to be sure (especially when dealing with conceptually complex material) that I am communicating with my reader as clearly as I know how to. I attend to word choice and particularly to syntax, doing my best to ensure that my sentences say fully, precisely, and comprehensibly what I hope the reader will understand. (For this purpose I sometimes deliberately cultivate parallel structures and series to organize subordinate structures where appropriate.) For if my reader looking at my text cannot construct essentially the meaning I intended him or her to have, then I have not done the job I meant to do. I value imaginativeness in language when I see it and do not cast aside metaphor or irony when they will work for me. But I have an audience—usually people who are practicing their profession under difficult conditions, or members of the public trying to understand our profession—and in the limited time I have to finish my writing, I must be sure that my readers will feel that their contact with me has been productive.

I check my writing for one other feature: tone of voice. I want if possible to avoid the ponderousness and pomposity to which I feel I am always prone. Much of my writing in first draft is stand-offish. I try to use humor, irony, directness of statement, economy of phrase, metaphor—various resources of style—to deflate what might come across as pretense and to relax stiff solemnity. Usually I fail, as I probably have in this piece, and release writing that is audibly unattractive. I regularly fear that my readers will find themselves unenlightened by what I say for that reason alone, irrespective of whether I give them other reasons for feeling so.

Transactional prose? Yes, insistently and inevitably so. Composed by procedures that might enlighten others? Almost certainly not. Others who compose as I must the kinds of pieces I write will have their own values, procedures, emphases. Or perhaps others are wise enough not to face the insistent deadlines for their transactional prose that I face. Each writer operates in his or her own context, to his or her own beat. That is as it should be.

Nothing here, then, as predicted at the start, from which a writer or a student of writing or a teacher of writing can learn. That is, unless the reasons for the unimportance of how I write may be instructive.

Andrea A. Lunsford is professor of English at Ohio State University. She has written numerous articles on rhetoric and composition studies, particularly in the areas of basic writing, cognitive studies, and nineteenth-century Scottish rhetoric, and is coauthor of Four Worlds of Writing *(2nd ed., 1985),* Preface to Critical Reading *(6th ed., 1984), and coeditor of* Essays on Classical Rhetoric and Modern Discourse *(1984).*

Lisa Ede is associate professor of English and director of the Communication Skills Center at Oregon State University. She has published a number of essays on rhetoric and composition theory. "Audience Addressed/Audience Invoked: The Role of Audience in Composition Theory and Pedagogy," coauthored with Andrea Lunsford, received the Conference on College Composition and Communication's 1985 Braddock award.

Essays on Classical Rhetoric and Modern Discourse, *coedited with Robert Connors and Andrea A. Lunsford, received the Modern Language Association's 1985 Shaughnessy medal. As Mina Shaughnessy Scholars, Lunsford and Ede have conducted research on collaborative writing; a book-length report of this research is forthcoming.*

COLLABORATION AND COMPROMISE: THE FINE ART OF WRITING WITH A FRIEND

Andrea A. Lunsford
Ohio State University

Lisa Ede
Oregon State University

Talk is central to our collaboration in a way that it seldom has been for us as individual writers. We find ourselves talking through to a common thesis and plan, talking through the links in an argument, talking through various points of significance or alternative conclusions. Talk is also central to our planning, which must be both more explicit and more detailed when we write together than either of us is accustomed to when working alone.

In this essay we hope to describe what happens when two people, each of whom has a fairly extensive history of writing alone, decide to collaborate on professional writing projects. We are those two people —friends who first coauthored an essay almost by accident, liked both the process and the product, and have continued often to write together. As the following discussion will illustrate, melding our two styles was less difficult than melding our originally quite diverse composing processes. Though our writing together will always involve a delicate balancing of tensions, the process of collaborative writing has changed both the way we write and the way we think about writing. To help illustrate the nature of that change, we will first each briefly describe our individual composing processes. We will then discuss how we write together, a process that involves both collaboration and compromise.

WRITING ALONE: ANDREA

Most of the professional writing that I do results from an "assignment" of some kind: I have agreed to give a conference paper, contribute a chapter to a book, or write a journal article. But in one respect, such "assignments" or invitations are themselves the result of questions I have asked myself, questions which eventually led me into certain areas of study and research: What constitutes development in writing during the college years? What happened to the rhetorical tradition in the nineteenth century? Why do we think of writing almost exclusively as a solitary process? For me, then, the writing process begins almost always with curiosity. What follows is generally a period of intense concentration and brainstorming, followed by a lot of reading, some of which is apparently desultory. I rarely take notes as I read, but my internal eye is watching for what I call the "shape" of whatever I want to write. This process of conceptualization is extremely important to me; during it I envision the direction of any essay, article, or book—where it will go and how it will get there. I can write without going through this internal and largely silent process, but I am uncomfortable doing so and will avoid it if possible.

Once I see—internally—the shape and direction of an essay, I commit them to paper, usually in a series of schematized jottings. From this point on, I write quickly, anxious to see each sentence appear, to see if my conceptualization will pan out. At this stage, I prefer to write for as long a stretch as possible and will finish an entire draft if I can. If not, I aim to complete a draft of a section and to begin the next section before I stop, since it makes it easier to pick up the thread of my argument the next day. I seldom take breaks and am very irritated by interruptions during this stage. I still prefer to write first drafts in longhand, and I always write sitting cross-legged on the floor or on the sofa in my study, *never* at a desk. Generally, I cast each sentence or series of sentences roughly in my head and then write them, revising as I go and writing "metadiscourse" notes to myself in the margins ("Expand this point"; "Give an example"; "Fix syntax," etc.) And I include bibliographical citations in the first draft—I can't face the boredom of doing a list of sources after the essay is finished.

As I've already suggested, revision is a constant in my writing process, beginning as soon as I start to think about my subject and continuing throughout the drafting stage. I often read aloud to myself, revising for rhythm and sound, particularly if I am writing a conference paper or address. My completed draft, which I often know by heart, most often looks like a road map with arrows and cross-outs and such indicators as "See over" or "Go to next page, paragraph three." As I type this draft, I may make further revisions, and I may revise the typescript one or more times. But often I can type a finished copy from my much-revised and often-recited handwritten draft. I hate typing and am just in the process of learning to use a word processor, which I will probably also hate in spite of its flexibility and powers. Only if I can manage to use it while sitting cross-legged on the floor will the computer become an integral part of my writing process.

WRITING ALONE: LISA

When I write professional articles, my strongest inclination is to proceed slowly, carefully—even cautiously. (Letters, journal entries, and routine memos are another matter: I zip through these fairly speedily.) As an undergraduate, I allowed myself the pleasure of polishing each sentence before I moved on to the next, even though I might finally toss half of them. During, but especially since, graduate school I learned to push myself, forcing ideas down, leaving words and sentences alone until later. I can now, if I have to, write professional articles and essays with some speed. But my inclination, my desire, with any important scholarly project is always to write slowly, stopping often to monitor and reassess what I've written.

The impetus for my writing comes from a variety of sources. Sometimes, like Andrea, I accept "assignments" and thus willy-nilly find myself with a task I must complete. But the questions that catalyze my research also come from my teaching—my interest in audience began that way—and from my personal experience. I am aware of two broad stages in my composing: information gathering and writing. But they're not discrete. I generally make a number of notes as I read, for instance, but I also do so as I write; and as I write, I often realize that I need to return to a source to find or clarify information. I find it difficult to separate planning and revising, except in the broadest, most obvious ways; for as I write I'm constantly both making changes in my writing and recasting my plans for the rest of an essay, often in notes at the top of the page or on scrap paper. If I have time, I like to type sections of an essay as I go; I seem to need to see a relatively clean typed copy to be able to distance myself from my writing.

When I write I am most aware of my struggle to shape meaning: to say what I want to say about a specific topic. But I am also aware of being engaged in a dialogue with others who have written compellingly on my subject. These people become a particularly important audience for me, whose expectations and standards I want to try to meet. But since the world of composition studies is relatively small, I sometimes also find myself envisioning a very specific person as I write. ("What would X think of this?" "This may answer what Y said in that recent article.") And I am aware of the constraints posed by the means of publication. I don't sit down simply to write my thoughts on Chaim Perelman or audience; from the start I am aware of writing an article on Perelman for a scholarly journal in speech communication or on audience for *College Composition and Communication.*

Like many writers, I have my rituals. I have always preferred to write at my own desk, which I have, ideally, both physically and emotionally cleared—paid all the bills, written the most overdue letters to friends, made neat lists of what I need to do in the next few weeks or over the quarter break. (I used to have to clean the house and bake bread before I could begin writing, but I've broken myself of those habits.) I am easily distracted when I write, especially by noise. I write almost everything but letters or routine memos longhand; the latter I compose at the typewriter or, more recently, at the word processor. (I love the way word processing simplifies editing, but I can't imagine ever composing anything important at the computer.) I feel happiest when I have a chunk of time—two days at least—in which to work on a project of any magnitude. And I write best in the morning. If I'm at my desk and writing by 9 A.M. that's a powerful signal to me that this will be a good day.

WRITING TOGETHER: COLLABORATION AND COMPROMISE

As the preceding brief summaries suggest, our composing processes when we write alone differ considerably. Lisa writes slowly and synthetically; thinking through writing is essential to her. Andrea writes more quickly. And even more important, she is more analytic; she does in her head—by simply sitting and thinking things through—what Lisa often needs pen and paper to work out. Andrea most prefers to write in one long spurt; stopping for any reason is an irritant and a serious interruption of her writing process. Lisa likes to stop often to reread, rethink, and if there's time, type up what she's written. Lisa, in other words, thinks and writes in stages or segments; Andrea, in one single extended burst of energy. Andrea can write almost anywhere—except at a desk!—and has, in general, fewer writing rituals than Lisa. Lisa tends to fret over her writing; Andrea is more businesslike.

We are, in other words, from this perspective as different as the proverbial tortoise and hare. How have we managed to write together, and why? One powerful impetus, and subsequent reinforcement, for our collaboration is our friendship. We enjoy being together, and even though we spend much of the brief periods we're together—a weekend during the term, four to six days over Christmas, a luxurious two weeks in the summer—working, we always find time for jokes, shopping sprees for exotic foods, and laughter-filled late-night dinners. Before we coauthored our first essay, we had coordinated several workshops, so we weren't strangers to collaboration. We knew that we shared a similar attitude toward professional commitments: if we agreed to finish a project by a certain deadline, we generally would. We also knew we could count on each other. In addition, we shared a number of intellectual interests: what, for example, constitutes the "new" rhetoric? and how might research on audience affect the teaching of writing? And finally, of course, we came to share an interest in the phenomenon we were experiencing—collaboration.

Looking back on our four years' experience as coauthors, we are surprised to note the relative ease with which we have modified or given up some of our writing habits or rituals in order to collaborate. Andrea now willingly, if not enthusiastically, takes more frequent breaks when writing and will even type up parts of a draft to please Lisa, if necessary. Lisa, on the other hand, now writes faster and for longer, more sustained periods than she was accustomed to doing alone. Important as such changes in habits are, however, they do not reflect what we believe to be the single most significant change in our writing processes demanded by collaboration. What for Andrea is largely a lengthy internal process of conceptualization must now be made external and explicit. And what for Lisa is largely a silent conversation with colleagues must now become a concrete verbal conversation with an all too unideal Andrea. (Yes, Andrea wrote this sentence, against Lisa's protestations.) *Talk,* then, plays a vital role in our collaborative writing. In fact, . . . talk is central to our collaboration in a way that it seldom has been for us as individual writers. We find ourselves talking through to a common thesis and plan, talking through the links in an argument, talking through various points of significance or alternative conclusions. Talk is also central to our planning, which must be both more explicit and more detailed when we write together than either of us is accustomed to when working alone.

Although we generally organize our projects so that we can divide up tasks and do part of the work—gathering information or writing a section of an essay or chapter—alone, most of our writing, especially final drafts, has been done together. This presents a number of practical problems, which we'll discuss shortly. But the advantages, especially given the role face-to-face talk (which can only partly be simulated over the phone) plays in our writing, make the effort to be together not only worthwhile but essential. When we are working, whether in Vancouver, Corvallis, or Seattle's University Inn, our halfway meeting place, we usually stake out different rooms to write in. But we move constantly back and forth, talking, trading texts (one of our favorite collaborative strategies is to revise one another's writing), asking questions. Often, when one or both of us is stuck, we'll work together on the same text, passing a single pad of paper back and forth, one of us completing the sentence or paragraph that the other began. By the time that most essays are finished, we simply couldn't say that "Lisa wrote this section, while Andrea wrote that." Our joint essays are truly collaborative efforts.

This collaboration is a crucial factor in our coauthored projects, from the earliest point in our composing through the final editing process. The simple physical act of meeting to work, for instance, has come to serve as a powerful writing ritual for both of us. However we feel individually—tired, cranky, concerned with other projects or issues—once we're together (after the 8-hour drive or the quick airplane flight) we know it's time to work. We have already commented on the importance of talk in our joint composing process, especially in the earlier or prewriting stage. Throughout our writing, however, we are much more aware of the way in which our joint ideas and understandings enable us, via the crucible of our conversations and collaboration, to discover new meanings—meanings simply not available to us working alone. Finally, we believe that we feel somewhat less ego involvement with our coauthored essays, that we are more willing to loosen our proprietary connection or hold on our "own" words. This latter point may be reflected both in the care with which we alternate our names as first authors—we thought that listing our names alphabetically would indicate that we were equal collaborators, but were quickly disabused of that notion—and our ability to negotiate differences in our individual styles, such as Lisa's love of dashes or Andrea's fondness for periodic sentences.

As we mentioned earlier, our collaboration has presented a number of practical challenges and problems. Since we live 400 miles apart, our need to be physically together at certain crucial times in our composing process requires careful planning. (As we write this in December 1985, we are also deciding when and how we can meet the following summer —and discovering a number of difficulties, even though we're planning six months in advance.) Money is also a constraint. Without the support of our departments, which have generously paid for our numerous long-distance telephone calls, and, more recently, our FIPSE-funded Shaughnessy Scholars grant, we simply could not have afforded to meet as often as we have, and hence would have been forced to limit our collaboration. Pragmatic constraints have also affected our research and writing. We try to have duplicate copies of important reference materials, for instance, but must often pass books and articles back and forth, with the attendant inevitable confusion. ("Do you have the Grimaldi?" "Where did we put that article by David Bartholomae?" "Did you remember to make me a Xerox of Lynn Troyka's essay?") We must also take much greater care keeping reference notes and bibliographic references straight, especially in articles with numerous citations. Finally, we simply could not collaborate without photocopying. We are constantly mailing copies of notes, references, and drafts back and forth. One of our standard jokes involves our usually desperate efforts in Seattle to find a quick-copy center open early Sunday morning so we can Xerox what we've written over the weekend and begin our separate journeys home and arrive in time to unpack and prepare for Monday's classes.

We will soon be faced with a new practical challenge: Andrea will begin in fall 1986 teaching at a large Midwestern university—5–7 driving days, not 8 hours, from Lisa's university in Oregon. We have of course discussed the problems this move will create for us as coauthors. We will almost certainly, for instance, have to commit ourselves to fewer joint projects, especially those with immediate deadlines, since we'll no longer be able to meet in Seattle in an emergency. We have both recently acquired personal computers, however, and we hope that these, and modems, may alleviate some of our anticipated difficulties. We expect, then, that our joint composing process will have to change. But we expect also to keep writing together. Collaborative writing has taught us too much for us entirely to abandon the practice of writing together; it has taught us how to read each other's illegible scrawls; how to be patient and flexible; how to listen to and criticize a draft over the phone; how to laugh, not cry, when one of us announces that something the other has just written is not quite right. Most important, perhaps, it has taught us what we know as writers but often forget: that there is no simple, single, static writing process. Rather, there are writing processes—repertoires of strategies and habits that writers can learn, and change, if they have a strong enough motive for communicating. We view our writing processes, then, whether single or collaborative, as flexible and multifaceted, as rooted in various rhetorical and social situations, as growing and changing—even as we grow and change.

Steve Lynn is currently director of the Writing Center and assistant professor at the University of South Carolina at Columbia. His Ph.D. is from the University of Texas, and his M.A. and B.A. degrees are from South Carolina. In addition to writing classes at various levels, he teaches courses in the history of rhetoric, eighteenth-century literature, and the teaching of writing.

He has recently finished a book on Samuel Johnson's composing strategies in the Rambler, *and he has published on eighteenth-century rhetoric and literature in* Eighteenth-Century Studies, South Atlantic Review, *and* Teaching English in the Two-Year College *as well as in* The Task of an Author, *a collection of essays on Samuel Johnson edited by Prem Nath. He claims to be the best bluegrass guitarist of all the rhetoricians in Columbia, South Carolina.*

HEURISTICS AND AQUATICS: WRITING WITH A PURPOSE/RIDING WITH A PORPOISE

Steve Lynn
University of South Carolina—Columbia

My impression is that I know a whole lot more about how I initiate writing than I know about how I keep it going and finish it. The more I get into a project, the more the adrenalin flows and that project becomes the world I inhabit.

I write for twelve hours a day, every day, beginning at 5:35 A.M., producing clear, orderly first drafts based on meticulous, thorough notes that are logically organized, cross-referenced, and always at my fingertips. I usually write after my seven-mile jog through the wilderness terrain that surrounds our two-story stone-block house I built myself in the mountainous national forest that President Reagan created at my suggestion over the protests of all the major oil-producing companies.

Although this opening paragraph is, of course, slightly exaggerated in spots, it does point toward some important facts about the way I write, at least some of the time. Thinking about this essay, I wrote that passage to have fun. When my wife, Annette, chuckled a bit when she read it, the challenge began: how could I work that paragraph into the essay? I worked on that problem for about two days—meaning that I consciously thought about it for a few minutes every few hours or so over a two-day period—and the best way I could think of to include such erroneous information was to concoct a quiz in which I would ask a question, offer three or four statements about my writing, and ask the reader to select the right answer. I thought this too would be fun to write, and it was; but I began to think, after I had made up several hilarious (to me anyway) questions and answers, that maybe this was a bit silly, and not at all what Waldrep wanted. So I ditched that plan.

During this gestation period I also came up with another sentence that I tried very hard to use: "Talking about how one writes is sort of like talking about anything one does in private, in relative silence, behind a closed door." This sentence, even though it seemed humorous, also didn't seem to be going anywhere that I was supposed to go, so it disappeared too. Of course, there it is, just a sentence ago, so one could point out that I did in fact manage to use both those bits after all.

This instinctive search for a starting point in humor or wit is typical for me. Perhaps I don't really like to get started writing, and this approach entices me. Perhaps I'm insecure about what I'm doing, how I'll be perceived, so I try nervously to make a joke. Or perhaps (and this gets my vote) I just like to please my audience, no matter what I'm writing about, and I think my audience especially values humor. Certainly this shaping at the point of witticism does not come about because I fail to take my writing seriously. If anything, I take writing too seriously, investing too much time, too much ego, in its results. I do better, it seems, when I'm not trying so hard.

Sometimes, of course, this urge is unfortunate. In the case of this essay, for example, it appeared to be obscuring the assigned topic, although one could also say that it led me to it, eventually. Anyway, this approach often seems to work nicely. For example, I have just finished an essay called "Sexual Difference and Johnson's Brain." The essay was written mostly because I couldn't use that title unless I had an essay to go with it. Why do I like the title, and where did it come from? I was reading an essay about Einstein's brain, which is (no kidding) sitting in a glass jar somewhere in Kansas (neurologists studied it, could find nothing unusual about it, and so set it aside and forgot about it). At about this same time I read the rather thorough autopsy report on Samuel Johnson, the eighteenth-century literary colossus, and so I began to wonder what Johnson's capacious brain would have looked like. Would it have been as unremarkable as Einstein's? And I thought, "An essay on Johnson's brain would be strange, wouldn't it. Yes, it would be as bizarre as a feminist/deconstructive perspective on Johnson." Thus the title popped into my head as a kind of incredible, unwritable essay: exactly the kind of thing I like. A few weeks later I needed to propose a paper for a conference, and so I pulled "Sexual Difference and Johnson's Brain" out of the semi-organized pile of notes on my desk, made up the skeleton of an argument, and got myself committed to invent an essay to go with the title.

For me, this is a typical story. I begin with a desire to write—to get tenure, to get raises, to see my name in print, to appease John Calvin, but mostly to please myself and an imaginary audience—and then focus that desire, oftentimes, with a title. I write many more titles than essays, because I am only one person working eight to twelve hours a day (including teaching, research, and a heavy helping of administration), and because about seventy percent of the titles are too silly even for me or they don't lead anywhere—yet anyway. I do save titles and sometimes consult my list or my note piles to see what I want to work on next. In the case of the "Sexual Difference" paper, to my genuine surprise and relief, when the time came to produce the paper, two months before the conference, things started to aggregate to the title every time I looked into Johnson's work: I noticed a recurrent interest in Amazons, a character named Hymenaeus who is in search of a wife, a wide-ranging fascination on Johnson's part with sexual identity and androgyny, and on and on. Things that I already knew about Johnson, such as the baffling evidence of a sado-masochistic relationship with Mrs. Thrale, took on a new significance. As I came across these passages, I marked them or typed them out or made notes.

I finally started the essay one evening, as the deadline approached, when I was rereading *Rasselas,* Johnson's great *Bildungsroman,* in order to discuss it with undergraduates the next morning. When I came to the marriage discussion between Nekayah and Rasselas, where Nekayah says "We differ from each other as we differ from ourselves," I felt that such a Derridean opening had to be analyzed on paper. First the analysis seemed to write itself, and then the analysis turned into the essay, rolling out faster than I could type it onto the screen. Not everything I write starts so well, but at some point in writing virtually anything longer than a memo, I will experience a stretch of time (or nontime it seems) when the writing is exhilarating, gratifying, when I'm barely aware, in a sense, that I am writing, when the adrenlin is pumping and the text seems to be shaping itself and surprising me. I gather most if not all writers experience this. I hereby dub it "the writer's high" and propose a major research grant to see how it relates to the endorphin-produced euphoria that runners experience. (Anyone contributing funds to this grant will receive a free copy of the questions and answers mentioned earlier.)

Sometimes my starting point for writing seems not to be an arresting title or an amusing idea, but rather a surprising observation, oftentimes only a sentence. For example, one day while working on Locke's *Essay on Human Understanding* and eighteenth-century rhetorical theory, I had this feeling that an idea was about to appear. I picked up my pencil to see what it would be, and I wrote, really without thinking about it (so that's what your problem is, I hear you saying!): "Locke's principle strategies in the *Essay* are erasure and deformation." In retrospect I can speculate that this sentence emerged as a way of getting to several examples in Locke's text that especially interested me: for instance, Locke's discussion of classifying is supported by the example, which he has seen himself, he says, "of the issue of a cat mated with a rat," a phenomenon that accords with other cases Locke has read or heard about; among these odd, class-defying hybrids, Locke mentions a man-hog (half man, half hog). I wanted to talk about these examples because it seemed strange to think of Locke's great mind building his monumental work on such bizarre examples. So that sentence was my entrance, even though I didn't know when I wrote it, consciously anyway, where I wanted to go.

Often when a project is getting under way I will find myself putting two or more unlikely or previously unrelated things together, as in the "Sexual Difference" essay, making the kind of hybrids Locke thought to be so epistemologically significant. For example, I was doing a survey on eighteenth-century rhetorical theories at the same time that I was working on the structures of Johnson's *Rambler* essays. I put the two together and wrote an essay on "Johnson's *Rambler* and Eighteenth-Century Rhetoric." Then I started thinking about how the kinds of composing strategies in current process pedagogies might be theoretically organized, and I saw a way to illuminate this classification by referring to (what else?) Johnson's *Rambler* and eighteenth-century rhetoric. This was, as my colleague Carolyn Matalene pointed out after the essay was rejected, trying to go too many different places at once. So I took out the contemporary composition stuff and sent the essay to another journal, where it was accepted.

If the impetus for a piece of writing doesn't come from humor or crossbreeding, then it probably comes from opposition. (Probably all these forces are at work much of the time.) I recognize myself in much of what David Bartholomae and Cyril Knoblauch especially say in the first volume of *Writers on Writing* (*WW I* hereafter). I also often write "against the grain," deriving energy from a text or a critical position that I plan to unravel or oppose. I like to test positions, even positions that I admire or agree with. The better established the position, the more I enjoy searching for fissures, gaps, omissions, inconsistencies. A chapter in my book on Johnson disagrees rather pointedly with Knoblauch's reading of Johnson's *dispositio,* even though I find Knoblauch's argument seductive and eloquent; still, I thought the evidence offered a contrary interpretation, and so I wrote the chapter, taking an opposing position, partly to see if it would work and to see what would happen if it did. At this point I'm not sure who's right, and I'm eager to see what other Johnsonians think. Like Knoblauch, "my writing depends significantly on dialectic" (*WW* 1, p. 138).

In other words, an instinctive writing strategy for me appears to be to see how much trouble I can get myself into and still get out. A crucial aspect of my preparation, then, involves extensive reading, for I've got to line up the positions I'm going to question or dismantle or incorporate or recuperate. The texts I'm working with have to be marked up with colored pencils (erasable), and the pages dog-eared or marked by an index card, or a clothespin (they're very nice for marking places and holding materials). Usually I take notes, first on 5 × 8 slips of paper, and then on index cards when the slips start looking too large, and then on the slips again when the cards seem so cramped. Thus I usually end up with an unruly pile of cards and slips that don't stack very well. I keep thinking I'll stick to one or the other, but I never do. I like to write these notes using a tricky fountain pen, until I start paying more attention to my calligraphy than to what I'm writing. Then I'll switch to a pencil or a Bic pen until my eye catches the beautiful fountain pen lying neglected on my desk. Recently, I've also started to take notes with my computer.

My impression is that I know a whole lot more about how I initiate writing than I know about how I keep it going and finish it. As I've already suggested, the more I get into a project, the more the adrenalin flows and that project becomes the world I inhabit. I've never been enough outside of a project I'm really engaged in to know precisely what the shape of my activity is. But I will try to make a few observations here that I think might be of some interest.

• I used to think that I required absolute silence and uninterrupted concentration for long periods of time while writing. Although I am embarrassed to admit it, when I was writing my dissertation I insisted that my wife say "Question?" before interrupting me. That way, if I happened to be at a stopping point, I'd say "Okay," and we'd talk. But if I happened to be in the middle of an idea, I'd just say "Not now." Then, when I came to a stopping place, if I remembered, I would say "What is it?" If Annette still rememberd what she wanted, she would ask me again. I do not recommend this method as a technique for nurturing marital bliss.

But I thought it was necessary. I can remember telling a friend at about this time that writing for me was like building a gigantic house of cards: one could work for hours, days even, only to have the whole thing collapse unexpectedly with a momentary loss of concentration. However, about three years ago I started listening to classical music whenever I was just typing or writing something unimportant. I also started watching/listening to television when I had some especially boring and mindless task to do, using the TV to keep me awake. I began to notice that I really wasn't distracted by these distractions, that my concentration, surprisingly, improved, so I decided to try writing serious things under playful conditions. It worked. Not only have I come to think I can work in the midst of pleasing sounds and even entertainment, I have come now to welcome a few interruptions, usually—as long as I'm working more than I'm pausing. These breaks, I have found, can provide a fresh perspective, a renewal of energy. Sometimes when I'm working on a problem and I'm called away, I've noticed that instead of the house of cards falling down, someone usually seems to have continued building it and even adding some foundation while I've been gone. In fact, I can't ever recall really, finally, losing an idea or train of thought; although I sometimes might forget for a moment what I was doing, I could always recover it.

• This confidence in my ability to write without an antiseptic environment has recently matured significantly because of a particular incident. Computers, like everything else that works well without complaining, tend to get taken for granted. So, periodically, they break down, just to get our attention. It is interesting how many of those writers in *WW* 1 report suffering disasters and yet in the same passage sing the word processor's praises. Anyway, my computer managed to eat the copy *and* the backup copy of a twenty-page article, leaving me with only eight pages of hard copy. I thought, as I was writing it, that the essay was perhaps the best thing I had ever done. When most of it was lost, I was certain. I mourned for a few days, thought about giving up the project, but decided I could still finish what I had more easily than I could start something else from the beginning. So, I set about to reconstruct the essay as best I could. Really, I had little faith that the second version would be as good as the first; but as it turned out, I think it may have been better. Although I had been telling my students for years that there's a lot less inspiration involved in writing than most people think, that time and effort are the real keys, I am afraid I never really believed it myself. This experience, along with my discovery that I can write with music and distractions, has made me feel that I control my writing more than I thought (if I could only control my computer), that even though I depend on forces I don't quite understand and can't always analyze, these forces do attend to my wishes.

• Speaking of my computer, I shifted almost immediately with surprising ease to composing with one. I used to think that important stuff had to be written out in longhand, and that less demanding writing could be done on a typewriter. This isn't amazing, I know, but it does offer one more piece of evidence suggesting to the computer-wary that composing on one may be easier than they think. Even hunt-and-peckers may find they can write better and faster with a PC.

• To be sure, I don't always type in *everything*. I also use some scratch sheets to sketch out, or perhaps "outline," the shape of the whole essay or the next section. This outlining consists usually of a few phrases arranged vertically. I might write only fifteen words all told, but the rest of the essay is somehow locked in those words, if the arrangement is right. Sometimes, when I run out of things to say, I'll look at the sketch, studying a phrase to see what other words might be hiding in it. Sometimes I redo the sketch when it doesn't make sense or I think of a better sequence or more ideas.

• Until I get the adrenalin and the words flowing, I'm restless. I'll get a pile of cookies, a bowl of popcorn, a cup of tea, a coke, a sandwich, a candy bar in a three-hour period. I've even seriously considered chaining myself to my desk, but for certain practical reasons never have. Perhaps this physical and culinary roaming is essential to getting started. I catch myself studying my study, and by the time I've finished a project of any size, rearranging the furniture is one of my rewards. My goal is to have every object in a ten-by-ten room at my fingertips. Sometimes, when I'm really stuck, I'll clean my office a bit. But that is a drastic measure. Generally I straighten up when my parents come to visit or I can't find something.

• As I write, especially as I revise, several people are looking over my shoulder. Although I've never been able to turn around fast enough to see them, I can sense their presence. It's a somewhat odd assembly, with different interests in my work: Karl Beason, my high-school English teacher, who first demonstrated for me what fun writing and language could be; Donald Greiner, whose comments on undergraduate essays first made me think I might be able to do what I'm now trying to do, and whose teaching remains for me a model of what that is; my mom, whose frowning smile gently nudges me out of my daydreams and draws my attention to the list of unfinished projects taped to my light; George Geckle, my most exacting and most patient reader, who kept telling me over and over again my ideas were good, but my style error-riddled and uneven; John Trimble, who showed me how to revise by working steadily on one of my sentences for fifteen minutes, while three of his students waited in the hall. And many others, including George Brauer, Jim Garrison, Benjamin Dunlap, James Kinneavy—it's a real crowd back there, but generally they're well behaved, although right now they seem to be cringing a bit. These presences are crucial to the way I write, for they have helped to shape what it is I'm aiming for, thus determining what I do and the fact that I do it at all.

And now I believe I can sense that Tom Waldrep has slipped discreetly into the back of the room, indicating with a nod and a glass of champagne that I've used up about all my available space and time. But Tom, since I've said titles are so important to me, can't I explain the one for this essay? No? What do you mean it's obvious? In Volume 3 maybe?

Elaine P. Maimon is associate vice president and professor of English at Beaver College (suburban Philadelphia), where she also directs the writing-across-the-curriculum program. She has coauthored two composition textbooks, Writing in the Arts and Sciences *(1981) and* Readings in the Arts and Sciences *(1984), has contributed widely to scholarly journals, and is a frequent speaker at professional meetings.*

From 1980 to 1984, she was director of the NEH/Beaver College Summer Institutes on the teaching of writing in the humanities. Currently, she is director of an NEH project designed to promote alliances in the humanities between Beaver College and local school districts.

THE VOICES OF A WRITER'S MIND

Elaine P. Maimon
Beaver College

The essential factor for me in writing anything that is not rou-
tine—that is anything from which I expect to learn—is to create
a conversation in my head. I need to hear voices to whom my
writing is a response. I want to feel part of a conversation.

I

Then I went back into the house and wrote,
It is midnight. The rain is beating on the windows.
It was not midnight. It was not raining.

—Samuel Becket *(Molloy)*

Midnight. The house is finally quiet. It is time to try that magic transformation from random notes to a connected draft. I sit before my Adam Coleco, a toy computer lacking even a single disk drive but equipped with a letter-quality printer, enough to lure me into the electronic age. The ease of computer writing invites me to chatter with my fingers. But because this machine is a primitive model, I must print each page or face the prospect of losing precious thoughts into thin air. (As if on cue, as if the screen were responding to these words, the Adam goes crazy at the command to insert a phrase and after giving me one minute, during which I frantically try to copy down as much as I can see of what I have composed, clears the screen completely.)

For years I wrote with a ball-point pen on lined yellow pads, and when I am not using the Adam, I still do. But I cannot say that I am in any way fixated on ball-point and yellow pad, since I am now composing on plain white paper until I have the nerve to try the unreliable computer again. (My children have appropriated all the yellow pads and all but one of the ball-point pens and have effectively sequestered these and all other useful household tools—scissors, Scotch tape, calculators

137

—in unspeakable places in their messy rooms.) Parents learn flexibility in their writing habits.

I do not need a special place or time to make preliminary notes or read background material and write responses. But when I wish to write sustained, connected discourse, I must find time, quiet, and will. Of the three, the will to write is often the hardest to find. A busy person can become fully occupied with numerous less demanding tasks: telephoning, reading, filling out checks, even writing routine letters. One of the most effective ways to avoid giving shape to ideas is to postpone connected writing by prolonging the process of research and preliminary thought. Reading for a project puts me in direct touch with others who have grappled with the same issues and eases the loneliness of sitting solitary at my writing table. In short, the essential factor for me in writing anything that is not routine—that is anything from which I expect to learn—is to create a conversation in my head. I need to hear voices to whom my writing is a response. I want to feel part of a conversation. In Volume 1 of *Writers on Writing*, David Bartholomae talked about working with other people's words. I write this essay alone in a quiet house at midnight, but I hear Bartholomae's words and Ed Corbett's—and Virginia Woolf's.

Actually I began this essay several weeks ago, when I started to read *Writers on Writing*, Volume 1. I keep that book near me now as I write, and I feel happy to be a Volume 2 writer who has the advantage of such good conversation. But my colleagues' essays have done more for me than just ease the loneliness. From reading the work of these immediate forebears I have caught the variety of tone and the possibilities of form. Most important, I have found reassurance in the risks they have already taken. Contributors to Volume 2 have the luxury of extending a tradition.

II

So naming and the problem of identity cannot
be dissociated. So literature and the problem of
identity cannot be dissociated.

—Geoffrey H. Hartman
Saving the Text

Hearing voices makes writing possible. I can understand why writers personify inspiration—the creative spirit within—as a Muse—something outside ourselves. For me, the Muse speaks in many voices, making writing of any kind a social activity. I invoke the Muse by conversing with other people—in person, by telephone, by reading, by imagining, and by remembering.

At times I believe that some of the voices I remember are part of a collective unconscious, voices telling stories. Before societies could read and write, stories transformed groups into communities. Gathered around a fire, primitive people listened to the voice of a storyteller. The fire provided warmth and protection from outsiders, and so did the story. Communities became cultures because they knew the same stories. Voices telling a story, what we might call the narrative impulse, established the fundamental motive, I believe, for reading and writing.

"You have a way with words, Scheherazade," says her sister Dunyazade in John Barth's *Chimera*. Scheherazade, like the primitive listeners around the fire, keeps death at bay by understanding the narrative impulse. The sultan participates in her composition so that he, too, is revitalized. The teller of tales and the active listener, wedded in organic dialogue, voices half-remembered, reverberate in my imagination as I read the narratives of others and as I respond with stories of my own.

I hear other voices when I read and write. These are less distant than those of the primitive storytellers, but they are from just as long ago in my biographical past. I hear my mother's voice reading me stories. One story, in particular, was about me, or at least about someone with my name:

Elaine the fair, Elaine the lovable,
Elaine, the lily maid of Astolat,
High in her chamber up a tower to the east
Guarded the sacred shield of Lancelot.

My earliest memory is my mother's voice reading that story. The English language and Tennyson's use of it in particular became for me the mother tongue indeed. In this childhood idyll, I soon could read one word, the heroine's name. Reading and writing became extensions of other sorts of tender familial communication, touching, being in touch.

Outside the household was a larger world of books to which my mother resorted periodically for replenishment. One bookstore in particular stands out in my childhood memory. In Philadelphia, where I grew up, there was a place called Leary's, a shop for old books, some rare, some merely well used. My mother went there about once a month, and each time she would remind me that the giant Gimbel's department store had to build around little Leary's because Leary's would not move. Such, she said, was the power of the book. When Leary's was finally torn down in the 1970s, the owners found there an original copy of the Declaration of Independence. Many years before that, I knew that Leary's held unfound treasures.

At five, before I entered first grade and learned to read for real, I had a ritual at Leary's. While my mother browsed, I would quite importantly approach a salesclerk and ask to see a book by Mr. Tennyson. The astonished clerk would find the book for me and watch as I scanned the table of contents for the one word I could read.

I take time to tell this story in an essay about how I write because of the profound, in fact definitive, influence reading and writing had on my earliest identity. I wish to conjure up a remembered voice that has been the matrix of my imagination. Remembered voices become an inner, creative conversation to make writing possible. We transform the world outside into an inner realm where the memory and imagination meet to create expression. Thus we give back what we have taken in, give external form to what we have internalized.

III

There is no authentically temporal discourse,
no timely utterance, except by resolute acts
of writing. . . . Writing, as an individual
or collective process, defers utterance of the
definitive *parole* or password—from generation
to generation.

—Geoffrey H. Hartman
Deconstruction and Criticism

My theme is voices. I write as part of an ongoing conversation. Time and quiet merely create appropriate conditions under which I can hear the voices that give me the will to write. I seek solitude so that I can be in closer touch with the voices that make writing possible. I tell my students about these voices. Effective teaching, I believe, involves helping others to internalize generative voices. A successful teacher creates an environment in which peers become colleagues who help each other enter the community of educated people. I have already made this point in print:

> Experienced writers can tolerate the solitude of the silent library because they have learned not to be alone there. Writers hear the voices of colleagues asking questions about the formulation of ideas, reminding them about absent readers, pointing to potential dissonances. Inexperienced writers hear voices, too, but these sounds are too often mocking and disdainful, "You can't write," they chide. Or they ask the student's preoccupying question: "Do you belong here?" When writers hear the

voices of colleagues, they can talk back to them on paper, and that dialogue can drown out the voices of self-doubt and discouragement.

("Knowledge, Acknowledgement, and Writing Across the Curriculum: Toward an Educated Community," in *The Territory of Language: Linguistics, Stylistics, and the Teaching of Composition,* ed. Donald McQuade, Southern Illinois University Press, 1986)

Some of the voices I hear when I write are those of my own earlier selves. To prompt this dialogue between self and soul, I often reread material that I have already written, to search for notes of harmony and dissonance. I have long believed that, for good or ill, what I have written is what I know. I remember exactly when I stumbled on this revelation. It was the night before I was scheduled to take my Ph.D. comprehensive examinations. For weeks I had lived in the library stacks, reading for eighteen hours a day, until the eyestrain made me give up contact lenses forever. During those weeks of study, I found, like Tantalus, that the more information I devoured, the more famished I became, discovering each day new abysses of ignorance. Finally, with only one day left, in desperation, I made a pile on the living-room floor of all the English papers I had ever written, from a freshman theme on *The Sound and the Fury* to essays written for that semester's graduate courses. Shoring these fragments against my ruin, I read through them all. When I took the examination the next day, those powers that watch over writers sent an omen, a question on *The Sound and the Fury.* We are what we write, and we can learn from listening and responding to our own former voices.

Besides listening to my own voice, I have, as I write this essay, actively sought the advice of friends and family. When I was still in the stage of making notes and brainstorming, I was fortunate enough to serve as a consultant at the 1986 CCCC winter workshop in Clearwater, Florida, where three other potential contributors to this volume were also consultants. The four of us engaged in several productive conversations about our writing processes. Joining also in that good talk were James Slevin and many other participants in the program that Rosentene Purnell had planned so well. One of the major voices influencing this essay was Edward Corbett, whose paper called upon the participants in the winter workshop to remember the early influences on them as readers and writers. At the first session that I conducted after listening to Corbett's paper, I asked participants to record in their journals what they could recall of these formative experiences. Trying to be a good discussion leader, I refrained from seizing the privilege of sharing my own journal entries and instead let the lively discussion proceed without my contribution. Such unnatural repression developed into the portion of this essay about Leary's bookstore. Ideas shared in conversation and thoughts left unshared have both contributed to this essay.

If I had been able to remain in sunny Clearwater with that congenial group of colleagues, I would not have inflicted interruptions on my husband and my daughter, both of whom have been reading this work-in-progress. My daughter saved me from an acute attack of self-doubt by telling me that the essay was not as boring as she had expected it to be. My husband, as always, provided encouragement and some excellent stylistic suggestions. Later, my colleague and sometime coauthor, Barbara Nodine, read and commented on a completed draft. When Janice Peritz read a version of this essay, she heard the voices of Samuel Beckett and Geoffrey Hartman and helped me to put my ideas in this broader literary context. Donald McQuade heard a discordant voice intruding in the draft he read and chided me emphatically about this nervous academic tone. In one last revision I tried to repress that apologetic voice.

These acknowledgments name the voices that have talked this essay into being. When my students write, I compel them, too, to name the voices that they hear. Whenever students in my classes go public with their writing (i.e., whenever they submit a paper for a grade), they must preface the document with a page of acknowledgment. This acknowledgment is the talisman of my theory and pedagogy. Not only do students give credit for help received, they also learn, I hope, that a writer never works alone. On pages of acknowledgment, students affirm their identities as writers by connecting themselves with an intellectual community. When writing and reading are perceived as social activities, acknowledgment becomes knowledge, as the students' prefatory narratives give witness to creative interdependence.

As much as writers are interdependent, members of a community, we are also individuals, varying infinitely one from another, especially in those strategies we can successfully employ while we are waiting for the Muse. Unfortunately, I have found no technique that always works for me even within the writing of a single project. I have observed, however, that my writing gains momentum as I get deeper into a particular task and that the hardest part is getting started on the translation of rough notes into first draft. I have also found that I demonstrate one consistent habit, although I doubt that this practice actually helps my writing. I ignore the voice that tells me that I am not hungry. No matter how firmly I resolve not to, I eat while I am writing, especially late at night, when I substitute the food for sleep. As a consequence, I put on "pretzel pounds." I can say with some assurance that if I ever gave up writing, I would be diminished: I would lose at least ten pounds.

Aside from this consistency, I find that my writing practices vary within a single project and, more particularly, from project to project. Sometimes I start writing a draft without a specific plan in mind. More often, I have a shopping list of points I wish to cover or images I want to invoke. Once in a while, I make an outline from rough notes. I deem myself to be an experienced writer because I have learned flexibility and the capacity for systematic variability.

My theoretical and pedagogic commitment to writing across the curriculum manifests my belief that inexperienced writers become experienced by learning to hear many voices: to shift perspectives, to read various genres, and to write in different contexts. *Writing in the Arts and Sciences* and *Readings in the Arts and Sciences* are not designed to teach students to become junior-grade scientists, sociologists, or historians. Instead, my coauthors and I have designed these texts to give students juxtaposed experiences in the different rhetorical moves that scientists, sociologists, and historians make. In this way students can experience from the inside the essential principle of experienced writing: contextual variability. Hearing different tones in varying contexts, students learn to speak in many tongues.

Experienced writers know how to size up a situation so that the form of communication they choose will most effectively communicate what they want to say. They understand how to identify themselves as members of the appropriate community by making tactful selections of genre, style, and tone. A research report that sounds like a diary entry will not be taken seriously as a research report. A diary entry that sounds like a legal brief may not accomplish the purpose of self-exploration. In light of this belief, I teach students to begin a writing assignment, as I begin one, by analyzing purpose and audience and then deciding who they will be in the text and who they want the reader to be.

At the same time I believe that the impetus for all writing, no matter what public form it eventually takes, is primarily narrative and autobiographical. People learn what they think about anything by telling themselves stories about it. Every form of writing—the research report, the case study, the book review—is to some extent a transformed autobiographical narrative. James Britton's influential emphasis on expressive writing has inspired numerous writing-across-the-curriculum programs, including those that I have developed, to encourage students to use journals, letters, and other writing-to-learn activities to tell themselves stories about their scholastic work before attempting to compose public documents.

In the instance of the particular public document on which I am now working, I have had the luxury of presenting autobiographical narrative in close to its natural condition. This opportunity has enabled me to focus on features of my writing processes that are less available to my contemplation when the major portion of my energy is devoted to transformations from the narrative. In this project, I have seen plainly how important it is for me to find a metaphor, that is, a vehicle for transporting something abstract into the realm of the senses. In the case of this essay, the presiding metaphor is the human voice, transforming the silence and solitude of the writer's isolation into the sociability of culture.

Writing this essay has reminded me of the debts I owe to the many voices who have conversed so patiently with me. The only way to repay such obligations to the past is to work even harder to include in the conversation of educated people those sons and daughters who never had a chance to visit Leary's. As a writer and teacher of writing, I hope that I, too, will become a voice in the minds of younger writers.

Richard Marius is director of the expository writing program at Harvard University. He received his M.A. and Ph.D. from Yale University in Reformation studies, and has taught at Gettysburg College and the University of Tennessee. He was one of the first five graduates of the University of Tennessee School of Journalism, and for five years worked on a small newspaper in Tennessee. A frequent contributor to numerous journals, he has had two novels published by Alfred A. Knopf, The Coming of Rain *and* Bound for the Promised Land. *He has written biographies of Martin Luther (1974) and Thomas More (1984), and is presently working on another novel.*

HOW I WRITE

Richard Marius
Harvard University

I am a compulsive writer. I not only love to write; I must write. If a day passes when I have written nothing, I am depressed. If I am expecting to write and something interrupts and keeps me from my task, I feel useless and lazy and somehow spent no matter what I have accomplished otherwise or how much good I may have done in another part of my working life. But several hours of writing leaves me in a state of euphoria. It may be lousy stuff. But it is there, and I can make it better tomorrow. I have done something worthwhile with my day.

My writing goes through several stages, but it does not pass through a linear progression. It is a stumbling, often disorganized, always difficult business. At times I am not sure when the process begins. It ends only when I am pressed flat against a deadline and someone takes my work away from me.

First seems to come a swirl of ideas that revolve in my head at the oddest moments. Someone has asked me to write something—like this essay or a book review. Or I decide on my own that I want to write something. Sometimes in a conversation someone suggests that I write something, and I take the suggestion to heart and do it.

Once the general topic comes into my mind, the most ordinary daily experiences are filtered through the writing task. Someone will say something to me. Or I will overhear a remark. Or I will try to explain something to a friend. I will read something seemingly utterly unconnected with what I am writing about, and suddenly I will see a connection—a nugget of information, an insight, a comparison, a metaphor. Some of my best thoughts come to me when I am riding my bicycle back and forth between my home and my office four miles away. This is dream time, one of the happiest periods in my day. Sometimes the general shape of what I want to write comes into my mind in the midst of pulling a hill or while pausing at a traffic light. Sometimes a sentence comes to me, or a metaphor, or even a word that I want to use, and I repeat it with the rhythm of the pedals.

I write both fiction and nonfiction. The process is somewhat different for each, but there are probably more similarities in the two than differences. In fiction I find character more compelling than plot. The fiction I like best builds characters who may do surprising things. But on reflection I find continuity between what characters do and what they have already done.

When I am writing fiction, I think about my characters and keep my eyes and ears open for the characters around me. I listen to the way people talk. I watch their gestures, their expressions. Above all, I look at what they do and how they see other people. And I try to incorporate these observations into the characters I am building. No character springs fully formed into my head. But as I write day after day, I see my characters more and more clearly. I hope they become more subtle, more complex, more familiar. I keep notebooks on them, writing comments to myself about them, who they are, what they do, why they do things (though sometimes I do not know).

Nonfiction requires a writer to pay careful attention to the evidence—to the incidents in a nonfictional narrative, to the logic of an analysis, to the details of a factual description. Getting it right in nonfiction is different from getting it right in fiction—though even as I write these words I find that the borderline between the two sorts of writing is more hazy for me than it might seem for others. The most interesting nonfiction that I do is biography. And building a character in a biography has many affinities with building a character in a novel. The evidence for the biography is intractable in a way that the ideas for a character in a novel are not. But descriptions of places, narratives of events, and analyses of causes may appear in both the novel and the biography.

For both fiction and nonfiction, the most important part of the process is the act of writing itself. I am a compulsive writer. I not only love to write; I *must* write. If a day passes when I have written nothing, I am depressed. If I am expecting to write and something interrupts and keeps me from my task, I feel useless and lazy and somehow spent no matter what I have accomplished otherwise or how much good I may have done in another part of my working life. But several hours of writing leaves me in a state of euphoria. It may be lousy stuff. But it is *there,* and I can make it better tomorrow. I have done something worthwhile with my day.

Most of my writing begins in a notebook. I usually carry several notebooks around with me, notebooks stowed in the capacious shoulderbag I carry on my bike commute and onto airplanes and to meetings. You never know when you are going to have some writing time or when an idea is going to strike. (I wrote part of this article during a lecture by a deconstructionist critic who, I decided, had nothing interesting to say. The other day I managed to write a fair chunk of a chapter in my current novel while a Harvard faculty meeting was droning on.)

I devote the notebooks to various subjects. I write both drafts to be reworked and thoughts about my subject that I have no intention of putting into the final draft. When I am writing fiction, I find it valuable to think about characters or purposes by writing out my thoughts about these matters. And when I am writing nonfiction, I find it sometimes helpful to stop and to write myself a few paragraphs to help me think of just what I want to be doing in the piece.

At some point I sit down at a keyboard, prop the relevant notebook in front of me on a stand, and start to pound away at a draft. I used to work at a typewriter, starting with an ancient Royal Standard that my typing teacher in high school sold me for $50 after students had beaten it more than half to death over the years. (I still have it and until the advent of computers wrote all my first drafts on it.) I used an even more ancient Underwood at the little newspaper where I began to work in high school and where I continued working throughout college.

I should pause a moment over my newspaper experience; it was a great way to learn to write. The most important thing about newspaper journalism is that it must communicate. You must find a common level of discourse so that your experience, your thoughts, your story can be quickly picked up by people in a hurry who do not necessarily have college educations. You must be simple. You must tell stories. You must use active verbs and nouns that convey something of sense experience. You must attribute sources. And you must get it all right because if you don't get it right, somebody is going to call you up on the telephone or come in to see you and rip the skin off your bones.

Composition teachers nowadays try to be gentle with students, and I suppose they should be, though I despise the touchy-feely attitude of many composition specialists. But all writers must eventually discover that everybody is not going to like their work, especially if they get something wrong. Newspaper readers make a more demanding audience than most writing students can imagine. And I am glad that early in my life I learned that there was an audience out there and that someone was likely to care deeply about what I said about seemingly the most ordinary things. Report the wrong second prize winner in the Garden Club's contest for the best dry arrangement, and see what happens. You don't get a friendly composition teacher writing in the margins of your paper, "Are you sure?" You get an outraged gardener sometimes weeping on the telephone or, worse, standing over your desk shaking a mean looking trowel in your face.

Newspaper writing also teaches you some things about process. You often have to write fast for a newspaper. Farther along in this essay I will say some things about revision and its pleasures. But every writer should learn to write rapidly, to get the words out on the page, to make thoughts run from one into the other, to fall into the patterns of repetition that make writing flow smoothly from idea to idea. I am glad that I once learned to produce a story in a half-hour if I had to do it.

Newspaper writing also teaches concentration. It pains me to see my academic colleagues demand a perfect environment before they can write. They have to have uninterrupted hours stretching ahead of them and minds free from cares, or they cannot sit down to write. Some of them almost require Proust's cork-lined room or perhaps just the right kind of soft music playing in the background. And of course they must have just the right desk and just the right chair. Many of my colleagues tell me they can write only in the summer when they are not teaching. Or they have to go off to Yaddo or the McDowell Colony or to some other remote place where they are utterly undisturbed for hours at a time and a flunky brings food to their door.

On the little newspaper where I worked, we had to write with the Milhe Vertical press rattling and banging on the other side of a pasteboard wall, with townspeople coming and going in the shabby office, with the telephone ringing, with friends saying interesting things to each other a couple of desks away, and with the reek of ink and newsprint and *foul* coffee and stale tobacco smoke in the air. I have never lost the ability to concentrate no matter what is going on around me. (As I write these lines, my fifteen-year-old son is hammering uncertainly at his piano lesson a short distance away. I am dimly aware that he is repeating the same difficult passage again and again. But I write on without feeling distracted.) If the atom bomb goes off in my neighborhood when I am writing, it is going to have to knock my house down before it interrupts what I am doing.

Having extolled the necessity of now and then writing rapidly, I must say that my favorite part of writing is revision—going over and over a text until it comes out "right." Before my conversion to the computer, I used to type a draft through a page at a time, typing every page over and over before going on to the next. Then I typed a second draft in the same way, running the words through my fingers again and again and again, throwing my discarded papers into the trash, placing the stuff I liked in a "keep" pile next to the typewriter. And almost always there was a third draft, worked through with the same laborious process. As I wrote, I read aloud in a soft mumble, testing the words with my mouth as I produced them with my fingers.

My big biography of Thomas More, published in 1984, came to 1,052 pages of typescript in its final draft. It was the last book that I shall ever write on a typewriter and with that method. While I was working on it, a woman from Ohio flew to Boston to protest a D we had given her sister in our writing program. I shall call the sister Henrietta, though that was not her real name.

She was furious about the grade we had given to Henrietta. She berated me for an hour. Finally she said in final proof of our unfair grade, "Henrietta wrote this paper twice, and you gave her a D for it. It is not fair to give a student a D who has written the paper twice. You have to give *some* credit for hard work."

It was late in the afternoon, and I had been working at a difficult part of my *Thomas More* all day with many interruptions. My trash can was filled with discarded pages. I picked it up off the floor and upended it on my desk. A storm of papers poured out over the desk top and showered onto the floor. I dug out nine different drafts of one page and spread them out before Henrietta and her startled sister. "Look," I said gently, "this is what real writing is. We are not judging your sister on any standard that we do not use for ourselves. We all take pains, and you don't get credit for anything until you get it right."

The woman from Ohio sat back in her chair and looked at her sister. "Well Henrietta," she said, "maybe he's right."

My discovery of the computer has changed my process. I now edit from the screen most of the time, though sometimes I print out a draft and sit over it with a pen. But usually I sit down at whatever it is I am doing, call up the file onto the screen, read it over quickly from the beginning, then read it over again making insertions and deletions and shifting paragraphs around in the magical way that computers allow. I change sentence forms, play with words, add thoughts, erase failures.

Some things hold constant in my progress from the typewriter to the computer. I still read everything aloud. I have a fundamental conviction that if a sentence cannot be read aloud with sincerity, conviction, and communicable emphasis, it is not a good sentence. Good writing requires good rhythms and good words. You cannot know whether the rhythms and the words are good unless you read them aloud. Reading aloud is also the easiest way to see that prose tracks, that it runs on smoothly from sentence to sentence, idea to idea, section to section within the larger whole. Reading aloud also makes the mind consider connotations of words and perhaps above all their relations to each other.

This long process of revision allows me two benefits. The first is stylistic. I love words. I love dictionaries. I love putting the right words together. What nouns require adjectives? What nouns most adequately convey the meaning I want to express? What metaphors can I design to make my meaning more vivid? What sentence forms make for the greatest efficiency of communication? What words are not necessary? What am I repeating that I have already said? Where am I being overbearing? Where am I not being vigorous enough? The best way to answer these questions is to think about them—and many more—over the time needed for good revision. I read all sorts of things. And if I read something and find a word I like, I may call up some part of my file and insert that word at an appropriate place.

I have already mentioned the newspaper reporter's vivid sense of audience. In my teaching I have always told students that they must write for an audience. Student writers need to learn that they have to interest someone. All too often they come out of high school thinking that the main goals of writing are to fill pages to the required number and to be correct. They can do all these things and be as dull as soap. The trick is to make someone want to read what they have to say and enjoy it and learn from it. Real writers are performers who, like pianists and singers and baseball players and ballet dancers, want their audience to rise to them in a mingling of admiration, pleasure, and something I can only call *participation.* A real writer wants readers to live through an experience the writer has, to identify with it, to *feel* with it in much the same way that a baseball fan thrills to a solid single hammered down the line with the bases loaded or to a great shortstop play that saves a game.

I write especially for my editor and for a few other good friends. I respect them and want them to respect me. I want them to enjoy my work. I often will think of one or the other of them when I am setting something on paper. I want them to think that I am fair, that I am reasonable, that I have worked hard, that I am interesting, that sometimes I am funny without being unkind, that I am confident without being arrogant, that I know how to use the language. Above all, I want them to read my prose with the feeling of participating in it. My editor said that she wept every time she read my account of the death of Thomas More. I wept over the keyboard as I wrote it in each draft of the book. When she told me of her own tears, I felt a marvelous triumph of a sort that made those three drafts worthwhile. We had participated in the same event both intellectually and emotionally through my prose.

But I suppose that in my own high middle age, I now write mostly for myself. I sit here and push and pull my prose into something that seems just right to me. I fall on words that I like, and I resolve to use them. I think of a good metaphor and feel a wonderful satisfaction at being able to incorporate it into something I am doing. I scribble thoughts in my ever-present notebooks and feel tremendous pleasure at shaping those thoughts into good prose.

It is perhaps a bit misleading to speak of writing for myself as though I were the center of the universe. I am a pretty good reader, reading at every opportunity and reading critically. So when I say I write to please myself, I mean that I write to please the sort of reader

I am. No one ever pleases everybody. I have read enough to know that important truth. But by this time in my life, I am confident of my ability to please some of the people I am trying to reach, people who share my particular taste, a taste that has been formed by the reading that I have done since childhood. Revision gives me the chance to play with style, to try different things, to look at them, to keep some, and to discard others. The computer allows any writer a facility in that playfulness undreamed of by our spiritual ancestors. And I love it.

The second benefit I get from revision is the demand that I learn more as I write. Most of my students and many of my colleagues believe that research and writing go on in two discrete parts. One does the research; later one writes.

My process is something else. I began my biography of Thomas More after working for more than a decade editing More's works as part of the great Yale Complete Edition. I knew much about him when I began. But as I wrote, the narrative form showed me many holes in my knowledge. And I had to fill those holes with substance. More wrote a history of the infamous King Richard III of England. I had read that little book many times before I started writing my biography. I could have summarized what More had to say about the usurper king and the supposed murder of the little princes in the Tower—one of the great mysteries of English history. But then I wanted to know what other people had said about Richard in his own time and then what people thought of children in that time and then of all the people around the king and of the general political and social situation when More wrote the book long after Richard was dead. My touching one part of the story raised other questions that I thought had to be answered. So my writing drove me to other reading.

Much the same thing is true of fiction. I write through one draft to get to know my characters, to think about them, to wonder what they might do to reveal themselves first to me and then to readers. And when I am done with that draft, I love to start all over again, putting my new knowledge to work in the new version. The point is that revising time is thinking time, and that the more thought you can pour into your writing, the better that writing is likely to be as long as you do not inflate the form until it loses its design.

This matter of design is important to the writing process. I am better at it in my nonfiction than I am in my fiction. My novels tend to sprawl all over the place. Sometimes I feel they are out of control, and I have moments where I must slash and burn. I control my nonfiction more carefully. I can see that one thought leads naturally into the next, that I develop a pattern of repetition of certain nouns and verbs that gives coherence to the whole, that I cut out unnecessary repetition, and that my last paragraph has some relation to my first—one of the surest tests of coherence that I know. Revision allows me to arrive painfully at this coherence, and at the end of one of my essays, I think most people can state fairly clearly in a sentence or two what I have said. This process does not come easily. But it does come. And, as I said, it is much, much harder with a novel.

The design seems to come best after rapid readings that let me check the shape of things. It always helps to spread this process out over time. I think it is always a good idea to write something and then to put it aside for a while, to sleep on it, to think about other things, and then to come back to see it fresh. That fresh new vision will help a writer see the flaws in design that are likely to lurk within the work of anyone who has concentrated long and hard on a piece of prose. Robert Pirsig in his classic *Zen and the Art of Motorcycle Maintenance* speaks of the "*a priori* motorcycle," the motorcycle as it is in itself. We know that motorcycle only as an ideal construct in our minds, since we can never see the motorcycle all at once. Then there is the motorcycle we see from various angles, a motorcycle that we can see only in parts according to our particular view. From that particular point of view, we assume that there is a whole motorcycle, a complete entity. But in fact that assumption may be false.

I like to say that there is an *a priori* book or essay that we have in our minds after we have worked on something for a long time. That is the piece of writing that we think ought to be there. But over against that ideally complete piece is the actual manuscript (or computer file), the thing that we see as a physical presence when we pick it up and read it. We often discover that the ideal manuscript we conceive in our minds is simply not there as we have assumed in the real manuscripts that lie on our desks. Sometimes we have to rest our minds a little while before we can achieve the critical freshness that lets us see our manuscripts as they really are and not as we assume them to be.

Many of my friends write outlines before they start writing, and I often recommend some sort of outline to fledgling writers. But I must confess that I cannot recall ever making a preliminary outline in my life. Sometimes I make lists of points I want to cover, jotting those points down in my notebook. But a list is not the same as the outline I was required to present for papers when I was in college. Then I always wrote the paper and figured out an acceptable outline afterward. My teachers loved outlines, and I thought it best to humor them.

In the end I have to give my manuscripts up. In early 1984 my editor sent back the copyedited version of my final Thomas More manuscript and called me every day for two weeks to see how I was getting along at checking out this final part of the editing process. At a certain point she asked me, "How many pages have you rewritten?" "Only forty-two," I said.

She sighed in disgust and told me that if I did not send the manuscript to her by Express Mail that very afternoon she was going to fly to Boston the next day and take it away from me. "You are going to be embarrassed, and I am going to be furious, and I am going to charge it all off to your royalties account," she said.

She was angry then, and I sent the manuscript off—and passed into a deep depression. When something of mine is in print, I can only rarely bring myself to read it. Once in print, it is unchangeable. To me it is almost dead. And since I cannot revise it any more, I really do not want anything else to do with it. I have never read a book of mine through once it has been published. People often write me letters asking questions about this or that in the book. I can barely make myself open the book to see what they are talking about. I read the reviews somewhat listlessly. I do not believe the good reviews, and the bad reviews make me angry. The only way I can be happy once a book is gone is to start another book.

Then the pleasures of writing begin all anew, and the world itself seems to take on a new form, and a new and glorious light of opportunity shines on every precious moment that I work at the new creation.

*An award-winning English teacher at the
University of South Carolina at Columbia,
Carolyn Matalene teaches undergraduate
writing courses and graduate courses in
the composition and rhetoric program.
She is also the writing coach at* The State
and The Columbia Record *newspapers.*

*Of special interest to her is the way in
which setting affects writers and their
writing. She has written on contrastive
rhetoric and is currently editing a collection of articles by teachers who teach and
study writing in a variety of nonacademic
settings, "Teaching Writing in Different
Discourse Communities." Here, as in her
essay in Volume 1 of* Writers on Writing,
*Matalene avoids describing her own com-
posing process; that's because she finds the
cultural and social and now technological
influences on how writers write endlessly
interesting.*

THE GREAT DEBATE: YELLOW PADS OR GREEN SCREENS?

Carolyn Matalene
University of South Carolina—Columbia

The thesis of this study then is that most (not all) converts manage the conversion to composing at the terminal because they can plan before writing, not just by writing, or because they can at some point form a mental image of the structure of their text. And the longer the converts have been composing at the computer, the less interested they are in frequently printing out their texts. They do most of their revising on the screen and are often content to leave blocks of writing as long as fifty pages on disks alone.

The availability of inexpensive microcomputers and easy-to-learn word-processing programs has allowed academic writers to change their writing technologies from scribal to keyboard, from yellow pads to green (or amber) screens. Accompanying this technological transformation, however, is a range of reactions from anger to bemusement to elation, from expressions of the direst stylistic apocalypticism to vibrant belief in the achievement of the textual millennium. Individual responses commonly range from confessions of guilt, remorse, fear, paranoia, jealousy, and outrage, to professions of freedom, celebration, playfulness, surges of creativity, risk taking, and vastly increased productivity.

In this study I attempt to classify and order some of these responses, to provide information about the composing processes of highly productive academic writers, to describe the ways academic writers both visualize and conceptualize texts, and to report on some attitudes—positive and negative—toward the new technology.

The participants for this study were chosen not only because I know them and they were too polite to refuse my inquiries but, more important, because of their high level—in some cases extremely high level—of productivity. All of the writers interviewed were highly sophisticated text processors and text producers, and all were highly articulate about their own composing processes. (Some were highly vocal about how other academics compose and why their texts are so terrible.)

Ten of the subjects were members of a large English department at a state university, and except for one assistant professor and one graduate student (included because of his publication record), all were at the associate or full professor rank. To provide some ethnographic contrast, a number of subjects in another discipline were interviewed: three professors, at the assistant, associate, and full professor rank, in the government and international studies department were included in the study. These writers were also highly productive, though of course most members of the English department would consider their texts something other than literary. Two other academic writers were also interviewed, both full professors, one in the foreign languages department and one in the history department.

In addition, two senior editors at a local publishing firm were interviewed in order to include some professional evaluation of texts produced on word processors. One edits *Contemporary Authors,* the other the multivolume reference work *Dictionary of Literary Biography.*

The writers interviewed, it soon became apparent, needed to be classified into three rather than two categories. Some academic writers write only on yellow pads, sending their revised pages to secretaries for typing and retyping. These writers I call *scribal.* (Some writers revealed themselves as scribal in Volume 1 of *Writers on Writing,* among them Joseph Comprone, Richard Graves, William Lutz, and Tom Waldrep.) Many academic writers now write on yellow pads and then type their texts into personal computers; usually revising printouts or hard copy, they are using computers as supertypewriters. These writers are called *transitional*—though as composers they are largely scribal. Some writers—not always the youngest—have thrown away their pads, sold their typewriters, and now compose entirely at the terminal. These writers I label *converts.*

Of the writers interviewed, only two were fully scribal, never, ever using a computer. Both of these writers compose on yellow pads, without outlines, proceeding from the beginning of the book or article to the end. One of these writers, Donald Greiner, revises his yellow pages after reading them aloud, types his own third draft on an electric typewriter, revises that, gives these pages to a secretary, revises again, and gives them back for retyping or correcting. Greiner can imagine using a computer instead of his typewriter for stage three, but he can never imagine giving up his fountain pens—two Schaeffer white dots, purchased in 1962 at Mincer's Pipe Shop in Charlottesville, Virginia. He loves his pens and his pads; he loves the rhythm of running out of ink every five pages and stopping to refill his pen.

A strong sense of the physicality of writing, of words coming from head, through hand, out of pen or pencil, onto paper in long lines, eventually filling page after page and pad after pad, was expressed by the writers who compose scribally. They like the feel of their pages, the heft of their pads. They cannot imagine changing.

Matthew J. Bruccoli, an extremely prolific writer, perhaps best known as the biographer of Fitzgerald, Cozzens, and O'Hara, believes that the physical act of writing is more than a feeling or a preference, it is what makes writing good. "Since people started writing with those goddamn devil machines," he said, "I have noticed a pattern in the books and articles submitted to me: paragraphs in which sentences do not connect because they are stuck in by pushing buttons instead of with the fingertips. I see more serious structural problems—paragraphs in higgledy-piggledy order—because writers are moving sentences and paragraphs with buttons! I have now reached the stage of paranoia in which I have convinced myself that I can recognize a published book written on a word processor. If I keep hitting paragraphs that do not follow, I become convinced that this is the work of a lazy, irresponsible writer, a writer who would not be this bad on paper because of the discipline imposed by making insertions with the fingertips!" The physicality of fingertips holding pencils, making revisions on paper, constitutes for Bruccoli what writing must involve. Seven days a week from 7 to 10 A.M. he writes with a Number 2 pencil on every other line of a yellow legal pad. On his desk was a great pile of yellow pencil stubs, looking burnt out and used, like a mass of cigarette butts. His handwritten pages get typed by a secretary, revised and retyped, revised and retyped, through a total of five drafts. Everything Bruccoli writes is handwritten, then typed and retyped by a full-time secretary. (Bruccoli's students tie up the department's Qume printer for hours, painstakingly inserting page after page of expensive bond so he will think their words were typed, not processed.)

Not many faculty members who are not administrators have a full-time secretary, however. Perhaps having one is the ultimate academic status marker.

Certainly for transitional writers, freedom from secretaries—from approaching them hat in hand humbly requesting attention—freedom from consigning precious pages to the delays of secretarial pools, and then freedom from the endless proofreading to catch the inevitable new errors introduced when the old ones were corrected, and especially freedom from performing one's own secretarial drudgery, cutting and pasting and whiting-out and typing and retyping drafts, such freedom is what word processing is all about. The transitional writers interviewed all typed; many had in the past typed their own final drafts of dissertations, books, and articles, not feeling their work was ever really safe with secretaries. Now they are totally (sometimes ecstatically) in control of their own texts. They view computers as wonderfully efficient, almost magical supertypewriters. But still only as typewriters, providing a powerful new technology but not a new writing mode.

The transitional writers, like the scribal writers, still write words by hand onto pages. They too love their pens and their pads. David Cowart could not imagine giving up "the hallowed instrument." He has two. One is a German Lamy ball-point, but his favorite is a Parker 75, given to him by his grandmother and made of precious metals that compensate for its leakiness. Jeffrey Helterman, author of four novels as well as a quantity of scholarly and critical work, likes to buy new brands of felt-tips before a project, then likes to feel the growing stack of unlined white paper he writes on. John MacNicholas, a playwright, writes his first drafts on yellow pads, knowing that for him yellow pads have an irrational talismanic appeal. "Writing is so difficult," he said, "Structures that have worked are not to be casually jettisoned."

The transitional writers (and there were more of them than I had expected) tend to be keeping the structures that have worked. Helterman, for example, after trying the PC, went back to his felt-tips and white paper because his style lost its complexity, subtlety, shading, on the word processor. It became bare and spare, architectonic; writing on paper allows him to be painterly, to achieve depth and texture, to be more three-dimensional. Writing on paper and seeing or holding several pages at once is for these writers the only way to grasp what they call "spatial relationships" or organizational patterns. "It's analogous," said Joel Myerson, another highly prolific scribal composer, "to the difference between a digital clock and a clock face. With a digital clock you lose the connection of time and space." MacNicholas said he might be able to compose at a computer if he could see one hundred and fifty lines at a time.

Similar difficulties in maintaining a sense of the text as a whole from what is visible on the screen are reported in a study conducted by Christina Haas and John R. Hayes ("What Did I Just Say? Reading Problems in Writing with the Machine," *Research in Teaching English* 20 [1986]; 22–35). Their study of sixteen "computer-writers" indicates that "locating and retrieving information is easier from hard copy than from some computer displays. Apparently, it is easier to perceive the spatial structure of the text when reading from hard copy than from such displays."

Somewhat surprisingly, none of the transitional writers in the English department writes from an outline. (In fact, I couldn't find anyone in the English department who does write from an outline; maybe that's why they're there.) Instead they begin drafts with sentence one, followed by sentence two, and so on to the end. They seem to visualize their texts initially in linear ways, as long strings of sequential sentences. Their composing process then involves constant addition; an initial string of sentences becomes a complex tapestry of text by a gradual accretion of ideas. Not until late in the drafting and redrafting process do these writers begin to see their texts as hierarchical structures. As the hierarchy emerges, they revise and reorganize, using lines and arrows, writing inserts on the backs of pages. These writers plan by writing, not before writing. For them, the green screen is much too small to enable them to see the entire structure developing; they need large blocks of words on pieces of paper. The words in the file that are not visible seem to them to be gone—like the time before and after 6:28 on the digital clock.

After they type their drafts into computers, they are likely to limit on-screen revising to surface features, changes in words or syntax. Serious revising is done on printouts; changes are marked or added to hard copy and then entered into the word processor. Many of these writers mentioned their urge to print out, to get "safe" hard copy, and their desire to see and hold the pages. (Haas and Hayes report similar attitudes even among the most experienced computer-writers.) Several believe that printing out the text provides a powerful motivation to write and to revise. And of course, because copy can be made clean again so easily, revising carries no costs, requires no trip back to the secretary.

Some of the transitional writers cannot imagine giving up their longhand composing processes; again and again they mentioned the physicality of the act of writing. But some transitional writers are finding that the drafts on their pads are becoming sketchier, more like outlines, less likely to be written in complete sentences. Will they one day give up their pens and pads entirely? Maybe, maybe not.

Whether they do or not and how easily and how successfully they manage the conversion seems to have to do with visualizing a text as a hierarchical structure, rather than as a linear string of sequential sentences. It is possible that the sooner in the process that a writer can see the text as a structure rather than as a sequence, the more likely is that writer to compose successfully at the screen. David Cowart, a transitional writer who is thinking seriously about selling his Oriental rug to buy a computer, often outlines his writing *after* the third draft. That would seem to be the point at which he moves from a linear to a hierarchical understanding of his text. This transformation probably does not have to do with a transformation from writer-based to reader-based. None of these writers is engaged in writer-based wandering around; rather, they have large goals in mind when they begin. They reach these goals sequentially, additively, by moving from the beginning to the end, often starting back at the beginning over and over again. Thus the line of the text gradually becomes a more and more complex skein. The point is that their sense of structure emerges from the text, not before the text.

Ina Hark now composes entirely at the PC, which classifies her as a convert. But Hark said she wasn't at all sure that it was a good idea. The computer lets her play endlessly with sentences but doesn't seem to help solve structural problems, which are less likely to get worked out at the terminal than on legal pads. Hark's sense of text is decidedly linear, "a wandering thread through a labyrinth" she said, and thus achieving structure on the PC requires many drafts, many printouts, and sometimes a return to pen and paper.

The true converts, however, those who have burned their pads and broken their pencils, are usually writers who have a clear sense of the structure of their text before they begin. Elizabeth Joiner, for example, a foreign language professor and textbook author, was taught by her English teacher to outline first. So she does. She purchased her IBM PC before she learned to type; after it taught her to type, she started composing her sentences on the screen from the very careful outline she has always used.

William Kreml, a political science professor, is working on his fifth book, a theoretical study, "Relativism and Democracy." On the floor of his office was a huge sheet of brown wrapping paper, covered with columns of irregular scrawl, the plan for the entire work. Here was a writer who indeed began from a hierarchical structure and self-consciously so. Kreml said, "I have a very nonlinear mind. Very spatial. The computer has freed me from the linearity of the typed page. I think of what I put on the screen as embryonic, not final, I can play with it. I can move it around. I can also work on several chapters at once." Clearly, Kreml visualizes his book as a structure not as a string. Or to use a painterly metaphor, he can separate his canvas into portions and work on single sections. The scribal composer, in contrast, seems to be thinking in terms of linguistic or temporal sequences rather than shapes, always inclined to go back to the beginning to add a thread of a different shade.

Metaphors get pretty shifty when writers (and researchers) talk about the composing process and computers. One writer's liberation may be another's enslavement. For Kreml the computer is spatial, the page is linear. For Jeffery Helterman, the computer is rigidly linear, only the page allows three-dimensionality. Perhaps these different conceptualizations are the result of different learning styles, different frames of mind. Howard Gardner might classify Kreml's intelligence as spatial, which means being able to describe and re-create the physical world, to form internal mental images. Gardner might classify Helterman's intelligence as especially linguistic, highly conscious of words and of the relationships of words in context. Gardner believes there is compelling evidence that these two kinds of thought are separate: "To the extent that language were to be considered a visual medium, it would flow much more directly into spatial forms of intelligence; that this is not the case is underscored by the fact that reading is invariably disturbed by injury to the language system, while, amazingly, this linguistic decoding capacity proves robust despite massive injury to the visual-spatial centers of the brain."

At any rate, questions about the linearity of a text versus its hierarchical structure did seem to make sense to these sophisticated text producers. All agreed that texts are eventually structured hierarchically, but they had different feelings, metaphors, processes, and time frames for achieving that sense of structure.

Steve Lynn, who is highly articulate about his composing process elsewhere in this volume, now composes entirely at the PC, using paper only when he is in trouble—and then he might draw a diagram "to get a spatial grip." He begins writing at the beginning; but he saves his text often, reading it again and again from the top down, adding more and more, and then he begins to understand the structure. Lynn, clearly a convert, can move comfortably from a linear to a hierarchical sense of text on the screen and be highly conscious of the transformation; this level of awareness about achieving form may be what makes possible a successful conversion to composing at the terminal. Graduate student Mike Taylor, a short story writer and free-lance journalist, proceeds similarly with the same self-consciousness about structure. Interestingly, Taylor talked about the top and the bottom of his file; for him the words that aren't on the screen aren't gone. They are above or below.

The thesis of this study then is that most (not all) converts manage the conversion to composing at the terminal because they can plan before writing, not just by writing, or because they can at some point form a mental image of the structure of their text. And the longer the converts have been composing at the computer, the less interested they are in frequently printing out their texts. They do most of their revising on the screen and are often content to leave blocks of writing as long as fifty pages on disks alone. The transitional writers want pages frequently to work out structure on paper; the converts seem confident of the structures from which they are writing.

Paula Feldman is a convert who has gained not only a new mode but also a new field; she now writes books about word processing and conducts workshops to convert others. (Faculty members, according to Feldman, take four hours to learn what freshmen can pick up in fifty minutes.) Feldman said that in her own writing she does indeed begin with a hierarchical structure; furthermore, as an experienced computer user, she now thinks of text structure in terms of the computer's graphic capabilities and in terms of increasing the visual impact of a text. Feldman's sense of hierarchical structure seems highly sophisticated. Is this a result of writing at the computer or of the kind of mind that she brought to the computer? I would suggest the latter; for some writers computers work, for some they don't.

Certainly the elation of the converts—the feeling of freedom, risk taking, playfulness, even joy—is not shared by the transitional writers. Converts, furthermore, insist that they are writing more, and most believe that they are writing better. Scribal composers are doubtful.

Are they really writing more? It is hard to imagine productivity greater than that already achieved by these scribal composers. (They certainly make their untenured colleagues nervous.) Matt Bruccoli can write 2,000 words in a morning; Jeff Helterman once wrote 180 pages in two weeks, though he usually manages about 500 words per hour; John MacNicholas on a good day can manage 20 pages of script in three hours; Joel Myerson has never spent more than two days on an article and can produce 40 pages of typescript in that time. Ironically, Myerson, Helterman, and MacNicholas all felt the computer was too slow for their composing processes, but they also felt word processing had tremendously increased and eased the production of finished copy. MacNicholas, for example, reinvented twenty percent of his last play while it was in rehearsal; with his KayPro he was able to present the actors with clean copy in less than three weeks. In a previous effort, one week's reinvention of a script had taken him an entire month of secretarial drudgery.

Has the computer really increased the productivity of academic writers? That depends on who you ask. No, said Karen Rood, editor of the *Dictionary of Literary Biography.* The academic writers with whom she deals don't seem to be producing that much more; they just have a different set of excuses for not meeting deadlines. And for some, composing at the word processor means structural disaster; writers who don't bother to print out and edit hard copy often repeat themselves, wander, and lose the point. (Linear texts don't always turn into hierarchical structures.) Lee Jane Hevener, a member of the highly productive government and international studies department, said yes, a lot more is getting produced but a lot of it doesn't really need producing.

Are the transitional writers and the converts producing texts of higher quality? That also depends on who you ask. "It's the end of style," said Matt Bruccoli, "Just as TV ruined reading, computers have ruined writing." "Nonsense," said Paula Feldman, "Computers are the beginning of style."

What's bad about computers? Nothing, said the converts, it's all good news. But being involved in the computer revolution is not without responsibilities for humanists, said Paula Feldman. It's mostly good news, said the transitional writers. Joel Myerson likes the versatility of formatting allowed by computers; a single spaced, double-sided manuscript, for example, is a lot fewer pages to schlepp on airplanes. And clever users can make end runs around department Xerox budgets—at least for a while. But the potential for real abuse exists, said Myerson, pointing to the absence of protocols for changing texts on disks. Who is to know who did what if editorial changes are not restricted to hard copy? If editors have access to disks, how can an author maintain control of his or her text or even figure out what got changed except by a tedious process of collation?

Computers are not all good news, said some; in fact, they are bad for us. The more we sit at terminals, the more human interaction we give up, and the more we are likely to give up. Do you want your kid to go to school to a screen? If you let a computer in your house it will start to watch you—just like the TVs Nixon was planning. Don't laugh; the folks in the Pentagon aren't. Though at the moment they are mostly worried about making sure their own PCs are shielded with lead foil—because disks can be read by spies with the right radios. Computers are bad for your eyes, bad for your neck, bad for your structure. And furthermore, said Bruccoli, "People who try to make writing easier are committing an act of impiety." But Bruccoli knows his complaints are like those of the fellow in the carriage house who said Henry Ford's cars smelled bad and were noisy.

These days, a fleet of computers is the new departmental status marker. The government department's last chairman made his reputation as an administrator by getting a PC for every faculty member. That is pure status. And now macho is determined by the size of your memory, the complexity of your software. In the English department, however, the pressures are more old-fashioned. Do you use the computer or don't you? If you don't, you're obsolete. Most of the converts and transitional writers interviewed started at the PC because of social pressure—because of fear, not curiosity. In English departments there is a lot to be afraid of these days; the compositionists are more and more vocal, the deconstructionists are more and more pervasive, and now computers too. That computers are easier to master than deconstruction seems to constitute much of their charm.

How widespread are computer-produced texts in our profession? The two editors estimate that one-third of their contributors are now using computers to produce final copy. Myerson said using computers is generational. Many older faculty members say why bother? But he estimates that up to fifty percent of younger faculty are at PCs.

For rhetoricians, word processing seems to be good news indeed; as Don Murray says, a word processor is a great new writing toy. But surely blanket recommendations are not in order. Computers are liberating for some, fearsome for others; a powerful technology we can use to help writers think both about their writing and about the methods of the mind that produces it. It's our job to know enough about both to encourage matches of mind and machine that help rather than hinder.

Susan Miller is associate professor of English, adjunct associate professor of educational studies, and director of the writing program at the University of Utah. She has published articles on composition theory, rhetoric, and literature, and the first writing textbook whose title included the word "process," Writing: Process and Product *(1974). She was contributing author to the seventh edition of* Writing with a Purpose *(1980).*

Miller has recently completed two manuscripts—an anthology, The Written World, *and a critical study of the historic development of rhetorical theory in relation to changing writing processes,* Rescuing the Subject. *She is currently researching a study of the politics of composition and literacy in American higher education.*

REBELLING AGAINST THE ALL

Susan Miller
University of Utah

Writing is at once a way to be myself and a way to hide myself, and it always was. I was writing columns in high school under another name, Sam. I was writing themes in college, sounding like I had grown up in a family who always went to college, not as the coal miner's daughter I was. I am. Even now, I suspect myself of not showing who I am, really. But now I have the joy of understanding that I am not constructing a text to imitate me, but a text that will create new parts of me. I really am whoever I am in my writing at this moment. The writing—both the act and the words—is constructing a me, not vice versa.

I heard last week that the man who invented the ball-point pen had died. He was Italian, I think, with a name as unfamiliar to me as the name of this year's French Nobel laureate for literature, and I wanted, when I heard of this death, to take everyone by the shoulders and cry out—SEE? THE BALL-POINT PEN. INVENTED ONLY IN THE SECOND WORLD WAR. TELL ME ALL ABOUT COMPOSING PROCESSES. TELL ME ABOUT HOW WRONG-HEADED WRITING INSTRUCTION USED TO BE. THE BALL-POINT! ONLY SINCE 1942.

I get excited about what an act of writing means, about a little thing like a ball-point pen and what the egalitarian technology it represents has meant to empowering writers. It is such technology that allows us to entertain theories of writing as "process" rather than only as a product of prior thought. Writing may now be an act of rebellion—not just by virtue of what a product may appear to mean (often what the most conservative, establishment-supporting person would say) but the act itself. For me, an act of writing is, like the invention of the ball-point, rebelling against all the limits on us. Rebelling against entitlements. Rebelling against time. Rebelling against size, and scope, and even what we are.

Quintilian and the other rhetors didn't countenance writing as rebellion. The *Institutes* have only one chapter about writing as an aid to oral composition, and no one agrees about placing it. In it, he advised against too much revision. Considering that "writing" meant acquiring and mastering eight separate tools in his time, it is no wonder he praised it as a way to see, rethink, and memorize what the young orator would later say. But, he said, do not become too much of a perfectionist. Do you want, he said, to be better than who you are? That's probably what I mean by rebellion. Writing is a way to be other than who I am, whoever that WHO is at any particular time.

How I write has everything to do with why I am writing at a particular time, as well as with rebelling. But I should start with the rebellion. The one line I've read that explains what I mean by that word is in Joan Didion's preface to *Slouching Toward Bethlehem*. She describes how the interviews she made for the essays collected in that book usually went. She, small, nervous, and somewhat shy, would politely make appointments, appear, and ask questions. She says that the people she interviewed—the murderess who dropped her husband off a cliff in a flaming Volkswagon so she could marry up, or Joan Baez—never realized that it might not have been in their best interests to answer her questions. "Just remember," I remember her saying, "a writer is always selling somebody out."

Since I've been living and sometimes made a living by writing from the time I won a scholarship on the strength of an NCTE contest back when the dinosaurs roamed the earth, I have to come to grips with this conviction that I too am always selling somebody out when I write. I remember the first time my language was "corrected." I was standing in front of a Safeway in Tacoma Park, Maryland, every inch of seven years old, complaining to an older (twelve? thirteen?) neighbor friend that "every bitch and his brother" was in there shopping. I got the most appalled look, and, with that nasty superiority only children (or I would like to think only children) can muster, I was told that NO ONE used words "like that."

My mother, or my father, or a visiting stranger, had indeed used such words, which I was parroting, unaware of what they "meant." What did I learn then? I learned that words actually could "speak me," that I could become something or someone I had no real claim to be by using a particular word. Of course I also learned that there were two worlds of words, a "right" and a "wrong" world, and that I was going to have to watch carefully which one I would be judged to belong in. I began to court correction. If my subjects and verbs didn't agree, I would be told "how you say that" by my buddies. I read a lot, so at school I had an easier time at writing for the "right" world than I did at talking for the "right" world. But I began to see that whether I was writing or talking, my language would be working against capture—against other people's view of some implicit degenerative strain in my home and to preserve my fierce loyalty to that home.

Writing is at once a way to be myself and a way to hide myself, and it always was. I was writing columns in high school under another name, Sam. I was writing themes in college, sounding like I had grown up in a family who always went to college, not as the coal miner's daughter I was. I am. Even now, I suspect myself of not showing who I am, really. But now I have the joy of understanding that *I* am not constructing a text to imitate me, but a text that will create new parts of me. I *really am* whoever I am in my writing at this moment. The writing—both the act and the words—is constructing a *me,* not vice versa.

Another way to explain how rebellion and selling out characterize writing for me is to tell a story about authenticity. It appears at first to be a flattering story about me, but it isn't. I was at a convention, CCCC or MLA or NCTE, in some city—maybe even Chicago. A friend introduced me to a publisher. "This," she said, "is Susan Miller." And the editor, whose name I had heard for years, said, "Susan Miller? You can't be Susan Miller. She's a lot older than you are."

You are imagining the happy blush and wondering why I would tell such a story; but its point, as I said, is not self-flattery or self-indulgence, but authenticity. I was, you see, only the product of my writing in that moment of encounter. I immediately knew what the man meant. This editor was telling me that I had written with a voice of authority I didn't *appear* to have. But of course, no one else had written what he had read. And no one else looked as unlike that voice, in precisely that way, as I did.

The issue here is not self-indulgence, but self-alienation, the feeling that came over me after the first sociable smile. If I, if we, set as a goal writing "congruently," writing to show ourselves, who would we reveal? Only, I realized, the person writing at this moment, on this topic, for this purpose. But this editor was sure I had hidden "myself" by writing so authoritatively, so "straight." And I was, after polite disclaimers, experiencing not a moment of elevation but a moment of fragmentation as strong as any I've ever felt. I had a sudden perception of "Who was that masked woman, the one who wrote herself up?" I thought that I had sold "myself" out and only later thought that I had as much claim to the person who was too old to be me as to any other voice or appearance. I had not shown a "side" of myself in writing, but *that* self, reflected in one of Lacan's "outside totalizing images." *All* of me was remade in the acts of writing the editor knew.

Plato has, of course, already laid this out for us in the *Phaedrus.* How will we know, he said, the true voices of the Fathers of words if all we have is a piece of writing? For Plato, this was an essential (and I use the word precisely) problem—how can we know what the person really meant? But now, especially since 1942 and the portable ball-point pen, his troublesome problem has become instead a new celebration. How can I know my true voice? I can read what I wrote. The surface is the me—the words write me as I write them.

Writing is for me the supreme, and the amusingly rebellious, act of SELF-sacrifice. That is, it is the only thing I do that requires me to assert strongly, wielding that by now well-defined phallic splash that Derrida and the feminists variously disapprove of. I cannot be mealy-mouthed, coy, or finally even entirely polite in writing. Something must be SAID. But even as I inscribe the words, I know that they are going to write their own meanings. That "splash" back there, for instance. Is it a typo for "slash"? Can you read one word without thinking of the other? Without thinking of the physical possibilities—ink? Water?

So who wrote that word's meanings? Of course you did. I, sitting here late at night looking for some other word than "symbol" to follow "phallic," certainly did not think the thoughts you read. Writing alienates *me,* resists *me,* by virtue of its physical resistance to the speed of my thoughts. These are not, I would stress, PRIOR thoughts, but the thoughts that the act of writing brings about now that it is not a slow, eight-tooled, act of recording. And writing entirely "reveals" me—or so you thought. The act of writing, if not the text we read, winks at old debates about stylistic "monism" (the word is the man) and "dualism" (the man chooses the words to affect his effect—or vice versa). Instead, the act of writing shows us, now that the ball-point and even the word processor have made the act frequent, available, cheap, and easy, that "style" is both anterior and posterior to meaning. Style is not the dress of meaning nor the identity of the man, but the only thing we have. My style chooses me as I choose it. We are the surface we write, nothing more but nothing less. My rebellions, then, are acts of becoming, and remaining, curious about what I look like after the moment.

And as I said, this rebelliousness is mirrored in the ways my writing varies depending on why, what, and who I am writing at a particular time. Watching my writing processes go wrong has brought this home more often than I like to remember. After I won that scholarship to college, I got a C in Freshman English, an absolutely devastating grade. I just couldn't write. I didn't understand the new expectations of college, or the reason for writing themes about personal subjects while we were reading stories. But mainly, I wasn't yet a "college student." I hadn't written enough in college to become the person who could write in college—an utterly circular, but utterly precise, description. The same thing came up in graduate school—fellowship, failure. A "best student" in my college class had become one of the least of these after a mere three months' summer break. When I was trying to publish my first article, and then my first book, I had the same problems, each time with more anxiety.

I decided to devote the rest of my career to studying writing at just about that time. I was sure that the students I taught at a downtown commuter campus had only about the same chance I had had to choose between "right" and "wrong" linguistic creations of themselves. They could learn to write well enough to win the moral equivalent of the fellowship, or stay in lower-level jobs the rest of their lives. And I could, because I came from a family whose subjects and verbs often disagreed, help them see that they could enter new language-created worlds without entirely leaving home. But I didn't know as much as I do now about how writing makes us into the person who can write, only that I sometimes could, and sometimes could not, write.

It has taken ten years for me to understand, provisionally at least, that it is a newly difficult subject and a strange set of readers that throw me, and my students, off. When I now write documents that the legislators of Utah will read, I confront this strangest group of readers, for me, with newly difficult subjects, like funding. But I do it now with the questions I need answers for, primarily asking for a sample of something like what I now must write. I have become the successful writing student, not a successful writer, and I have become this because I am now used to the feelings of dislocation and uncertainty that new writing situations inevitably produce. It is not "practice" in the sense of drill and revision that has helped me, nor will that sort of repetitive "practice" help my students. Writing the same five-paragraph themes over and over has no discernible influence on how well students write exams or reports in chemistry; but writing notes in response to readings for the chemistry course seems to raise test scores in the course. They make the student more of "a chemist," a person who writes about chemistry.

My point is, of course, that I have become "a writer" by having to write, and wanting to write, essays, textbooks, articles, letters, memos, proposals, short stories, poems, critical books, and newspaper columns in six widely separated states for popular, academic, governmental, family, and friendly readers. I have become a person who is created through all of these different sorts of writing, just as a student can become "a chemist" by writing in chemistryland. And that language is not frivolous, for it is not the reading and writing only that comprise "chemistry," but also the proximity to others who "do" chemistry and their tools. The risks have to be taken in contexts, they can't be removed by "practice" before hand.

Now all of this is to say that I don't have "a composing process." I flagrantly move from one to another medium, sometimes for sheer perversity using a pencil so I can write slowly, thinking as I go. I write too much to think of a special time or place as "best." Sometimes I write everything in one burst; sometimes I write—even stories—in short snippets without a moment's thought about what will come next in between the times I have to write. I've had the experience of outlining everything and following the outline; and I've had the experience, the most dangerous I've ever felt, of sitting down to write the next ten pages of a book with not a thought in my mind. (I have also, having written ten pages, stopped and said "No, that isn't true," then written "It is not true that . . ." at the beginning and gone on in the next ten to correct what I've said.) I change and change and change, demanding the complicity of anyone who will read what I'm working on; but I may only write once and stop. I have two principles about writing:

1. It is only writing; it can be changed or I can write something else.
2. I only wrote it. Let other people decide if it is any good.

The "only"s in those sentences are the most liberating words I know. Like Orson Wells, who never saw a single film he made, I never reread after a "publication" of whatever kind. If I do, I accuse myself of stupid narcissism. After it is published, it isn't "only" writing, and I am bound to feel that I am no longer that person who wrote it, or not *yet* that person.

If I reflect on this description, I see myself as accumulating writing processes, not as having one. Any and all of the models for writing fit, including "think-write," the old, oral composition method that lasted through centuries until just about the time of the invention of the ball-point, as any reader of Warriner's knows. For me, the ontogeny of writing's technological and as well its social development since Greece has recapitulated the phylogeny of my own processes. I have gathered ways to write, and I answer with a blank "It depends" when asked for a favorite.

When asked to write about my composing process, then, I think of "composing" as something different from sequential actions I can teach. Sometimes I am the hero of the piece, the "person writing this particular thing." But sometimes my audience has the lead, and I am guided by conventions and languages they will find so transparent that they will think they could have written this themselves. And often the subject is the star; the problem at hand, the research or the speculation, becomes the foreground, while I and my readers fade, down left, down right. Within these possible categories, the *movement* I make as a writer, whether described physically as pauses and tools or mentalistically as stages of reflection and recursive rethinking, are not interesting parts of the process. Instead the action, actually the *plot,* defines composing. Burke had it right. Telling what has aroused and fulfilled a writer's desires would describe a composing process.

I fear mystifying a process of writing, on an analogy with the mystification of the Romantic, inspired poet. I have known "writers" who explain and forgive their own unhappiness on those extended critical grounds, and I have felt they would be happier if they would be happy, not imitate a popular image of what a writer is. So I also think that what a writer does, the only special thing about writing, is to write. Certainly studying what writers actually do, from their pauses and motions to their remembered thoughts, stays at a distance from understanding the amazing feat of negotiating an actual writing situation. Such an emphasis is like, for all its observatory interest, trying to discover whether the pistons in a car are, just NOW, up or down, by looking to see what direction the car is moving in.

More important, mystifying a process of writing is inevitably exclusionary. Focusing only on writers' actions excludes the memory, the source that has constructed this essay. It can exclude a writer's sense of mastery, no matter of what, that supplies the store of "materials" that the ancients expected anyone composing to draw on. Finally, I would fear, it may exclude unentitled writers like me. They may once again, as they have been when belleletristic polite learning defines the entitled, be left out if they have missed a current ideology of writing instruction. A totally fluid, electronically processed text may exclude the writer who is too poor to master and use the computer's processes, just as expensive parchment once kept the poor from producing a perfect product.

Some people, even the young, sometimes do sit down and write well in one continuous action, make a few corrections, and have done with it. For me, aging has made this reactionary act more possible; for I now am more likely to begin thinking about something I know I will write months ahead of time, forget it consciously, and find it simply "there" when I begin to feel the pressure of production. I do not assume that this is mysterious, simply that I do not understand it. Language can work on me, and me on it, outside the physical or mental set of actions I can describe. I know this, but I do not know how it happens nor how to understand it. It is my writing process, more and more frequently. I cannot practice or teach it, but I assume that I must credit its possibility, depending on whether writer, reader, or subject is taking the lead in a particular spectacle of writing.

I note with interest that the ball-point, and the concept of portable writers and writing it represents, has been around precisely as long as I have. *I* in that sentence is not of course only "me" but all who necessarily came late to stable characterizations of traditionally honored sources of language. We are constructed "subjects," made from our writing and its results. We do not claim "established" voices nor presume that writing will merely reinforce our presence and display us to a world that already cares what we have to say. Whatever our politics, we understand Marxists. We are, as you know us, direct results of a new means of production that was once so cumbersome that it was reserved for slaves (the early Greek dedicated word processors) or those who had the leisure and wherewithal to hone a quill and acquire the hand of a gentleman.

Portraying my unstable writing processes as rebellious versions of a self composed of language, not as the actions of a stable self who composes language, may be unsettling. Many people deeply concerned with both the research and teaching of writing do not share my problems. They began "to write" with more surety about who they were and wanted to be. They projected themselves in their writing and happily accepted the public identity their writing solidified for them. Many who have never doubted their place in an agreeing, agreeable, right world of subjects and actions are one person, not those who are newly becoming each time they write.

To answer their inevitable questions, I should point out that the variations I have described are not acts of impersonation, and certainly not acts of fakery. As I write to discover "what is going on in there," I do not mistrust it, but I know about it—in any of the senses of "knowing" from Plato to Polanyi—only by reading my words. At that distance, it is a wonder to me; I listen as I read.

But I must also admit that my composing processes, as I have described them, do implicitly critique a "prose of the center," privileged writing in hierarchical views of language communities. I have insisted that I stand outside an authorial canon in any genre and outside the constructed social practice of "authorship" which comprises common views of a superior writing activity. If I refuse to be an author, with a composing process, I set aside what many teachers call "real" writing in favor of an activity that is neither ritualized nor sanctified nor sanctifying. I announce that I see no more than anyone else might by virtue of writing, only that I write with more joy and sense of play than those who usually avoid it. And I claim that being an "author" or a "writer" is not so important as the play of written words that construct us each time we try to author-ize or authen-ticate them.

If I insist on being a "student" of writing, it is at least partially because students do understand how written words take them over, give them unfamiliar and sometimes bothersome new voices, and turn them into certain sorts of "students." I think it is very important for those of us who teach to understand what is at stake in our views of composing. It can itself be elevated and mystified to innocently re-create ideologies we would rather avoid. Elitist processes have the same effect as elitist products. Despite my own irritation at those who resist understanding and studying the complex process of writing, I think of students like me who may be bewildered at new prescriptions for composing. I hesitate, as I hope they will, before describing even my own write/right way.

*Lee Odell is professor of composition the-
ory and research at Rensselaer Polytech-
nic Institute. His major publications include* Writing in Non-Academic Settings
(1985), Research on Composing *(1978),
and* Evaluating Writing *(1978). He is
presently beginning a three-year study of
the thinking processes writers engage in
when they try to formulate their ideas.
The study will include public-school students in grades 1–12 and will try to deter-
mine how thinking processes vary according to (1) type of student, (2) academic
discipline, and (3) classroom context.*

*In other work on writing in context,
he has conducted several studies of how
adults compose job-related writing and of
how adults' composing processes might
influence the teaching of writing to undergraduates. He also serves as consultant
to a number of colleges and universities on
writing across the curriculum.*

CONSTANTS AND VARIATIONS IN MY WRITING PROCESS

Lee Odell
Rensselaer Polytechnic Institute

Writing, for me, is almost never a straightforward, dispassionate matter of presenting information or defending conclusions. I assume—indeed, hope—that writing will entail an interplay of cognition and affect, of rationality and emotion, of conscious, disciplined effort and intuition and inspiration.

I have always envied poets. Not only do they get to read—to *perform* —their works, they get to talk about them. They get to describe all the intellectual and emotional turmoil that led to the completion of a poem; they get to explain the genesis of a particularly apt phrase or compelling metaphor. Those of us who do more prosaic stuff only occasionally have the opportunity to read our work to an audience and almost never have the chance to talk about how we produced it. The closest we come to this is when we have to respond to a hostile questioner who asks, in effect, How could you possibly have come to *that* conclusion?

For me, this is frustrating. The process of composing occupies enormous amounts of my time and energy. And the drama of this process sustains me and pleases me in ways that no finished piece of writing ever does. That may be a comment on my completed writing. But it is, for me at least, also a comment on the richness and importance of this process. I have not always felt this way. For a long time it seemed to me that the only good piece of writing was a finished piece of writing. But I now feel that once a text is in its final, typed form, I am no longer interested in it. When the published version arrives, it usually goes direct from my mailbox to my bookshelf, with perhaps an appreciative glance at the type style or layout.

Since accepting the invitation to write this essay, I have worked on a number of other projects, ranging from papers to be presented at professional meetings to personal correspondence to memos and reports intended for administrators and colleagues at my university. My comments in this essay will be based on those projects, including—perhaps predictably—my efforts to write this essay. This way of proceeding has the advantage of allowing me to be very specific in answering the question "What do you do when you write?" However, this specificity forces me to acknowledge that much of what I do varies widely from one piece of writing to another, even from one moment to the next in the process of writing an individual piece.

In all this variation, there seem to be few constants. Like many other people, I am never completely sure that I know what I want to say until words actually appear on the page. Prior to that time, ideas usually seem only half-formed, no matter how much I have thought or talked about them. Until I write them down, ideas lack shape and refuse to hold still while I examine them.

CONSTANTS IN THE WRITING PROCESS

Beyond asserting that the act of writing is my principal medium of discovery, I can't think of any generalizations that would apply at every moment of the composing process or to every type of writing I do. There are, however, two further generalizations that apply to much of the writing I do. The first is that the sound of writing is often very important to me. Thus I very frequently imagine myself speaking the words I write, in effect performing them and using that performance to help me sense where I need to revise and/or edit. The second generalization is that, for a certain kind of writing, I have very strong preferences about the circumstances under which I write.

When I'm working on relatively long pieces in which I am trying to formulate ideas that mean a great deal to me, I always write in my office at home, with a stack of legal-size yellow pads and a half-dozen or so freshly sharpened 2½ pencils. And not just any 2½ pencils; there's one brand that has exactly the right feel against the yellow pad. Other brands write too smoothly. And I never use a pen for this sort of writing. Ink seems too permanent. There is no way to erase it, and it seems wasteful to throw away pages written in ink. Ink is for final copy. Once you write something in ink, you're stuck with it.

I could, I guess, work in my office at school. But it's not a good idea. I like to get up from my desk from time to time, wander around, stare out the window. Although I don't usually use those short breaks to plan what I'm going to say next, my mind is, at some level, still engaged. It doesn't seem to be directly focused on the task at hand, but it doesn't want to be focused on anything else. At the office, there are simply too many unmanageable distractions. For example, one campus phone call can lead to another and yet another. By the time I get back to work, all momentum is gone. So it's much better to work at home. If someone calls with a complicated question that will take a lot of thought, I usually resort to claiming that the answer is to be found in materials which, regrettably, I have left in the office on campus. Or I refer the caller to my department's administrative assistant, the person I would probably have to consult with anyway.

VARIATIONS IN THE WRITING PROCESS

Apart from the constants I have just described, about all I can predict about my writing process is that it will vary greatly. Fortunately, I can anticipate (and prepare myself for) at least some of the kinds of variations that will occur. I know, for instance, that I can anticipate wide fluctuations in my emotions, in my need for closure, and in my ability to use relatively systematic inquiry procedures. However, it is very difficult to predict exactly when these fluctuations will occur, although in retrospect they seem not entirely random.

Emotion

Writing, for me, is almost never a straightforward, dispassionate matter of presenting information or defending conclusions. I assume—indeed, hope—that writing will entail an interplay of cognition and affect, of rationality and emotion, of conscious, disciplined effort and intuition and inspiration. This is usually true of even the most mundane types of writing. For instance, in writing short, routine letters and memos, I usually jot down a note or two (or underline key terms in a letter I'm responding to) and wait (usually very briefly) until an attitude or feeling begins to form. Then I begin to write, usually without planning what I will say, trusting, instead, that there will appear on the page some words that bear upon that attitude—perhaps simply conveying it or, more likely, giving it clearer shape or perhaps causing me to revise it or abandon it altogether. If the subject of the writing is not terribly important or if the intended audience is a sympathetic friend, I may consider the writing finished once my attitude seems well expressed. More typically, I hope, the feelings are tempered by careful reflection, either while a draft is being produced or after the draft is completed.

Specific Influences. As a writing task becomes more complex, so does the role of emotion in the writing process. Sometimes, my feelings are focused on a very specific aspect of a text, acting, along with my sense of performance, to shape the text at the moment it is being written. For example, I almost began this sentence with the phrase "Take for instance. . . ." But every time I start to use *take* as a synonym for *consider,* I remember the following classroom episode: A college student was engaged in a classroom debate about the economic prospects for small cities in the South. "Take Bessemer (Alabama), for instance," she began, only to be cut short by a professor whom we both admired greatly: "And just where, Miss ———, do you propose to take Bessemer?" There may be other reasons for not treating the two terms as synonyms, but the scorn, the derision in that professor's voice is still reason enough for me.

Another example: When I began trying to write this paragraph, I wrote and then crossed out two successive topic sentences. Neither of them was inaccurate, but for some reason neither felt right; there was something about the tone of each that put me off and that made me think it might have the same effect on a reader. I wanted to go on with the paragraph, but as sometimes happens, I couldn't—not until I was more comfortable with the point from which the paragraph began. Eventually, I came up with a third sentence that said pretty much the same thing as did the first two but that, somehow, felt better. Curiously enough, that third sentence has now disappeared; it became unnecessary when I combined this section with a passage I wrote earlier. But the important point is that this third sentence served an affective purpose as well as a conceptual one; it enabled me to feel that I could go on with the paragraph.

More Extensive Influences. Thus far, I've been talking only about the way emotion influences what happens at specific points in the process of putting words on a page. But the composing process extends well beyond those specific points. And so does the influence of emotion. A really productive two or three hours of writing can lead to a kind of euphoria that takes me well beyond the passage I have been working on. When I am pleased with the progress I appear to be making on one section of an essay, it's very likely that I will begin to get ideas about how to proceed with other sections; and as one essay starts to take shape, it's almost certain that I'll think of ways to proceed with other writing projects, or even start dreaming up new projects. When this begins to happen, the margins of my yellow pad fill up with notes—brief phrases that at the time seem to me too valuable to forget, brief instructions to myself as to how to develop the new section or new project.

This euphoric momentum is likely to continue well beyond the time actually spent writing, buoying me up when committee meetings or administrative chores seem especially tedious, even consoling me somewhat when a class doesn't go as well as it might. When the writing is going extremely well, there's a good chance that the euphoria will last for several days. There may be brief periods when things don't go smoothly, times, for example, when a passage just won't work out right. But those seem only minor irritations, small obstacles that are swept along in a general surge of accomplishment—connections are getting made, ideas are coming clear; one troublesome passage can't hold me up for long.

That, of course, is the good news. The bad news is that for every moment of accomplishment and gratification, there are long periods of anxiety, uncertainty, fear. There is never any guarantee of finding something that seems worth saying or of saying it in a way that seems appropriate. Consequently, there is always the awful possibility that the yellow pad will stay empty or that it will fill up with material that won't satisfy me or anyone else.

Fortunately, the terror, the misgivings, the uncertainty are at least occasionally replaced by the confidence, the sense of well-being I've already described. These extreme emotional states seem to alternate with each other, so that the composing process reflects an ebb and flow of emotions that is surprisingly reliable, if not entirely predictable. When I reach one extreme, I no longer believe—as I once did—that I am destined to enjoy or endure that extreme forever. The euphoria always diminishes, but then so does the terror. On the face of it, this observation is just common sense. But it took me a long time to learn that such common sense might be borne out by the complexity and confusion of my own writing process.

Closure

In lots of ways, I am a very goal-directed person. I need to have clear objectives and some reassurance that I have a chance of achieving those objectives. Consequently, after experiencing a modest amount of uncertainty, I need some closure, some sense of where I'm headed and how I'm going to get there. Predictably, this need appears in my composing process at least as often as it does in other areas of my life. Sometimes I can satisfy this need by creating an outline that includes main topics and subtopics and that lets me see how everything fits together. Or I can actually begin producing a draft, starting at the beginning of a passage (a paragraph, a section of an essay or, less likely, an entire piece) and working straight through to the end, getting each sentence right before I go on to the next. These activities, of course, are very pleasurable. Both outlining and drafting encourage me to think that I may actually meet a deadline or, more important, that I'll be able to tie together some of the loose ends that have begun to drive me crazy.

But the need for resolution does not always serve me well. Sometimes I have to force myself to avoid achieving a sense of closure. At other times, I have to make myself recognize that closure simply is not possible, that I need to muddle along for a while and that I will be better off for having done so. This tension between achieving closure (chiefly through outlining and drafting) and avoiding it is one of the main factors in my composing process.

Outlining. At the end of one evening's work on this essay, I jotted down some notes about a possible structure for the entire essay: two main sections, each with two subdivisions. I have now revised this organizational plan, but at the time it provided a good bit of satisfaction. After all, my college teachers persuaded me that a detailed outline was essential for writing a piece of any length. And besides, I find a pleasant, reassuring sense of order and rationality in being able to see relationships clearly, especially when those relationships can be expressed—as in an outline—as categories, subcategories, and sub-subcategories. Indeed, there comes a time in the composing process when I cannot continue working on any part of a piece until I can explain to myself exactly how the whole piece fits together. However, that overall picture is almost never clear to me when I begin writing. In fact, it makes me nervous if an outline begins to form too soon. When that happens, one of three things is likely to occur, and two of them are bad. The first is that the outline is likely to be inaccurate; it presupposes categories or conclusions that prove to be untenable. This leads usually to disappointment and sometimes to a kind of paralysis: I try to force information into the categories suggested by my outline, the data won't fit, and the whole process grinds to a halt. I become frustrated and begin to wonder why I didn't go to law school. Or the outline may be absolutely accurate; the data fit into my scheme quite neatly—too neatly, in fact. When this happens, writing becomes one of the most boring activities I know; composing seems reduced to painting by numbers. The only real advantage to having an outline take shape early in the composing is that it provides an element of reassurance, a brief respite from the uncertainty and chaos that seem to characterize my writing process.

For me, then, writing entails a process of alternating between seeing the big picture and becoming immersed in very small points. I don't trust any organizational plan—whether for an entire essay, a section of an essay, or even a paragraph—unless I have been through this process a number of times. (How many times? Enough so that it feels right. Enough so that the emerging structure will withstand close scrutiny.)

Drafting vs. Provisional or Exploratory Writing. While in the middle of trying to write this chapter, I was asked to help write a report that described and justified my department's plans for growth over the next few years. I approached it the way many students approach their writing assignments. I set aside a single evening to work on my section of the report, determined to force myself to produce a draft by the end of the evening's work. I began by writing the first sentence and fiddling with it until I got it right. Then I went on in the same manner to the rest of that paragraph, then to the next, and so on until the report was complete—or at least ready to be read and revised by other members of my department. Although there was some fumbling and there were a few times when I went back and reworked a passage I had previously considered finished, I proceeded in a fairly neat, linear manner. I completed point A before going on to point B, B before going to C, and so on. At every step of the way I had to feel that I knew exactly what I wanted to say and where I was headed.

The morning after drafting the departmental report, I returned to working on this chapter. Specifically, I was working on this section of the chapter, which I eventually decided to identify as "Drafting vs. Provisional or Exploratory Writing." For most of the morning, my writing process was not nearly so focused and linear as it had been the night before. I began the morning's work with the vague but strongly felt notion that I wanted to get at some sort of distinction between two types of writing processes. But the distinction seemed so complex that I wasn't at all sure where to grab hold of it or how to present it in a way that wouldn't be filled with jargon. Consequently, I began the morning's writing with this sentence "What I want to do now is contrast the writing I did last night with the writing I'm going to do this morning." That sentence seemed all wrong, even as I wrote it. But I knew that in order to be able to write anything at all, I would have to forgo some of the pressures that had served me well in the previous evening's work. In effect, I had to tell myself: "Just write something. Don't worry. It won't appear in the final copy. You don't have to know where it's headed. You can come back and fix it later. Just get to work." I knew that much of this writing would be unusable, and that it might change direction at any time. Further, I knew that it would be impossible to give myself a deadline. When I began the morning's work, I could not have told myself: Before you stop for lunch you must have completed the section "Drafting vs. Provisional or Exploratory Writing." Nor did I expect to draft as many pages of text as I had the night before. (The evening's work on the report produced about ten typed pages; the morning's work on this section of the chapter—plus three subsequent hours or so of tinkering—produced four typed pages .)

These two examples are to illustrate, if not define, the terms *drafting* and *provisional/exploratory writing*. The former is relatively linear, rational, goal-directed. The latter is tentative; goals may emerge, change, or even disappear. Much of this provisional writing never appears in a draft. Indeed, it is never seen by anyone else. I do not mean to suggest that these two types of writing are mutually exclusive or that one is inherently more desirable than the other. However, they are different, and they arise from quite different situations.

Drafting is possible for me only when I have a sense that my task is relatively well defined and when I feel a strong need to achieve some closure. I always hope that the process of drafting will entail enough small discoveries to keep the work interesting. And sometimes, of course, the drafting will force me to rethink an entire section or even an entire essay. But when I begin drafting, I do not expect to come to major new insights about either audience or subject. For example, I was able to produce the planning report in the manner I have described only for these reasons: (1) I have had a lot of experiences with the audiences for my report; I know a good bit about their values, the questions they will ask, their notions of what constitutes a well-written report. (2) The subject matter of the report had been thoroughly hashed over in any number of formal and informal conversations. (3) I was tired of thinking about what members of my department have come to refer to as the GDP (the God-Damned Plan); we have considered possibilities and weighed alternatives until it's time to make some decisions and get the GDP out of our lives. At this point, drafting was not only possible, it was essential.

By contrast with drafting, provisional/exploratory writing occurs when my task is relatively ill-defined. For example, when I began working on this section I was not at all certain as to what I wanted to say. And I am still uncertain about my audience: If you are still reading at this point, why? What are you trying to learn from this? How do you plan to use it?

These questions notwithstanding, my morning's work seemed productive enough to justify this further comment: I frequently have to move back and forth between drafting and exploratory/provisional writing. When I began my morning's work on this section, I proceeded in a very exploratory manner; things had no focus; notes appeared on the page in a very associative, sometimes apparently random, sequence. Eventually there came a point where lots of ideas were bouncing around in my head and on the yellow pad. I could *almost* see how things fit. In fact, things were going so interestingly that I almost stopped writing, rather than continue work and risk finding out that my ideas weren't nearly as wonderful as they had seemed. But again I was facing the combined pressures of an approaching deadline and the need to get some resolution. I had to go back and tidy up, tie up loose ends, bring things into focus. So I went back, started at the beginning of this section and proceeded line by line, trying to get things right as I went along.

If I had tried to do this at the beginning of the morning's work, I would almost certainly have finished the morning with little to show for my efforts, other than perhaps a paragraph or two of unsatisfactory text and a strong sense of frustration. But if I hadn't ended the morning's work by drafting, I probably would have had to start the whole process all over again the next time I sat down to write. I will have to do this anyhow, but I'd rather do it with something new, another section of the essay.

The Process of Inquiry

In much of the writing I have previously published, I have described conscious intellectual activities that can help make the process of inquiry relatively systematic. These activities are important for me; they provide a structure and guidance that, as a writer, I find necessary. In the last couple of years, I have become increasingly interested in ways inquiry is influenced by social processes and in ways systematic procedures interact with nonsystematic processes—intuition, luck, timing. The effort to write this essay has forced me to think about ways all three of these matters—systematic procedures, nonsystematic processes, and social interaction—influence my own writing.

Social Interaction. The composing process, and specifically the process of inquiry, is not limited to those times when I am at my desk, writing on a yellow pad. Composing is very much a social process, although perhaps not in ways one might immediately assume. It is, for example, unusual for me to sit down with someone and try to talk through the substance of what I want to say in a piece of writing. About the closest I have come to doing this is in the discussions that were part of the departmental planning process I described earlier. And even then, the substance of those discussions was not always reflected in the report. Those discussions served to help me start thinking about the subject and identified some of the main choices the department seemed to want to make. But by and large, I tried not to let those discussions serve as rehearsals for what I would say in the report.

And yet social interaction is essential to my process of inquiry. Often my research on nonacademic writing begins with interviews or with my listening to other people's discussions. And my choice of people to interview or group discussions to attend may be influenced by my overhearing a chance remark or by someone coming up to me and saying "You might not be interested in this, but I'm about to start writing a. . . ."

Sometimes the influence is more oblique. It often happens that a really stimulating conversation about one topic lets me start thinking productively about another topic, even though those topics are, so far as I can tell, completely unrelated. And sometimes the influence is very indirect indeed. Occasionally, prior interaction will emerge from memory at the most unexpected times. For instance, earlier in this chapter I mentioned a college professor's derisive comment when a student used *take* as a synonym for *consider.* That comment has influenced my stylistic choice in this matter and also has informed my thinking about the subject matter of this essay. But I didn't witness that episode; it was recounted to me by an aunt who had attended the same college I did and who had studied with a teacher who was nearing retirement when I entered college. The first time—but not the only time—I heard that story was almost thirty years ago, when I was a college freshman. Dr. Hunter would have been quite surprised to find his comment to a student in 1919 represented in this essay. But no more surprised than I am.

Usually the social interactions are a little more recent or clearly relevant than in the preceding example. My thinking about the planning report will surely be influenced (perhaps reinforced, perhaps changed drastically) by formal departmental discussions of that report. And there have already been a couple of informal conversations that make me want to go back and be certain that I have carefully considered all the options and have justified all proposed actions. Also, conversations about previous pieces of writing influence my thinking here. This is particularly true of conversations in which my dissertation advisor and I discussed my ongoing work on the dissertation. This advisor had the curious notion that a dissertation was not just an additional hurdle for a graduate student to jump. Instead, he felt that every word, every sentence must mean something and must stand up to the most rigorous kind of scrutiny. When I write, I still hear his voice: "Here you say X. Do you really mean X? Why couldn't you just as reasonably say Y or Z? If you really do mean X in this sentence, how does that square with . . . ?" That voice often guides my thinking about a piece of writing —sometimes my own, sometimes a colleague's, sometimes a student's. Often it frustrates one or more of us, forcing us once again to confront uncertainty, to do the hard work of rethinking a passage that had seemed completed. Yet when we listen carefully to that voice, our writing and thinking are better.

Systematic and Nonsystematic Activities. Throughout the composing process, there are times when I consciously try to be systematic in my exploration of a given topic. For example, when I've collected a large set of interview data, it's almost certain that I'll have to categorize the data, looking for similarities and differences among individual statements and perhaps relating those statements to theory or to what I've concluded about other interviews. However, my choice of inquiry strategies may vary from one topic to another and even from moment to moment in the process of writing a particular piece. Further, there is a complex interaction between the mental activities that can be directed systematically and consciously (e.g., by asking myself "How is this interview statement similar to other statements?") and the nonconscious, nonsystematic activities that seem to be directed by a mysterious array of forces that may (or may not) include such things as tacit knowledge, the Muse, blood sugar level, and barometric pressure.

Even though I can't be certain what these nonconscious forces are, I know that they operate, just as surely as I know that the conscious processes operate. Last fall, for instance, I kept a journal in which I tried to record and comment on the processes I went through while working on another piece of writing. After Christmas, I returned to that journal, not to add to it but to see how I might use it as the basis for this essay. When I began to reread the journal, I planned to do the sort of categorizing I mentioned earlier.

Fortunately, this plan has worked—up to a point. But the route from my early plan to this draft is very circuitous. Paradoxically, I began the systematic process of categorizing by relying heavily on intuition. That is, I began reading through the journal just to see what would strike me. But this reliance on intuition soon gave way to more conscious, systematic effort. Even as I allowed intuition to focus my attention on a particular passage, I began to ask whether the item seemed likely to represent a type of behavior. If the answer appeared to be yes, I found myself taking a still more systematic look at subsequent passages: Does this new passage seem to fit with the earlier one? If not, does it seem to suggest another category? This attempt to be systematic was still influenced heavily by intuition; in effect I was asking, "Does my intuition tell me that passage B might belong in a category with passage A?" I wasn't, at that point, trying to look for detailed points of similarity and difference among items. With this data, that more rigorous examination didn't seem necessary, although it often does when, for example, I'm trying to make sense of large amounts of interview data.

Eventually, this categorizing process led to thirteen categories. Intuition or perhaps simple indifference seems to have prompted me to discard some of them, and it now looks as though my analysis of my journal has led me, directly or indirectly, to three major categories: emotion, the need for closure, and the process of inquiry. Thus my journal has provided me with headings for three of the main subsections of this essay. But it has provided none of the data that are discussed in those sections. Instead, I have worked my way around to talking about writing I have done since stopping work on the journal. I don't know why this happened, for I had planned to write about the journal. But so it goes. I use conscious, systematic inquiry strategies, but my use of them is influenced by intuition, serendipity, and who knows what else.

The Attractiveness of Uncertainty

My last comment about the process of inquiry leads me to my real motive for writing this essay—or anything else, for that matter. For me, the process of writing satisfies a need to try to understand things that might not be completely understandable. This is especially true for a topic like the composing process. As should be clear to anyone who attempts to write about it, trying to know that process is filled with the same uncertainty that characterizes the process itself. That process is complex, messy, and elusive. And therefore, for me at least, it is perpetually fascinating. Writing about the composing process is not the same as being a poet who gets to perform and explain his work. But it will do.

James Raymond is director of freshman English at the University of Alabama; editor of College English; *author of* Writing (Is an Unnatural Act) *(1980); coauthor, with Ronald L. Goldfarb, of* Clear Understandings: A Guide to Legal Writing *(1983); editor of* Literacy as a Human Problem *(1982); and coeditor, with I. Willis Russell, of* James B. McMillan: Essays in Linguistics *(1978).*

In addition to articles and reviews about rhetoric and composition, he has published essays on legal writing and conducted numerous seminars for judges and attorneys in the United States and Canada. He has been an assistant dean of the graduate school of the University of Alabama and a series editor for composition textbooks published by Prentice-Hall.

TRUE CONFESSIONS AND OTHER LIES

James C. Raymond
University of Alabama

I don't believe in a single, optimum writing process—an algorithm we might teach students—because I rarely follow the same process twice. Even the impulse to write differs on each occasion, and the motive is never pure. My most faithful Muse is a department head who asks for a list of publications each year, a week or so before making her salary recommendations.

But he offered these reasons because his need to theorize, to turn everything into an impersonal truth, an eternal axiom, was as compulsive as his need to write.

—Mario Vargas Llosa
Aunt Julia and the Scriptwriter

Not long ago I attended a reception for writers at the National Arts Club, where the very well-to-do patronize, in every sense of the word, artists and the arts. On this occasion the patronized were members of PEN—the international organization of poets, playwrights, editors, and novelists, who had gathered in New York for an international congress. My arrival caused something of a quandary for the doorkeepers. The problem was that I was not a Writer, with a capital W, but merely a member of the attending press. In the end, I was invited to swill unlimited quantities of champagne and nibble *hors d'oeuvres* without end, but not to add my name to the guest register.

The doorkeepers, I think, decided wisely. Gradations of status are worth preserving. I don't pretend to be the sort of writer Norman Mailer had in mind when at the same PEN congress he spoke of his trade in metaphors that approached pyromania—lighting bonfires, explosions, votive lights, and luminescences of words. For me writing is more like walking through a bed of hot coals. Ordinarily I'd rather observe the ceremony than join it. But I do write from time to time, and I am happy to convey a list of observations in which other reluctant writers might find, if not utility, at least fellowship.

For me, it's usually a mistake to write first and select a journal later —as if an article could be solid on some absolute scale. Manuscripts are always judged in the context of each journal's imagined readers. The readers are implied, in large part, by silences in the text, omissions of information presumed to be known and of assumptions presumed to be shared. Manuscripts that presume too little are perceived as derivative —rehearsing information that everyone knows; manuscripts that presume too much are perceived as either esoteric or insufficiently documented. Because journals differ in what they presume of their readers, I find it useful to start out with a particular journal in mind. A corollary to this theory is that what one journal considers derivative, another might welcome as news. There is no universal audience, universally well informed—not even among scholarly referees.

Of course, I don't always follow my own advice. I wrote a report of the PEN Congress for the sheer fun of it, intending to produce something like a "Talk of the Town" but with no illusions that the *New Yorker* would want it. As a result, unsurprisingly, the piece was rejected twice before finding a suitable home. Had I followed my own advice and written for, say, the *Village Voice,* I would certainly have written a different piece, and probably better.

I've made similar mistakes in writing conference papers, hoping, like every paper reader, that some editor in the audience would approach the dais at the end of the session and request publication rights. Now, as an editor, I realize why conference papers are rarely suited for publication: not because their manner is too informal, but because the audience at any conference is subtly different from the audience of any journal. Even when I feel satisfied with what I read at a conference, I find that recasting it for journal publication would require much more than cosmetic adjustments. It is far easier to write with publication in mind at the outset and to make necessary adjustments at the conference.

I don't believe in a single, optimum writing process—an algorithm we might teach students—because I rarely follow the same process twice. Even the impulse to write differs on each occasion, and the motive is never pure. My most faithful Muse is a department head who asks for a list of publications each year, a week or so before making her salary recommendations. The PEN piece was an exception: I wrote it for fun—and for a tax deduction. I wrote *Writing (Is an Unnatural Act)* because I genuinely enjoy teaching composition and because, like every other textbook writer, I was sure mine would put *The Elements of Style* and the *Harbrace Handbook* in the shade they deserve. I wrote my part of *Clear Understandings: A Guide to Legal Writing* because my coauthor (Ron Goldfarb) and I had collected so many examples that the book seemed almost to write itself. And I am writing this piece because, like Llosa's scriptwriter, Pedro Camancho, I can't resist an opportunity to theorize.

I avoid footnotes whenever I can, and I am grateful to the MLA for making it possible to avoid them entirely. I particularly dislike notes that attribute a widely held notion to a single author, as if someone had acquired proprietary rights to "writing is a recursive process" or "Shakespeare is a good poet" simply by saying it in print. Graduate programs and freshman composition programs are partly to blame for requiring or rewarding papers so thoroughly tangled in references that the voice of the writer comes through only feebly and intermittently, like a distant radio station awash among the locals. The trick is to use previous scholarship to set up a context for a statement of your own, to avoid insufficient attribution as well as insufficient originality.

Among the scholarly pieces I have published, my favorite is the article on enthymemes in *Classical Rhetoric and Modern Discourse.* This piece began with close observation of a text—observation that was aided, I think, by postponing the commentaries until I had read Aristotle in two translations and revived my meager Greek to examine a few crucial passages in the original. Reading the text before the commentaries gave me a chance to carve out a small but original space for myself, trusting in the probability that when I read the commentaries I would find none that laid claim to exactly the same territory in exactly the same way.

I like to write from examples. It took me nearly seven years to collect the examples in *Writing (Is an Unnatural Act),* nearly ten for *Clear Understandings.* To write a defense of the new MLA documentation style, I needed to locate half a dozen tedious passages in social science journals to use as counterexamples. That took about twenty minutes.

Whenever I write, I imagine not only friendly readers but a cast of monsters Maurice Sendak might have drawn, fuzzy beasts with bulging eyes and buglike proboscises, looking over my shoulder, laughing their mischievous laughs at solecisms, contradictions, platitudes, and misprisions of fact. When I catch them laughing, I remedy the problem. But I always worry they might have sniggered without my noticing, or suppressed their laughter until I left the room to warm a cup of coffee.

I don't organize my papers. I plot them. The plot involves a sequence of revelations through which the implied writer gets the implied reader to react in a predetermined manner. The sequence varies with the subject and the audience. My defense of the new *MLA Handbook* begins with examples of the sort of antistyle my fondest colleagues fear we'll all be writing if we adopt the new MLA form. The readers' role is to be persuaded at the outset that I understand their fears, and then to discover that their worries are bogey monsters after all. The report on the PEN Congress has a chronological plot and three chronological subplots; the readers' role is to be informed and entertained rather than disabused of some illusion, and to discover, gradually, that the suplots, which seem extraneous to the proceedings, are in fact a commentary on them.

I outline only when I feel overwhelmed by material that refuses to find a plot on its own. When material gets impossibly out of control, I print it out, spread it across the kitchen table, and operate with time-honored tools: scissors, tape, and colored pencils.

I am addicted to beginnings that read like beginnings and endings that read like endings, usually looping back to the beginning in some more or less subtle fashion. I like the appearance of closure, even when the point of the paper is the indeterminacy of something or other, a favorite theme of late. Between the beginning and end, the middle grows into a geometry that I *could* outline at any point as I write but usually don't; and until the last draft is in the mail, the order is subject to sudden, radical change. Sometimes, as in this case, the geometry dissolves in successive drafts, replaced by a more or less fluid sequence of associations.

I usually begin at the beginning, writing an introduction to an idea not yet completely formed. Addicted to a word processor, I find myself writing from the top down until I get stuck; at which point I return to the top, edit for style and for substance, revise what's there so as to better set up what follows, and continue writing until I'm stuck again. The process reminds me of combing out a head of long hair, just washed and thoroughly tangled. At first the strokes are short and painful. When I'm lucky, the tangles eventually get worked out and the lines are, as Hemingway might say, long, clear, and straight.

I edit for style from the first word of the first draft to the last of the last. I prune mercilessly, but I am no longer surprised that my best readers find more to cut away. I avoid repetition of words, phrases, or rhythms unless they are functional or inevitable. I read aloud, especially when I've revised too much to hear the rhythms and echoes plainly in my head. I imagine that I like a plain style, but no interesting style is ever really plain. I am bothered by sentences that lie on the page, complacent and inert, merely signifying without taking the trouble to delight either by some internal twist or by participating in the rhetoric of their neighbors. I trash sentences, paragraphs, sometimes whole sections the moment I notice them sneaking by on content alone. Even so, sluggards survive my inspection because these are hard times, and the better sentences seem to go to Norman Mailer and others higher up on some Muse's list. If I am afraid to delete a sentence or a paragraph permanently, I send it to a limbo in my word processor; the limbo file for this paper is larger than the paper itself, most of its contents condemned by a yawn the attending monsters could not suppress. What now appears as the beginning of this paper spent about three weeks in limbo, released only moments before deadline.

I don't keep a journal. And yet I found myself keeping a journal at the PEN Congress because I felt it would be useful in writing the specific sort of piece I had in mind. In it I recorded quotations from the speakers, observations about colors, sounds, and textures—sense impressions of every sort—just what the textbooks advise.

I don't keep a bedside notebook, but I do keep a computer in the next room, and I often find myself at work from 2:00 A.M. till dawn. Normally I write when the mood strikes; but when I have a large project, I make a schedule and stick to it, even if I feel inspired to write past the time I've set for stopping.

It would be nice if we could make writers out of nonwriters simply by telling them how we make decisions during the relatively small portion of the project in which we actually set down words. But much takes place between drafts as well as in the years that preceded them, when we learned the rhetoric of form in stories told or read to us as children, when we stored random information that unexpectedly turns up years later as a metaphor or controlling insight, when a vibration transmitted from knee to brain as we jog along a sidewalk jostles something subconscious and spews up solutions to problems we could never solve by method.

Techne is, as Linda Flower might say, the porpoise's fin. The conscious control I have over my writing is limited, ad hoc, and serenely unsystematic. By far the more important part is luck, inspiration, serendipity, prior reading, chutzpa, and the advice of friends.

Having made all these confessions, I realize how right Flower is to mistrust writers' retrospective revelations about their own work. All writing is posturing. In this case, afraid to appear too many removes from the PEN writers, I have discussed only what I publish, ignoring the letters and memos that consume half my time as a writer. Perhaps I should admit that when I write a memo to the registrar, a response to a manuscript, or an application for sabbatical leave, I am creating a persona for myself, a role for my readers, a reality no less fictive than those created by Mailer, or Llosa, or Pedro Camancho. And no less candid or contrived than any true confession.

David H. Roberts is associate professor of English and director of composition at the University of Southern Mississippi, where he also directs the South Mississippi Writing Project. A former director of the Baptist Language Center in Zambia, he has served in administration and instruction at both Bluefield State College in West Virginia and Bluefield College in Virginia.

Roberts is president of the Southeastern Writing Center Association and serves on the executive committee of the National Writing Centers Association. His honors include a 1985 research award from the National University Continuing Education Association and several grants to support writing research and training at the University of Southern Mississippi.

YOU CAN'T ARGUE WITH A SICK MIND

David H. Roberts
University of Southern Mississippi

I write to be read. I used to keep a journal. I wrote it as though it would be read after I died, but it was read a few years ago (long before I die, I hope) and now that it's been read, I don't write in it any more. Although I wrote in the journal for it to be read but was disturbed when it was read—and I write articles to be read, but they often are not published—I still say I write to be read. Maybe I just harbor the illusion of being read.

I am what Carolyn Matalene would label a "convert" to word-processing composing. I am now a thoroughly evangelized, indoctrinated, and baptised convert to composing on the computer. Bear with me while I give a short testimony.

Giving up pens, pencils, and paper at my conversion was easier for me than it is for some people because I began composing at the keyboard during my second attempt at college, in 1968. I had to have typewritten papers for my English professors, so I learned to type as a 23-year-old college freshman. Total conversion to computer-aided writing came 17 years later, after a harrowing experience: typing the final copy of my dissertation on an IBM Selectric—text, tables, statistics, and bibliography—all without a correction key. (Anyone reading that dissertation today can verify that there was no correction key.)

My first computer came into the house two years after that experience, an IBM PC clone. I was so firmly converted when I took the plunge that I agreed to split the proceeds of a house in Virginia my wife and I had just sold. "Listen, I'll give you $3,000 with no questions asked if you'll just let me buy this computer," my sick mind reasoned. "I can't argue with a mind like that," she responded. So I bought it on faith. Real faith. To prove my conversion, I *gave away* my electric typewriter.

So, here I am, sitting in my office at home, with a small desk light on and the amber letters on the screen reflecting in my glasses. I just moved a paragraph that begins, "I am sitting at my computer . . ." from the beginning of this essay to a space just below this sentence. I don't know where that paragraph, a bit of freewriting I did a couple of days ago, will end up. Maybe I'll alternate-F4 it (computereze for "crumple it in a ball and throw it in the fire") before the essay is finished. I don't know.

I am listening to a Joe Walsh album with the same title as this essay. I can't write in silence, so my ears are stuffed with blue sponge covered earplugs and Joe's guitar is so loud I can't hear the phone in my desk drawer when it rings. My wife calls. Luckily, the drawer where I keep my phone is still open after the last call from the English department secretary, who was wondering when I would be on campus today. I told the secretary that I was working on a project and that I might be in tomorrow. I can't hear the phone, but I see the flashing light. My wife wants to know if I can meet her for a sandwich on her lunch break. She asks if I'm making headway on this essay. "Sure." I lie because I want her to be proud of me.

I rescan a lot and revise and move around and rewrite. Each day I work on a piece of writing I begin by rereading all that I have written before. I can't just pick up where I left off without first rereading. I write for different lengths of time, taking short and long breaks: sometime minutes, other times days. I'm going to stop soon and take a shower because Midge, the secretary, said that I have a 10 A.M. appointment. Then lunch at Subway with my wife. Then I'll hang around the department for a while. About 2 or 3 this afternoon I'll reread all I've done so far and begin again. Meanwhile, I've got to stop now and give my ears a rest from this loud music.

The music I listen to depends on what I'm writing and the motivation for writing. Some of my friends introduce me as "The Rev. Dr. Dave" because of my ministerial background. I don't write sermons any more, but when I did, I found inspiration in the rock opera *Jesus Christ, Superstar.* I haven't given up religion—just the pulpit. But I now find writing inspiration in the Joe Walsh album *You Bought It—You Name It,* and in B. B. King and other R & B or R & R classics. Occasionally the Muse is encouraged by Rimsky-Korsakov, Chopin, Handel, or Bette Midler. Or by the four Bs: Bach, Beethoven, Brahms, and the Beatles. Barbra Streisand's latest, *The Broadway Album,* is now playing.

I write to be read. I used to keep a journal. I wrote it as though it would be read after I died, but it was read a few years ago (long before I die, I hope) and now that it's been read, I don't write in it any more. Although I wrote in the journal for it to be read but was disturbed when it was read—and I write articles to be read, but they often are not published—I still say I write to be read. Maybe I just harbor the *illusion* of being read.

I also write because of a need to express certain feelings or to understand what I feel, for self-discovery, as in a journal, or to make myself feel good. My motivations for writing have not changed during my adult life, and those motivations can be expressed by examples picked from three decades of my life. Here are pieces I wrote when I was 20, 30, and 40. The tone, style, and quality vary, but the motivations are clear. One explores my mind, another attempts to please, another to hurt, and others to impress.

First, an exploratory piece—perhaps a prayer—from my journal when I was 30 and living in Africa.

12 November 1974, Luanshya, Zambia

What will become of my life? Why am I in Zambia? Why do I live? I know—somehow, I know not how—that God has a purpose for my living. What is it? Why, oh why, am I here in this place in this time and on this earth? Do I really believe in the purpose of God or have I deluded myself for lack of anything else to believe in? The way of Jesus sounds most appropriate, most reasonable and promising of all I've encountered, but I still don't know why I'm here. What has my total experience got to do with this moment—any moment? How can I put to use my talent and my experience? Am I still in preparation for some Divine Purpose, some mission God has in mind for me after my years-long training? Or am I missing the boat by waiting for proper passage? Do I get on before I know where it is going? Where, indeed is the long-sought port? My training, my education, my love, my motives, my personality, my ambition, my sensuous nature, myself: What does it all add up to? How can I place myself into the hands of the Future with any sense of security and warmth, with guidance and direction. I don't believe in proselytizing—why put me here, hear?

At times I write to make another person feel good, as in a strained note to my wife when I was 40 and we were approaching our seventeenth anniversary after a couple of rocky years.

September 4, 1984

Madonna,

We have a hard time of it, don't we? I still believe it's worth the effort, and I hope you do, too.

You're on a new job, working on a new degree, and trying to cope with motherhood and a seventeen-year-old marriage. My, that's quite a long time. And we have both changed. We have both grown. Apart in some ways and closer together in others.

I just want you to know, in the quiet of this morning, that I do love you and I want to keep our marriage going. I want you and the boys to have the best possible home. I will try to improve my part of it.

Love, D.

Other times I write to hurt people because I've been hurt, as in this excerpt from some bitter prose I wrote to my sister a few days after our mother's funeral. I was 40 when my mother died of Alzheimer's disease.

August 29, 1984

Nancy:

I should have known that I couldn't trust you. In all of the years of our mother's debilitating disease, in all of the suffering and the pain and the humiliation, in all of the years between our father's forced retirement, his death, and until our mother's death, I made but two requests. The first was not complied with, even though you agreed to it, so I should have known that the second would be ignored, too.

The second request was that the five years of the disease not be entirely wasted. I asked something that no one could gain from except all future generations. I asked something that could give us the satisfaction of knowing that our mother's humiliation and suffering would not be entirely useless. I asked for something that cost you nothing. I simply asked that her brain be sent to competent researchers so they might have definite help in breaking through barriers keeping them from knowing more about the disease. Well, I shouldn't have been disappointed—in the light of the past —to find that another simple request was not filled, though you had earlier agreed to do it.

Do I sound bitter? However bitter this letter sounds it is not a single percentage point of the hurt and the disappointment I feel. I only made one request. I wanted her last five years to be a sacrifice of love from this family to the world. I hoped that gift would bring us together; she would have wanted it that way.

It's clear to me that you are entirely responsible for making the last five years of her life a complete and total waste.

David

Sometimes I write to play with words and syntax, then marvel privately at what I've created, hoping it's like Whitman, Hopkins, or even Wolfe—and, knowing that I haven't made it, still feeling proud, as in this tribute to a college English teacher who died young. I was 30.

11 November 1974, Luanshya, Zambia

Have been reading some of the criticism Charlotte Adams Clay wrote on a paper or two I wrote for her English classes at Lander. I regret that

I did not listen to her more carefully and more often. I should have worked harder for her . . . Oh, Charlotte, how much you meant to me and how your death tore my bones and flesh. I was too young and naive to appreciate your all then: the wit, the learning, the drive, the creativity, the love for your students and your love for life. Oh, would that I had drunk full and deep of your many-flavored wine while I had the chance. How ashamed I am that I did not perform better for you—you who gave me a chance and inspiration when I was ready to let it all slide by me.

Oh Charlotte, how you lived for us!
How you loved us, would give for us.
You gave your love
    and I, for one, was enslaved.

How you heaped praise for creative phrase.
Charlotte, Charlotte. Adams & Clay.
Memories blaze
    with the warmth of your love
        our love never to be cooled
All our days.

Other times I write to play with rhetoric, usually with a pointed purpose in mind. When I was 20, I wrote my parents from Fort Jackson, South Carolina, after an unsuccessful attempt at college:

November 20, 1964
Fort Jackson, SC

Dear Mother and Daddy,

Only two and a half million seconds to go, and then my stay at Camp Jackson will be over! I still like Camp Furman better.

Here at Camp Jackson, we have too many counselors. Most of them wear stripes on their arms, and they don't allow us to call them "counselor" or "mister" so-and-so. We call them Sergeant. Some of the counselors wear silver or gold bars on their shoulders, and we must call them "sir."

We live in large wooden buildings called barracks, with 20 or 30 campers in each room. At Camp Furman, we lived in buildings called dormitories, with only two people in each room. The dorms were cleaner and warmer than the barracks. And while they were no quieter than the barracks, the dorms were more comfortable and pleasant.

At Camp Furman we had physical training twice a week. We played games: baseball, badminton, golf, and even bowling and camping. Here at Camp Jackson we have physical training every day, but it is really different: we do push-ups, knee bends and run a *lot*.

We camp here, but for weeks at a time instead of overnight. We shoot guns, which is exciting, but we also run around in the woods and get wet and cold. Sometimes we think the counselors don't like us very much because they are always yelling at us.

Here, we have to ask permission to go *anywhere*—at Camp Furman we just took off any time we wanted. And this is more of an outdoor camp than the other one. We all wear the same kind of clothes here, mostly boots, green shirts and pants, and hard, heavy helmets. At Camp Furman we could wear almost anything as long as it was becoming of "Furman gentlemen," as we were called. Here they call us, very drably, "troops."

Camp Jackson is very large and has many campers, and we don't get the personal attention available at Camp Furman. The counselors were nicer there and they didn't yell at us nor make us yell things like, "More sweat, less blood, Sir." Counselors with brass on their shoulders make us yell all sorts of things, and the counselors with the stripes ask us, "What is the spirit of the bayonet fighter?" And we must reply at the top of our lungs, *"To kill, and to kill without mercy!"*

At Camp Furman they taught us to love; here they teach us to kill. I don't like being taught to kill.

People here speak of Uncle Sam with almost the same reverence people at Furman spoke of God.

Many other things are contradictory: where they taught us love, they wouldn't allow minorities, but where they teach us hatred and killing, we have people of all races. Uncle Sam likes all people, but some people who claim to be Christian don't.

Well, for all but one thing, Camp Furman is far better than Camp Jackson.

Love,

David

Motivation controls the voice, tone, and subject of my writing, and as one might suspect, I pick the music to fit the motivation.

Let me turn your attention to form for a moment.

I usually have a fixed form in mind when I begin to write. No, that's not true. I have in mind that the piece I write will conform to one of several fixed forms by the time it's finished, but I don't think about it much at the beginning. I just write. Sometimes I freewrite, like I'm doing now, trying to figure out what I think.

I think, "I'm writing an article for such-and-such journal." or "I'm writing a letter to so-and-so." or "I'm writing ———." That's the extent of my fixed forms in the beginning. Finally, after discovering what I want to say, after discovering what I think—or, more accurately, what I think I can support—I rearrange on screen to suit the fixed form expected by the audience. Then I print a hard copy, turn off the music, and read to my wife, who is supportive and always willing to listen, but who is otherwise no help because she is too complimentary.

I write in a linear fashion and then rearrange, adding cohesive language after I can make sense of the rearranged essay, sometimes. Other times, I rearrange however much I've written, after letting it sit for a day or two, just to get my bearings—like turning this way and that to find my way in the forest before going further and getting hopelessly lost.

When I do get lost, I just save the manuscript on disk and hope to resurrect it later or cannibalize it for other essays. Sometimes I get so hopelessly lost that I alternate-F4 the entire manuscript, change tapes, usually to the Eagles' *Hotel California,* and start over, knowing that the line "You can check out any time you want, but you can never leave" means I can't stop writing—ever—even though it's ruining my life.

I have arranged and rearranged this essay. I've deleted and added. I've revised and re-revised, and still I'm not satisfied. And although I haven't proofread the essay or run my spelling program on it, it's time for a hard copy. It's time for me to read it to my patient, loving wife. As I read aloud, I'll find gaps and garbled thoughts. I hope to find them all, else you, dear reader, will be less supportive than my wife.

A final note: If you see me at a conference and ask how you, too, can experience a computer conversion and be freed from pens, pencils, and paper, speak up, my hearing's getting bad.

Barbara Tomlinson is assistant professor of writing and director of the Muir Writing Program at the University of California at San Diego, where she teaches in the undergraduate writing major as well as in the graduate program in composition studies.

For several years she has been working on a project concerned with how people talk about their composing processes in retrospective accounts, and particularly the metaphors they use to describe their composing. She is currently completing a book about the metaphors used by published authors in literary interviews. Articles related to this project have appeared in Written Communication *and* Metaphor and Symbolic Activity. *She has also published a number of articles on the teaching of reading and writing.*

ON EARTHQUAKES, LOST WAX, AND WOODY ALLEN: COMPOSING, COMPOSING, COMPOSING

Barbara Tomlinson
University of California—San Diego

To do important kinds of writing—to shape the deeper meaning, to push forward the main themes, to write about things that I don't yet understand—I need to be intimate with the text. I must feel myself wholly within the evolving text, and it within me: we are in each other's skin, blood, flesh, self. We—text and I—formulate the text within the collaborative matrix of self, text, and context. As I mark and shape the text, so the text shapes me, marks me, sometimes scars me.

In Woody Allen's *Sleeper,* our hero, having awakened from a cryogenic sleep many years in the future, comes through a bizarre series of circumstances to try to cook with the utensils of a futuristic kitchen. Needless to say, Allen doesn't quite have the knack for making futuristic pudding: the pudding swells enormously, surging up out of its huge bowl, overflowing, threatening to roll over him, to fill the entire kitchen, perhaps the house. Allen, daunted but brave, snatches up a nearby broom and whaps at the billowing mass, trying to beat it back into its bowl, trying to contain its pulsating, demanding, overwhelming mass.

That's what writing is like for me.

Sometimes.

At other times I sit at the keyboard, squishing out the last bit of toothpaste from my exhausted tube, wondering whether there's enough there to do the job, wondering what I'll have to do to get more —more ideas, more words, more connections, more recollections. Or, desperate for a few suggestions, I wait longingly for someone else's Muse to drop by (what with two kids in college, how can I afford one of my own?).

Most of the time, I write about composing processes and how people talk about them, particularly how they use metaphors for composing. In the book that I am completing now, I focus on metaphors that published authors use in literary interviews when describing their composing, and the way all of us—teachers, students, writing researchers— share these metaphors. We are handicapped when we talk about our writing processes, because writing events are ambiguous, and writing processes abstract, complex, varied, difficult to monitor, remember, and report on accurately. So rather than merely observing and representing our writing experiences, we must "construct" them. In effect, we all "compose" our conceptions of composing (so my working title for the book, *Composing Composing,* and the subtitle of this essay). And in doing so, we rely a great deal on socially shared knowledge—exactly the kind of knowledge that is conveyed by metaphors for composing.

Composing about metaphors for composing, I have come to realize the extent to which I compose *by* metaphor—and by difficult, inadequate, illogical, contradictory metaphor at that. I compose not merely by one metaphor but by many metaphors, some original, others adopted. I discard and take up metaphors as I work, moving fluidly from one to another. Sometimes I choose them voluntarily, and other times, as when I write à la Woody Allen, the metaphors are thrust upon me.

My metaphors for composing don't, of course, have equal status and don't function in the same way. I use some metaphors to comprehend and give shape to patterns of experience that are not easily labeled and identified. My earthquake metaphor works that way for me: There are times when I write that I have a growing sense of unease, of distrust, of discomfort. It is as though there is rumbling beneath the surface of the text, beneath the surface of my thoughts, my desk, my floor, beneath the surface on which I live. As I continue, focusing on the ideas I am developing, I feel uncomfortable deep down; I sense problems with things that I am not working *on,* yet working *into* and working *from* as I complete the surrounding parts. Though I don't know yet what is going wrong, somehow I know it is a geological problem, a weighty problem, having to do with how large parts of the text fit together, with the total structure of the text. I am standing on a fault line, feeling the tension, micromovements at a very deep level, as my newly reformed and solidified intentions and the text I have written *scrape* against one another, like two tectonic plates.

I don't know how I came to see those experiences as earthquakes, though they seemed deep, related to the fundament, independent of me, and potentially damaging. Now, with the earthquake label as a reminder, I am able to identify those vague stirrings and rumblings early on. Knowing what is to come, I can choose what to do about them: I have learned that it is better for me to wait, to let the cracks develop, not to examine what is causing the tension. As the cracks become fissures, I can begin to sense what is wrong with my current structure —what it is not going to do for me, why my increasingly well developed plans are incompatible with the old. But I forbid myself to give more than an occasional glance at my shaky ground; for when the upheaval finally comes, the solutions are usually evident. If I haven't become too familiar with the problem, haven't made previous attempts to solve it before the significant oppositions have formed, I can at that point artic- ulate what should be the new "lay of the land." So my world is firm once again—but only for a while, because I write, as I live, in earthquake country.

I use some metaphors for reassurance, to provide a positive view of difficult, discouraging, or uncomfortable moments in composing. For instance, on many occasions I have found myself needing to make a connection between sections of text that are relatively finished. To make logical connections that are related syntactically and lexically to both preceding and following sections is a highly constrained task, and because of the constraints I must work very slowly, very carefully, very consciously. I generally find the process a bit tedious. I concede that the link is essential yet feel that I ought *not* find writing it so difficult, since it is "mere connection"; it seems to *demand* my full attention without *deserving* it. I suppose I might call the whole thing "tediously demand- ing."

My frustration with this task has been much alleviated since I came across an appealing metaphor in an interview with Lawrence Durrell. Discussing one of his novels, he says: "the construction gave me some trouble, and I let in a hemstitch here, a gusset there."[1] A "gusset" is a small, irregular piece of material which is inserted in an item of clothing to reinforce it or make for a better fit. The small, irregular piece must connect the parts of the garment on all its sides, its edges invisible or inconspicuous. While it may be necessary to insert a gusset if some

---

[1]Lawrence Durrell (Julian Mitchell and Gene Andrewski, interviewers), in *Writers at Work: The Paris Review Interviews,* 2nd series, ed. George Plimpton (New York: Viking Press, 1963), p. 267.

garments are to look good, be strong, and fit well, undoubtedly it requires difficult, close work on detail—work that is "tediously demanding" in the same way as my writing of connecting links. Thinking of gussets helps me to write those connections: It reminds me that working small and fitting in *deserve* attention, not just because their result is valuable but because they are intrinsically difficult. It reminds me that the task is finite and identifiable, and that if I just keep working, joining the parts with small stitches of thought and word, the task will get done. And it breaks the isolation of my writing moments, reminding me that I share experiences with others—not only with Durrell and other writers, but also with tailors and seamstresses and other craftspersons who stick with slow, boring tasks so that something will eventually function well.

There are other discouraging moments when I can use the support of a positive metaphor, especially during revising. I revise extensively, sometimes doing major reformulation, sometimes minor lexical changes and surface corrections, but in any case writing many drafts. S. J. Perelman on one occasion claimed that he always needed thirty-seven drafts; once, when he did only thirty-five, he found the text to lack a certain *"je ne sais quoi."* Without an adequate number of drafts, my texts also lack a certain *"je ne sais quoi"* (but I don't know what it is . . .). Multiple drafts make for interesting developments, but also problems. Particularly disheartening is the moment when the course of revision leads me to throw out the last remnants of my early drafts. I tend to dwell on the waste of all that hard work, its uselessness, the gulf between me and "real" writers, my inability to get anything done efficiently, and eventually, my inadequacies as parent, friend, colleague, and citizen.

Clearly, this situation requires a strong counterargument. John Ashbery's metaphor of the lost-wax casting process has provided such a counterargument, not only for me but for several of my colleagues in similar situations. Ashbery, discussing his poetic process with interviewers in the *New York Quarterly,* indicated that his impelling initial lines "often don't fit into the texture of the poem; it's almost like some sort of lost wax or other process where the initial armature or whatever gets scrapped at the end."[2] The "lost-wax process" to which Ashbery refers is a method for making castings: A metal mold is built up over a shaped core of wax; when the mold is heated, the wax melts and drains away, leaving the mold ready to shape other materials—jewelry, sculpture, and so forth. The wax is essential to the process, unnecessary to the

[2]John Ashbery (Janet Bloom and Robert Losada, interviewers), in *The Craft of Poetry: Interviews from the New York Quarterly,* ed. William Packard (Garden City, N.Y.: Doubleday, 1974), p. 14.

product. Guided by the metaphor, I can reconceive the role of the early drafts, seeing them as powerful shapers of the final, more finished product.

I have also used metaphors in trying to understand or explain my sometimes peculiar writing habits. For instance, I write at night, often writing through until 3 or 4 or 5 A.M. I don't need to look far for the origin of this habit, given my children. During their early, deluded years they wanted to talk to me; during their teen-age years it was thirty phone calls per movie selected, five friends in for a day of wargaming, or inquiries about which chains to wear for Billy Idol. It seemed that the only time to write was when they were comatose. But now that they are away taking other people's writing courses, I find that I continue to write at night, and even all day and all night, working for many hours without interruption. Why? I have come to realize that it is the only way I can become *intimate* with the text.

To do important kinds of writing—to shape the deeper meaning, to push forward the main themes, to write about things that I don't yet understand—I need to be intimate with the text. I must feel myself wholly within the evolving text, and it within me: we are in each other's skin, blood, flesh, self. We—text and I—formulate the text within the collaborative matrix of self, text, and context. As I mark and shape the text, so the text shapes me, marks me, sometimes scars me. There is something in me that is never free from the mark of the text and its making. I too am the result of our collaboration.

To be intimately within the text is to forget myself in the writing, in the thinking, to focus so deeply on text and ideas as to lose myself, my connections, to exist only within the reality of the "context of the text." When I am successful, I have moved through a barrier into a different reality, as may occur at the theater or in dreams. Transitions into and out of this reality can be painful. Trying to get in, inveterately self-conscious, doesn't help, for I can't get in by conscious decision; only when I forget that I want to be there, in some way commit myself to the writing more than to my ego, do I find myself there. If I gradually emerge, fatigued, the transition is pleasant; but if I must "wake up" (or "wake through"?) suddenly, I am jarred, frustrated, disappointed. Still, long hours of writing and uncomfortable transitions are a small price to pay for this kind of intimacy. For once I exist only within the context of the text, committed to text, not self, then writing is not easy or hard —it is just what there is to be done, *everything* and *the only thing* there is.

Of course composing by metaphor isn't always safe (but what kind of composing is?). Though I am aware of the traps found in some of the most popular metaphors for composing, I find that I can still be seduced by their wrong-headed implications. I know that the idea of writing "blocks," for example, comes directly out of our tendency to use the "conduit metaphor" to describe communication. The conduit metaphor implies that a sender "packages" ideas and sends them through a conduit to a receiver who "unpacks" them.[3] In the case of writing blocks, the conduits from the source to the writer and the writer to the page are unable to convey the ideas. I'm not saying that the metaphor isn't "true"—I am sure it *is* true to many of our writing experiences. But I object to its primacy, first because it implies overwhelmingly that the opposite of blocked writing is *fluent* writing, writing that *flows* forth— a very limited notion of successful composing. And second because it doesn't seem like a very productive metaphor, providing a limited range of suggestions for helping writing along (mainly various forms of pushing and battering against the impediment).

Despite my dissatisfaction with the metaphor of blocking, I sometimes find myself behaving according to it, pushing against something, staring out the window beyond my computer, whining: "I can't get any ideas," or "Nothing is coming," or "This is coming out so slowly." You'd think I had never heard the word "heuristic," never heard of Peter Elbow, never thought of *creating* ideas in writing, rather than merely *receiving* them. I need to be vaccinated frequently with the essence of other metaphors so I won't absorb such dysfunctional views. I need to be reminded of writing as building and journeying and giving birth, as electricity and dictation and exploration, as climbing, as groping and fighting with recalcitrant texts. I need to play one metaphor off against another to understand and control the complex issues of my composing. Perhaps "vaccination" is a particularly apt term: I'm exposed to analogical diseases in the weak form, so I will be safe learning from and exploiting stronger doses of analogy.

Because of the principle of vaccination, I am not particularly concerned about delineating all the ways that individual metaphors are *not* like writing after all, though I remain alert for metaphors that have dysfunctional effects on me. It is more important to focus on the ways that metaphors are true or not true of *my experience,* rather than true or not true in an abstract sense. My metaphors *are* like writing in the sense I am trying to grasp or express. And they can be discarded at any time for metaphors that are *more* descriptive or *more* useful. I'm not worried about whether my metaphors, as figures of language, are real. Of course they are real if they serve my purposes. They are real at the moment I have used them for some purpose in conceptualizing or talking about my writing. If I find myself behaving as though writing

[3]See Michael Reddy, "The Conduit Metaphor—A Case of Frame Conflict in Our Language About Language," in *Metaphor and Thought,* ed. Andrew Ortony (Cambridge: Cambridge University Press, 1979).

should "flow" out of me, it is important to remind myself of other, more helpful metaphors. But it doesn't seem helpful to say that the metaphor wasn't true—that writing isn't like that or that it isn't real to me, that I didn't feel that way. To continue to write, to focus on writing, each of us needs to feel empowered. It empowers me to use my metaphors, not to deny them.

My metaphorical identification of my experiences brings them more fully under my control. The unifying label of each metaphor makes the reccurrence of those experiences familiar to me. Review of my favorite metaphors reminds me of my most effective writing strategies. The implications of my metaphors suggest ways of writing, avoiding problems, finding solutions, working through new tasks, keeping myself going. My metaphors for composing haven't finished educating me, however: I still have much to learn from them about the kind of writer I am, and the kind of writer I can come to be.

Some of the metaphors for creativity that writers use are shared by those doing other kinds of creative work—by scientists, painters, architects, musicians—and it is clear from these shared metaphors that creativity involves both active and receptive processes. I have been discussing primarily active metaphors here, partly because I am interested in their implications for controlling writing processes, but also because I seldom have had experiences of transcribing dictation, working in a trance, receiving a gift of ideas, or being a vehicle for others. Since I'd like to have such experiences in the future, I'm always primed for them. And on my bulletin board I keep the following inspiration, from an interview in *Crawdaddy:*

> "I didn't really write 'Shake Your Booty,'" KC confesses, eyes wide, his hand running through still damp hair. . . . "Some spirit came over the whole room. I mean, my hands were beyond human control. . . . Like an egg was cracked open and all this music came out." He shakes his head and says quietly, "Something much greater than me wrote 'Shake your Booty.'"

OUR TURN: AN AFTERWORD FOR GRADUATE STUDENTS AND OTHERS

David DeWitt
Stephanie Morris

Revenge impelled us. We talked excitedly of "showing up those malcontents" who had rebelled against English 701, the Theory and Teaching of Composition, a year before we had taken the course. Mike Taylor reported on that rebellion in the first volume of *Writers on Writing* in his "Afterword for Graduate Students." We plotted our possible rebuttal to his essay, deriding our peers' naivete and pseudo-intellectual desire for practicality (surely everyone knows that antitheoretical is pseudo-intellectual these days!). In the safe confines of our Humanities 215 office, we paused between evaluating student papers to eviscerate Mike's essay with pointed jabs, constructing pithy descriptive passages about our markedly different (i.e., positive) experience with 701 in spring 1985. We chuckled and said nasty things about those who had come before, speaking with the sort of enthusiastic, careless malice one enjoys because it will never be publicly consummated, never be publicly revealed . . . Wanton mutterings that would never be spoken outside the office. Oh, but it was fun.

Our work beckoned, so we quelled our exuberant discussion and let the chuckles peter out. Pause.

"Do you think Tom needs an afterword for the second volume?"

"Do you want to?"

"I don't know. Do you?"

"Let's go ask him."

Impulsively we scampered down to Tom's office, and impulsively we asked for the assignment.

We (with childlike enthusiasm): We want to write the afterword for your book.

Tom: (nose cast downward, smiling suggestively): Are you volunteering?

We: Yes!

Tom: Deadline is February 15. I'll give you a few more days if you need it.

Kind man. It was January 29.

Thus we embarked on an analysis of our experience with 701, an analysis that we hoped would reveal significant insights about writing, teaching, and learning. We were about to render publicly what had remained private, and it intimidated us. The reportage by Mike Taylor, a good and oft-published student writer, looked like an awfully well written account of his 701 experience. Our lack of credibility weighed down our spirits; who cares what two graduate students say when their essay is rubbing papyrus-to-papyrus with essays by the nation's most prominent rhetoricians? How pompous we were to assume the task in the first place! We, who once had so much to say, were at a loss for words. And collaborating was new territory; fears of either controlling the process or ruining it haunted us both, so we were noncommittal and silent. In short, we had writer's block.

A week after accepting the assignment, we sat again in our office, less cocky than before, bemoaning our lack of tangible progress.

In desperation, we decided to rely on the advice we gave our students: Write until you know what you want to write. Dutifully following Peter Elbow's wisdom like idealistic (fearful? lost?) freshmen, we turned to our respective desks and began freewriting "letters"—messages to each other about 701 and our essay. After five or so intense minutes, we ran out of energy and exchanged our scribblings. Below are highlights:

Stephanie:

> I think, David, it would be good to show our vulnerability. . . . I remember how THREATENED I felt by it all. I remember feeling jealous of all those freshman babes being spoonfed. I was convinced that either you can or cannot write . . . for to me, writing was survival: Writers were the fittest in the world of academe. All the heuristics and strategems that all the composition teachers could dream up were not going to help the weak ones. I was, or at least I thought I was, being realistic. Yes! That's part of it: Theories (including heurisitics, freewriting, etc.) were unrealistic. And I could not reconcile my own experience as a writer with all these concepts.

David:

> OK Steph—I have more confidence in the working of this project than you
> do . . . I really like the theme of dialogue—on all the levels (student-student,
> teacher-student, writer-writing, theory-practice, etc.). . . .
>
> Every practice bespeaks a theory. . . . Paulo Freire says even peasants have
> theories inasmuch as they practice something; their ability to objectify that
> theory is all that prevents peasants from also being intellectuals. We peas-
> ant (read "student") writers have theories, too; we must, 'cause we do
> write. . . .
>
> BRAINSTORM! Could we write this as a conversation—our form then
> equaling our point, re: dialogue 'tween theory and practice, writing the-
> ory and writing? (Highest form of rhetoric - Form symbolizes content.)
> Maybe . . . ?

Readings over, we sat and stared at each other. We began with the
usual quivering, hemming, and hawing that goes with verbalizing one's
reactions to another's intimate (raw?) ideas. Then followed a back-slap-
ping affirmation of each other. Triumphant cheers of "Yes!" resounded
through our office. We were exuberant about the dialogue-format idea.
It would exemplify the cyclical purpose of *Writers on Writing:* Practicing writers objectifying their theories naturally causes dialogue among
readers, who are practicing writers. Now we had a sense of direction.
Suppressing our egoistic enthusiasm, we realized that the letter writing
worked and decided to bend our Elbows (pun intended) again, this time
focusing on our specific relationship and shared experiences as cowrit-
ers, costudents, and coteachers of freshman English, somehow orbiting
around the 701 class and its concepts. Following are highlights of our
multipage notes.

Stephanie:

> I could hoot at Waldrep, and by golly, it was rewarding to hear a chorus
> of hooters complaining right along with me. So at the beginning of the
> semester, Tom was the alien zealot, and I know he perceived it. . . . My
> face betrayed my skepticism and rebellion. Rebellion is the key word. My
> soul got all worked up at Tom and his heuristics. I hated that word the first
> time he mentioned it, and he repeated it just to annoy me. . . .
>
> Nevertheless, Tom's lectures spawned lots of long talks in quiet little T.A.
> offices . . . David, we pushed, stomped, really beat up some of Tom's
> theories. The thing was, they always somehow got up when it was over.
> Got up and smirked at us. . . . I suppose, then, that this is one of the practical
> consequences of 701: It was disturbing. It caused dialogue. And the neat
> thing is that the dialogue still IS.

David:

> The excitement of our dialogue just runs amuck over my mental blocks! I make strong statements, create a specific intellectual/professional identity for myself, in your presence. . . .
>
> In all areas, our dialogue makes us incredibly strong and independent, yet honestly open-minded and joyously needful of the other's feedback. As writers, we really are fairly similar, despite appearances. Your writing is so passionate, so personal, yet formal and ornate. You're aware of your writing . . . it's baroque and shows great care and playfulness all at once. That intimidates me a bit because I always feel my writing is so unambitious compared to yours. Really. . . . Although I've been liberated from my old generic, journalistic form and try to obey my personal voice, I still hold to the maxim that writing is communication, and that communication, the message itself, should make the impression. Writing shouldn't be impressive; what's being written about is what should make an impression on the audience. . . .
>
> If it's a class that's worth a damn (and, I hope sometimes, if it's not), we both engage in a personal dialogue with the material. We can't separate Alexander Pope's and John Dryden's works from our feelings, theories, and world views; we have to decide if we agree or disagree, are provoked or bored, enlightened or confused. . . . How can one separate personal beliefs from intellectual beliefs? My mind is a part of me; my intellect is part and parcel of my personality. . . .
>
> Point is, a class without dialogue—between students and students, students and material, students and teacher—has no vitality. A theory that is not personalized, challenged and met on a personal, practiced level, is not a useful theory. A practice without awareness of the theories it bespeaks is rote, mechanized practice, unvitalized by dialogue. We can't deny the fact that we have a theory behind our practices; we can deny a dialogue between the two. To write without voice is to deny oneself, either out of ignorance or fear. To practice without (recognized) theory is to deny oneself, either by ignorance or fear.
>
> And Stephanie—our relationship as writers, students, and officemates is helping me embrace, or at least understand, the theories behind my practices.

Round 3 of the letter writing began. Highlights:

Stephanie:

> I really fancy your description of my writing. I guess my writing is baroque. (I think *I* am baroque!) Your aim is straight communication: a real one-on-one, gut-to-gut dialogue. You have a naked severity that my passionate exultations and ornate figures cover up. In this way your writing is human

and honest. I try to achieve transcendence. I want yesterday. You want tomorrow. Our writing gives us away.

I am not sure I agree with your statement that writing is communication, and that communication, the message itself, should make the impression. That makes perfect sense, but I don't know if I agree. I can't help but think of Ruskin; John Ruskin's words are sublime. His style incorporates the message, and therefore a mutuality of message and form emerges from the text; the reader's visual, intellectual, and aural senses are simultaneously stimulated, so that there is no separation of message and delivery. . . . I cannot separate soul from body.

Our dialogue is almost a living thing. It keeps growing, expanding, developing, changing forms (i.e., becoming print, and/or becoming memory to reinforce other dialogues, and/or becoming print and published and shared with all kinds of people). Our dialogue is animate as well as animated!

David:

I'm not sure I engaged myself with the theories as much as you did. . . . Perhaps because Matalene's Classical Rhetoric/Advanced Writing course had acquainted me with Christenson's cumulative sentence, Don Murray's teaching ideas, Aristotle's rhetoric, etc. . . .

I hate heuristics, too. They seem so juvenile to me. I hated writing my heuristic essay . . . I felt I was simply stating the obvious in specific (trivial?) language. The entire heuristic business to me is false theory, and to promote it as theory is false professionalism. As I sat in that room, talking about the Christenson "theory" or the Lindemann "theory," there was Patti P. Gillespie, my dramatic theory professor, whispering in my ear: "A theory is (a) comprehensive, (b) useful, (c) elegant, (d) based on evidence. These are simply random ideas about writing. Einstein, Aristotle: They had theories. These are mutterings. I just wanted to scream "Bullshit!" The land of writers and rhetoricians seemed like meaningless baby talk, trivialities elevated to seriousness simply to fill academic journals. Where's the beef? I wondered (before the phrase became a tiresome cliché).

I guess I really quit bitching like a baby and started purporting ideas with the final project. I started incorporating invention strategies within the broader field of creativity research and started really hitting on things I cared about. My vision became more comprehensive, and those "random ideas" that had frustrated me so were in my memory bank, ready to be plugged into my personal world view if applicable.

Point: I could distance myself from the material at first. But I couldn't distance myself from what I wrote about the material, from the students (you, Annette, Dana, Melissa) with whom I examined the material, and I especially couldn't distance myself from the teacher who so lovingly and genuinely embraced the material. So people were the key. ("We don't teach writing, we teach writers"—Remember?)

Writings over, and deadline approaching, we had circled back to our beginnings: There we sat in our office, talking. We felt spent; we'd put a lot of time and commitment into our letters; we'd said everything we needed to say, yet we wanted to say more because we hadn't said enough. And we talked about the thin line between personal experience writing and self-indulgent, prosaic wastes of space. The writer's dilemma.

Stephanie wanted to add how her dislike of theories turned one hundred and eighty once she started reading Erika Lindemann's *Rhetoric*. She was entranced with Lindemann's triangles, circles, and other geometric forms, which transfigured the practical and mundane into the theoretical and fantastical. To her it was like gazing at the stars: otherworldly, yet revelatory. David, remaining earthbound, wanted to proclaim Donald Murray's humbly written gospel *A Writer Teaches Writing*. A Murray proselyte, David has become a lecturn-thumping advocate of freewriting, conferencing, and other muscular, sweaty, wrestle-with-the-student approaches to teaching.

Although we were pleased with our conclusions, we despaired at still not having a starting point for our essay, or even a procedure for writing it.

By now it should be obvious what approach we took. We hope it's even obvious why. See, 701 isn't over for us. It exists in this essay. You rhetoricians, both professional and student, are part of our class. Even the antitheorists (a misnomer, certainly, for as we define it, the species antitheorist cannot really exist) will react, in some way, to this essay. As you've read, you've argued with, critiqued, praised, scoffed, and otherwise responded to our words and ideas. You own them now, and 701 lives.

And us? We're still talking about writing, teaching, and 701.

David:

> Stephanie, I like the essay. It's clearly from students, but that's its strength. Isn't it? And it's honest to the process so people can get what they want from it. Glad we did it. Love, David

Stephanie:

> Well, David, if we have been too enthusiastic, even annoyingly enthusiastic, with our pentecostal fervor swelling each word, well, then, so be it. I'm glad we did it, too. Love, Steph

ABOUT THE EDITOR

Formerly director of the Writing Center at the University of South Carolina, Tom Waldrep has just finished a five-year term as director of Freshman English. He has served on the editorial boards of several professional periodicals, including College Composition and Communication *and* Teaching English in the Two-Year College. *He was president of the Southeastern Writing Center Association (1984–1985) and has served as chair of both the regional executive committee of the SCETC (1981–1983) and the freshman English section of SAMLA (1984). Before moving to the University of South Carolina, Waldrep had taught in two-year colleges in Alabama and South Carolina. He is a frequent leader of writing and teaching writing workshops for businesses and public schools in Alabama, Georgia, and South Carolina.*